The Fourteenth of July at Nuremberg

GEORGES BONNIN

By the same author

Bismarck and the Hohenzollern Candidature for the Spanish Throne (1957)

Le putsch de Hitler à Munich en 1923 (1966)

Georges Bonnin

Georges Charles Bonnin was born at Les Sables d'Olonne, in the Vendée, western France, in 1920. The son of a solicitor, he was educated by Jesuits at Vannes and received a doctorate in law from the Sorbonne, where he was a colleague of Charles de Gaulle's son Philippe. After serving in the French Army when WWII broke out, he was rounded up by the Germans while trying to evade forced labour and was imprisoned in Toulouse.

In 1945 he was appointed an assistant to the political adviser to the French delegation at the Nuremberg trials.

The Fourteenth of July at Nuremberg

An Original Publication of Silver Egg Publishing

An imprint of Red Egg Publishing International

First published in the UK by Silver Egg Publishing

on 14th January 2016

www.redeggpublishing.com

Copyright © Jean Bonnin and Lynn Bonnin 2016

2nd edition 2017

Georges Bonnin has asserted his moral right to be identified as the author of this book

Cover design: Silver Egg Publishing

British Library Cataloguing-in-Publication Data

A catalogue record for this book is available upon request from the British Library

ISBN: 978-0-9571258-4-1

While every effort has been made to contact copyright-holders, if an acknowledgement has been overlooked, please contact the publisher. This book is sold subject to the condition that it shall not, by way of trade or otherwise, be lent, re-sold, hired out, or otherwise circulated without the publisher's prior consent in any form of binding or cover other than that in which it is published and without a similar condition including this condition being imposed on the subsequent purchaser

The Fourteenth of July at Nuremberg

GEORGES BONNIN

List of Contents

Foreword	9
Introduction	13
The Fourteenth of July at Nuremberg	21
Epilogue	328
History of the Resistance	336
A Final Consideration	339
Bibliography and Notes	341
Obituary	368
Notes and Acknowledgements	370

FOREWORD

My father, Georges Bonnin, began writing *The Fourteenth of July at Nuremburg* in the late nineteen-seventies or early -eighties. As well as being a significant addition to the historical material relating to the Nuremberg Trials and the Second World War, it is an important personal account of what took place.

In 1986 my parents retired and moved house. At the same time as they did this I went away to study Politics and Political Philosophy... When my parents moved they moved into a smaller house, hence some belongings had to be left in storage. One of the places they rented was the upper tier above a farmer's barn.

One day, when I'd returned home for the holidays my father took me to the barn to help him collect one or two things and to see if there was anything there I wanted. This, he told me, was the last time he was coming to the barn since he was going to cease renting it. And anything that was left the farmer could keep.

I picked up half a dozen books and my father did the same. Then as we were exiting this attic floor, about to descend the rickety wooden stairs, I turned for one last look over the many packed shelves of files and books that remained.

On the floor there was a wooden crate and on top of it a box, cascading from which to the floor were sheaves and sheaves of A4-sized typed paper. I asked my father what all the paper was. Indifferently, he told me that it was his manuscript of a book he had been writing. I recall feeling stunned, as my father's words did not quite register. When he then told me that there existed no copy anywhere else, I asked if it would not be wise of us to gather all the pages together and take them with us. My father shrugged. "We really should take them with us, Dad," I insisted.

I went back, stooped down, and saw *Le Quatorze Juillet á Nuremberg* typed on the first page (for my father had written the manuscript in French). Underneath this dishevelled pile was another, on the first page of which was typed *The Fourteenth of July at Nuremberg*: the translation. Translated by whom and when, my mother and I don't recall.

There were several piles of pages of each language version, which probably made up two or three full manuscripts of each. The pages were scattered across the floor. I grabbed what I could. I was youngish and probably did not completely grasp the significance of what was there. Whether what remained were different drafts or had extra pages I don't know. Had that episode happened today, naturally, I would have taken absolutely everything. Nevertheless, it exists! And I am glad that my father's last visit to that rented barn was when I was at home. For had I not been with my father on that last visit of his to the farmer's barn, this significant contribution to our understanding of that period would not exist.

As our proof-checker, reviser and friend Paddy Long said to me – the only shame is that Georges is no longer still around to ask him about certain episodes or to expand upon certain areas. If only we had begun the process of getting this book published ten or fifteen years earlier...

My mother Morfydd (Lyn) Bonnin and I present this as the invaluable and, as far as we are aware, unique personal account of a young lawyer and observer at the Nuremberg Trials. We don't know if my father would have altered it greatly or not. Nor do we know if there are any errors concerning dates, names or accounts. We assume not, but if anyone detects an inaccuracy we would be grateful if that person would contact the publisher so that, needless to say, amendments would be made for future editions.

Jean Bonnin

27th December 2013

Pembrokeshire, Wales,

United Kingdom.

INTRODUCTION

Two years earlier, almost to the day, I was arrested by the Gestapo, on 13 July 1944, near the Place Esquirol in Toulouse. A black Citroën stopped. One of the men, dark, small, puny, and nervous, said to me, "German police! Your papers ... They are false, completely false!" The two Gestapo put us into their car. My companion was a former school friend, encountered by chance that evening. The small, dark Gestapo officer warned me, "Do not try to escape – I am armed."

At Caffarelli, an army barracks in Toulouse now used as a prison, the Gestapo instructed us, "Pull down your trousers!" I saw my friend opening his fly and showing his penis. I did the same, wondering why on earth he would do such a thing without argument. The following day, I learned that the Gestapo wanted to know whether we were circumcised. We were not...

As I sat and watched as the weeks of the Nuremberg Trial passed, the memories of July-August 1944 superimposed themselves onto my impressions of the proceedings. These, despite the slight abstraction brought by their legal content, took on a very real meaning when I remembered my experiences as a prison inmate. When there was mention of the millions of Jews exterminated at Auschwitz and elsewhere, I remembered the faces of the hundred Jews I saw leaving our prison on 30 July to be deported by the last train out. Nothing has been heard of them since.

Memories of events of 1944 kept coming into my mind. If only I had known at the time that, a mere two years later, I would see Goering standing two steps away from me, that I would be present at his judgement and those of a handful of Generals and Admirals, I could have told my Jewish companions, "You are dejected, you have been on the run for so long ... but one day it will be the turn of the Goerings, the Kaltenbrunners, the Seyss-Inquarts, to receive their punishment, and I can tell you that on that day, I shall be there."

I observed at Nuremberg the "Great War Criminals" with the same interest as I had observed the Jews exercising in the courtyard at Caffarelli in the evenings. The Jews, as did the Defendants, chatted away in German, reminiscing of their past in a Germany that had disappeared. In both cases, death was waiting for them, not many weeks ahead.

The world of Caffarelli remained very real to me, perhaps more so than the world of the Trial. At Caffarelli I frequently had the opportunity to talk with our guards. They reminded me of the monitors of the various Catholic boarding schools where I had spent my youth; the monitors were priests of peasant origin, convinced they had a mission and with a strong belief in discipline.

The chief of the guards was *Unteroffizier* Muehlhausen. He belonged to the *Wehrmacht*, not to the *SS*, and was a man of about forty years of age. In civilian life he was a commercial traveller.

Muehlhausen came from Hanover, as could be heard in his pedantic pronunciation, of which he was proud. "We speak German as it is written. In the case of the word '*Spitze*' [point; peak], for example, we say '*Spitze*', instead of '*Schpitze*' as in the rest of Germany." He was a man who in his job would have inspired confidence. He had a round face, blond hair, and chubby cheeks that descended into jowls, always carefully shaven. He was a good soldier in the field, ready to leave at the blow of a whistle, his pack always impeccably prepared. He preferred to trust everyone, his men and his prisoners alike, although occasionally had doubts and disappointments. In his relaxed moments he would tell his men, almost threateningly, "*Ich kenne Sie alle ... alle*" ("I know all of you, yes, all of you"). There was in him something of the *petit-bourgeois*, a little limited and worried. He often told us, "Believe me, it is not in your interest to mix with the Jews."

By contrast, Hans the Berliner with his proletarian looks was a generous, open-handed character. He chose to spend his evenings with us and the Jews. He strummed away on his guitar, accompanying himself while singing "*Sie Sass auf der Banke ... an der Panke*". Frau Pick, also a Berliner, explained to me that the "*Panke*" was a river in Berlin and "*Banke*" Berliner dialect for "bank" (where "you sat", in the song). Frau Pick was a veteran among the Jewish prisoners. Because she was German, she was interned as early as in 1939 when the war started. Under Vichy, she was kept in a concentration camp then transferred to Toulouse by the Gestapo after November 1942, when the non-Occupied Zone was invaded by the *Wehrmacht*.

The other soldiers, typical of Occupation troops in 1944, were quite old, called up recently as a result of the last *en masse* conscription. They had only one thought: to get back home. A very tidy worker talked of his wife as a wonderful woman. When he arrived home of an evening, she had done all of the chores, washed the tiled floor and chopped wood for the stove. All he had to do was to sit down and put his feet under the dining table.

The most disquieting of the guards was a gangling peasant, a village braggart, who pretended to be able to shoot backwards over his shoulder with the Sten gun he had taken from the Resistance, a weapon dangerous enough even when used with care. He demonstrated this by leaning backwards, putting his face upside-down and holding the sub-machine gun at arm's length, his finger on the trigger. He boasted that no one would escape. When he accompanied deportation convoys to Germany, every single noise caught his attention despite the loud crashes of the colliding goods trucks. He stood as does a hunter, prepared to shoot.

My French "Aryan" companions at Caffarelli were not particularly *Résistants*. They had been arrested an hour or two before I had, in the course of a Gestapo raid on an illegal gambling dive. The aim of the Gestapo was to grab the money lying on the tables: it was a financial operation. When I arrived at Caffarelli, the Gestapo were processing them. "- And you, what do you do for a living?" "Nothing," the gambler replied. "You are very lucky," said the Gestapo. "I get up at five o'clock every morning and I can't find the time for everything I have to do during the day."

The man of leisure was nevertheless released. It was not long before I discovered that all of the Aryans arrested on that evening were in fact gaolbirds. One of them had been released from the civilian prison, Saint-Michel, only the previous day. I found myself mingling with a section of the Toulouse underworld. Their chief was Petit-Louis, a short-legged, rather fat man with a podgy baby face and blond hair. He was the owner of the gambling joint that had opened only a week earlier. He also owned a black-market restaurant serving thick steaks – without coupons – and had an interest in two or three nightclubs.

I spent the day of 14 July in Caffarelli finding my bearings among my companions, who had known each other for a very long time and who looked on me with suspicion, the only "stranger" in their ranks. When Petit-Louis noticed that I could speak German, he advised his men to be "extremely prudent" around me. In the Toulouse underworld Petit-Louis no doubt commanded respect, yet he was only a minor power compared to the big boss at the time: Lignon. All of those sharing the room were waiting, on this 14 July, to watch Lignon passing through Caffarelli in a landau on his way to the races. When they saw him over the wall, they shouted in enthusiasm; Lignon, a slim figure with a small moustache, responded by benevolently waving his right hand. He wore a white straw hat and held a cigar in the tips of his fingers. For several weeks, the prisoners placed their hopes in Lignon. "He could well make a deal with the Gestapo," they used to say. They thought he could have Petit-Louis released if only the latter were prepared to pay a high enough price.

Two years later, in July 1946, I saw Goering in the dock acting as just such a gang leader. Had he been tempted to "make a deal" with the Prosecution? I learned later that he had not been far from succeeding in doing so with the Americans. As this failed, he turned his full resentment against the

Allies. Goering decided to take his revenge and pose at the trial as Hitler's right-hand man.

Petit-Louis and one of his acolytes had been Warrant Officers in the French army. This tended to support the notion that the same qualities found in leaders in the eminently respectable institution were just as useful in the anti-society that constitutes the underworld. Petit-Louis' sense of leadership and organisation showed themselves on the very first day. He had read straight away the mind of *Unteroffizier* Muehlhausen, who issued his instructions during the roll call: "*Tadellose Ordnung, Kein Ungeziefer und so weiter...*" ("Everything is to be in perfect order, no vermin, and so on..."). Petit-Louis, who knew as much about army life as did any re-enlisted NCO, did not need to have it spelled out. Nobody was going to tell him what a barrack room inspection meant. He took charge: "For the roll call, as of now, I do not want to see one single wisp of straw in the gangways between the rows." We were sleeping on loose straw. Yet the gangways were drawn as straight as could be and with the greatest of care cleared of straw. A few minutes before the *Unteroffizier* was due to arrive, followed by two soldiers armed to the teeth, Petit-Louis himself would fetch an enormous can, which had two small holes pierced in the bottom. He filled it with water and walked along the gangways, swinging the can as if it were a censer, slowly back and forth and sideways at the same regular rhythm. He drew symmetrical figures-of-eight that covered the gaps between the bunks.

Petit-Louis would then make us line up in two rows, shouting "Right, smarten up!" "You," he ordered me, "As you speak German, you will stand in front of us and when the sergeant opens the door, you will order us in German: 'Attention!'" Actually, I yelled as best I could *"Stil-ge-stand-en!"*, the emphasis on the third syllable. With practice, I managed to give the instruction its proper rhythm. The trick was to balance the two stressed syllables, the first and the third, in such a way that the first was a sort of preparation for the explosion of the third – at the same time, not making it a parody. The *Unteroffizier*, on the evening of the 14 July, was overwhelmed at seeing our flawless presentation. His reflex response, in the same tone, was *"Ruehrt euch!"* ["At ease!"]. Then, in a much softer tone, he added *"Danke schoen! Danke schoen!"* ["Thank you very much!"]. He was visibly moved.

I turned back to look at my companions. Despite the command of "At ease!" they kept their chins jutting forward, their jaws clenched, their faces in the same fixed expression. At that time, obviously, I knew very little about them, except that the confectioner was a gambler who had finally lost it all: his shop, the family home, absolutely everything. His children would beg him not to, crying, "Daddy! Don't go out! Don't go gambling!" Another prisoner, still young, had made a fortune in the Belgian Congo, yet sympathised with the locals there. In Toulouse, he had bought the brothel considered the most chic, except for the one requisitioned by the Germans for their troops. A third man, nearly fifty, the mainstay of a café, used to spend most of his time in front of a glass of vermouth and a pile of saucers, watching women passing by. He suffered from prison life more than did the others because, deprived of his drink, he had to endure the kind of thirst he had never before experienced. He retained an air of respectability: from morning until night he wore a grey trilby and even a tie, whatever the heat – which could be stifling. He spent his mornings kneeling on the floor as if in deep prayer. Actually, through a hole in the floor he could watch the women below washing themselves. Petit-Louis used to say about him, with a kind of admiration, "He is more vicious than any of us." Another man, quite old, would walk around the prison grounds holding his umbrella; he was a bachelor who lived with his mother, and a friend of the judge at the Court of Appeal. 'Umbrella man' was responsible for encouraging Petit-Louis to open a gambling club.

At the beginning of a sitting at Nuremberg, the Marshal of the Court shouted, "Attention!" and the whole assembly would rise. I felt the urge to echo him with "*Stil-ge-stand-en!*" as at Caffarelli, and wondered whether it was feasible to compare Goering with Petit-Louis, Ribbentrop with the confectioner, and Funk with the vicious voyeur.

CHAPTER 1

The Political Adviser

I left the villa early for the French Kasino, a café in Zirndorf. It was a half-hour's walk and perhaps the best moment of the day. This corner of the Bavarian countryside reminded me of my native Vendée: the same hedges, the same wild apple trees. I enjoyed the freshness of the air. Later in the day, the sun would become a torture. I arrived home exhausted after a day's work. Nearer the village, the road was cobbled. It crossed a railway line, no longer in use. The streets were empty. I wondered if the whole village had been built after a Spitzweg painting, its gabled houses and their small, square windows and balconies overflowing with flowers just the type of houses in Advent calendars with one window to be opened each December day until Christmas.

A few days before, on the way to the Kasino, I wondered how to get hold of some money. The amount I had changed before leaving Paris would last no more than the next three days and my salary, due at the end of the month, was still a couple of weeks away. In fact, it was even further away than I could have imagined, as my salary did not reach me all the time I was in Nuremberg. Fortunately, our secretary, a twenty-eight-year-old (and to me therefore quite old), was kind enough to initiate me. "Nothing is simpler," she explained. "Every week you get your PX ration, which costs about 18 marks. It entitles you to two cartons of cigarettes and two pounds of coffee. You need only to sell one carton of cigarettes for 500 marks, or a pound of coffee for 50 marks, to be able to live easily for a week. Besides, you will have no difficulty in selling your goods, as they are valuable. There is a captain in the French delegation who has organised the black market – he used to be a journalist in Vienna. He must be making a fortune. Every weekend, he catches a plane to Berlin, where American cigarettes sell in the Tiergarten for ten times what they fetch in Nuremberg. Imagine the kind of profit he makes!" As she was rather generous, she even lent me 20 marks to pay for my first PX ration.

At the Kasino, the French prosecutors were sitting at various tables, enjoying a very full breakfast: porridge, eggs, bacon, potato pancakes – almost a 'full English' – ham, cheese, rolls and coffee. Only a glass of red wine was missing. Dubost, the person with whom I shared a room at the villa, had his own table by the window. He was head of the Prosecution team in the absence of Champetier de Ribes, who was in poor health and too frail to play his part effectively. Dubost once pointed out to me the table opposite where his favourite guest, a Soviet general, used to sit. The latter dreamed of a trip to France. Unfortunately, some weeks before my arrival, he had been so clumsy as to kill himself while cleaning his revolver.

Dubost was good-natured, large, sensitive and enthusiastic. He liked to court popularity with everyone: the Prosecutors, secretaries and *gendarmes*. However, when I arrived in Nuremberg he was going through an anxious period. Within a few weeks he would have to deliver his final prosecution speech and feared that, being thought a good chap, he was not – as he would have wished – going to be able to strike terror into the hearts of the Accused. To look more like a "tough guy" he had begun to shave his head. The roll of fat around his neck reminded me, rather, of the Germans of the pre-1914 generation. Dubost's table was raised above the others as if to remind all there that, as in a French court, the Public Prosecutor sits a step higher. On the floor below, his assistants Lanoire and Fuster ate breakfast with the rest of the delegation.

Lanoire was small, nervous and astute; he had a club foot. His task was to write for the Prosecution the final speech that Dubost was to deliver. Lanoire was conscious of the inherent difficulties: for one, he should not irritate Dubost. Also, he should align himself where possible with the other delegations and, at the same time, ward off possible criticism from the French press. They were represented at Nuremberg by journalists such as the vigilant Madeleine Jacob. Lanoire was worried to the point of obsession as to whether he should conclude the Prosecution's speech by asking for "the death penalty" or for "the supreme punishment". He had tried to sound out the other delegations, with no success. "Death" both fascinated and repelled him. The Soviets would no doubt ask for the death penalty, but which way would the British and the Americans go?

Serge Fuster was a very different character. Because his name was Serge I decided that he, with his thin face and pale blue eyes, must be of Russian origin. I thought he had a Slavonic charm, and could envisage him in the white tunic and round peaked cap of the Tsarist naval officers. This image was one I remembered from the film *Battleship Potemkin*.

Fuster had brought his wife to Nuremberg, as had the French judges. It seemed to me this showed how they thought regulations applied only to other people.[1] In contrast with Lanoire, Fuster was relaxed, amusing, non-conformist and open-minded, sometimes biting in his remarks yet never truly nasty. He was bound to come into conflict with the authorities some day; this actually happened many years later when, under the pen name of Casamayor, he wrote frankly about the workings of French justice.

Holding himself slightly aloof, Monnery, a sombre and sturdily built man, was a barrister, who had become Prosecutor for the occasion. He was present at the Trial from beginning to end, and seemed better informed than anyone else about what was going on in the other delegations. He understood English well, including American slang. He seemed almost embarrassed to have to express himself in French; his knowledge of German was perfect, and southern intonations detected in his French were in fact resurgences of a German dialect. I can remember a misunderstanding on the occasion of Monnery's questioning of Marshal Von Rundstedt, when he asked: "Could you tell us about the part played by the '*Gendarmerie de Campagne*' in France?" Von

---

[1] *Actually, regulations had been modified some months earlier, although the Quai d'Orsay seemed unaware of the changes. In March 1946, Telford Taylor, the American Prosecution's assistant, had been in Washington on a mission. He delayed his return as he could not take his wife back with him. Eventually, the US Army gave him permission to do so. At about the same time, in April, the American Judge Biddle and his principal assistant Wechsler brought their wives to Nuremberg and installed them in a luxurious requisitioned villa. Jackson, the US Prosecutor, nevertheless upheld the rule forbidding the presence of wives, and accused Biddle of undermining the morale of his administration. Rumour had it that Jackson did not wish his own wife to come; her arrival would disrupt his domestic arrangements at Nuremberg. See Robert E. Conot, Justice at Nuremberg, p. 363.*

Runstedt, misled by a faulty translation, nevertheless responded: "Well, the *'Gendarmes'* are in charge of maintaining order and security in the countryside..." Monnery, listening to Von Rundstedt without the aid of earphones, interrupted him to comment, "I think there has been a mistake in the translation. I prefer to use *'Feldgendarmerie'*."

At the Kasino I sat next to Gerthoffer's table. From my first day there, I noticed that by all he was approached with deference. He was a courteous magistrate, well groomed, and reserved in attitude. Gerthoffer had succeeded in modelling himself on the ideal of a magistrate according to statutory texts and tradition, yet he was not an *'homme de salon'*. He was active and efficient, and believed he could at this point in his career adopt the profile of an *'haut magistrat'*. Competent and hardworking, he would immerse himself in a task, identifying fully with the part assigned to him. Neither raising his voice nor leaving any doubt about the firmness of his views, Gerthoffer did not hesitate to voice criticisms of the French delegation of which he was nevertheless a member: the situation was going down the drain, magistrates did not bother to attend the sittings, and carelessness in the conduct of business was echoed in slovenliness in behaviour and dress. "Look at the British delegation, then look at you! Maxwell Fyfe requires that his assistants wear black jackets and striped trousers. The English know how to behave!"

Gerthoffer was that morning impeccable, as usual. His skin glowed, a narrow rim of hair bracketed his head, and he was wearing a white celluloid collar. Somehow, I thought I could detect in his voice, usually so calm and well controlled, a trace of tension betraying a repressed anger. This was surprising, as he was the type of Prosecutor determined to remain cool because he knew that by staying moderate and reasonable he would retain his effect. He would hit harder.

Although he spoke in a muted tone, he did so with the intention of being listened to by everyone present. "Some young Inspectors of Finance have just imagined that it was better not to court illegal gold dealings for, as they say, the more gold there is in private hands, the richer France will be. Where are we heading?" He shrugged his shoulders.

I listened respectfully to his acid remarks. I admired the loftiness of his utterances. I recognised the tone and the self-confidence of a well-informed top civil servant. However, Gerthoffer, suddenly sweeping his eyes over the room in a glance that embraced Fuster and the female secretaries, who were hanging on his every word, shot a new arrow: "Yes, Paris sends here young men who know nothing about Nuremberg!" I shared his wrath: such a move was indeed scandalous and unacceptable, another example of the incompetence of a Headquarters always ignorant of the needs of the combatants in the field.

Gerthoffer fell silent. I ordered another *Pfannkuche* (pancake) from one of the waitresses circulating among the tables. They wore the Dirndl dresses that German magazines, during the Occupation, proposed as models for the future European fashion. These were of floral patterned material; they had puffed sleeves edged with embroidery, and a square neckline. With their small white aprons, the waitresses wore the fresh-looking outfits of a typical farmer's daughter as they served my meals. For a week now – and for the first time since 1940 – I could eat to my heart's content. I thought, "If only my father could see me now!" He was always amused to watch me, as a child, eating heartily and sharing his tastes at mealtimes. I noticed Gerthoffer viewing me somewhat distantly and, as if to excuse myself, said, "I adore *Pfannkuchen* – they are new to me. I have been here only a few days." He did not answer, but looked away. For his breakfast, he was content with a cup of tea and a dry biscuit.

Conversations began to build up again, and I looked around to make sure that everything was as usual. To the left there was a retired colonel, here to work on translations. Next to him sat Zeitz, who had a grey and angular face. He spoke with a strong Germanic accent and had belonged to the Paris Gestapo during the Occupation, working secretly for the *Deuxième Bureau*. Now, he had been sent to Nuremberg as an 'expert'. The colonel had given up the idea of correcting Zeitz's French, as the latter rejected any form of contradiction or correction. The accommodating colonel was making conversation with Ginette, a blonde secretary, overweight and not in her first youth, and a good sort. She cast on all men a tender, almost motherly glance. Fuster also took an interest in Ginette: "Well, Ginette, how are we going to celebrate 14 July?"

Soon after, there was a certain wavering in the crowd. Zeitz looked to the right then to the left, as calm as a bird of prey waiting unhurriedly for a victim. He then got up quickly, carrying the ubiquitous thick, black briefcase that German soldiers and officers had with them day and night during the years of Occupation, when the war had become for them a matter of administration. It was assumed to contain files and documents, although I always wondered whether it did not also hold a few slices of black bread, a piece of *Speck* [ham] and a bottle of wine unearthed in the course of some expedition.

Zeitz was always the first in the bus that took us from breakfast to Nuremberg. He had taken it upon himself to make us leave on time – at exactly a quarter to eight. He used to sit next to the German driver and tell him: "*Mach doch Musik!*" ["Make some music!"]. The driver sounded the horn and we would all, including a chattering group of secretaries, pile out of the inn.

While the bus was making its way between the potholes, the French, revived by a breath of fresh air, were again murmuring and complaining. They would not admit it, but actually they were quite content. To them Nuremberg meant adventure, food galore, cheap living, small-scale coffee and cigarette trafficking and, as a bonus, the excitement of war and the scent of victory. I absorbed greedily the landscape rolling by: the colours of the houses, the shapes of the trees. Nuremberg was, to me, a sort of private victory. During all of those years of studying towards my degree in France I promised myself to go and see Germany one day; this would happen only at a time of my own choice and not when called up for the STO (*Service du Travail Obligatoire* [Compulsory Work]), no, not as a factory worker.

I was slightly disheartened by the impression that Gerthoffer had very little empathy for me, particularly as I was quite willing to admire him as much as did the clerical staff: a respectful admiration towards an '*haut magistrat*' [senior magistrate] who also had the ways of an '*haut fonctionnaire*' [senior civil servant]. It seemed increasingly obvious after my few days there that his comment "Paris sends us young men who know nothing about Nuremberg" was directed towards me, because I was the only one he could have meant. But why take it out on me? I played no active part in the Trial although was indeed present, it is true, at the sittings of the Court. Sometimes I was the only Frenchman to attend. My sole activity was to write each evening an account that would become the reason for a "telegram" to the Quai d'Orsay.

During the first few days, I had to compose a relatively long "letter" ("letter" sounded more modern than the traditional "despatch") on the examination and cross-examination of Schacht. This activity appeared innocuous. Why, then, was I blamed for my ignorance of Nuremberg? Admittedly, in just one week I had not been able to absorb everything that had been going on for the past nine months – and no one expected me to do so. Also, thinking it over, I wondered whether the French magistrates at Nuremberg were really that brilliant. Some of them could understand neither English nor German, one of the reasons that kept them away from the courtroom. The famous "simultaneous interpreting" system used for the first time at Nuremberg supplied only incoherent translations, judging by the translations from Russian into French. Fortunately, I could listen 'live' to the other languages.

Did the French magistrates have a great body of work to do behind the scenes? I doubted it very much. During the whole of my stay until the end of the trial, the French delegation played almost no active part – with the exception of the famous final Prosecution speech, which took less than one morning. The bulk of the work was done by the British, whose delegation gained in prestige with every day that passed. It included Maxwell Fyfe and several able barristers, aided and abetted by a team of researchers. In the background could occasionally be distinguished some real experts on Germany, such as Wheeler-Bennett.

The American delegation was supported in all fields by a powerful organisation. This included a number of German refugees, some of whom had left Germany only on the eve of the war. It would not have been easy for the Accused to throw dust in the eyes of those refugees, who knew the Nazi regime only too well. However, the American Prosecution at this stage was somehow sidelined since its leader, Jackson, lost face earlier on when he failed to dominate Goering in the course of an examination. By the time I arrived, Jackson had to all intents and purposes left the trial. He was trying to get himself invited to Paris and other capital cities in order to improve his image. Jackson's place at the trial was virtually left to his deputy, Dodd.

On the way from Zirndorf to Nuremberg, we passed a 'cemetery' of American tanks, estimated at between three and four thousand of them. They stood there in perfect condition, condemned to rust on the spot now that the war had ended. Every Frenchman, seeing this for the first time, had the same reaction: "If only we had had this mass of tanks, deployed in the right place, in June 1940, we would have smashed the Germans and never have endured four years of Occupation."

Our bus reached the suburbs of Nuremberg. Zeitz, next to the driver, pulled from his black briefcase a file that he consulted, feverishly adding pencilled comments in the margins. Germans cannot stop working... The suburbs were almost intact, except for a few houses here and there riddled with bullet holes. In stark contrast, the city centre within the walls had been virtually completely destroyed by an air raid.

Now as we drove over the cobblestones, the trams passed close by, packed full of passengers. It was as if we were travelling along a 'corridor' lined with five-storey buildings, austere and heavy, referred to by the Germans as "barracks". The Law Courts were no less austere, but they appeared more haughty and triumphant. The flags of the four participating nations flew from the four giant flagpoles at the front. It was always a pleasant surprise to see the French flag. Not so long ago, who would have thought it possible? Inside, whitewashed arched corridors met at right angles. The sounds of footsteps on the granite paving slabs reverberated along the corridors. Was it a monastery or a prison?

At last I reached the office of Lalouette, political adviser to the French delegation and my 'boss' at Nuremberg. He was still a young diplomat who, through his current position, carried some weight and had reached the rank of *Conseilleur d'Ambassade*. At his side this morning was his very young and charming assistant, the Vice-Consul François de la Gorce. Both had made their careers under the Vichy regime, of which they were willing – with an element of caution – to talk. De la Gorce was reminded of the poor meals of carrots and swedes; Lalouette spoke smugly of his past as General Secretary at the Résidence in Morocco: "I was able to have a few pieces of furniture sent from France," he confided to us, proud as he was of this *tour de force*. He was still in Morocco when the Allies landed, and wasted little time before joining his old regiment. In the story of these events of November 1942 there was, however, a 'black hole' between the landings and the time when Lalouette found himself again in the uniform of a cavalry captain in the Army, gallantly pursuing the Axis troops in North Africa. De la Gorce used to say, "He had difficult postings during the war."

Between the end of the war and the Nuremberg Trials, Lalouette spent a few months in Dublin, time enough to rig himself out before embarking on a new element of his career. He was wearing a rather gaudy grey suit with large checks, obviously of Irish origin, yellow shoes with triple soles, a green silk tie, also Irish and patterned with a design of small, stylised flowers and arabesques copied from the stained glass windows of the Middle Ages, and a shirt with wide blue and white stripes. Were it not known that all of his clothing came from Dublin, Lalouette could have been taken for a prosperous businessman. His stocky figure was waiting for me as he stood in front of his desk, blocking with his solid form the view out of the lower part of the window. He was careful never to be seated when a visitor came in; this was so as not to be caught in a position of inferiority. He looked me up and down, weighing me up as I approached. It was as if he were commenting, "You are not very well dressed." This was true. During the whole of the war I was able to buy only one suit, and believed the material to be made of a mixture of recycled rags and cellulose. I used to have two good suits from pre-war days. The Gestapo went to collect them from my landlady, Mme. Person, three days after my arrest, saying, "We are here to fetch M. Bousquet's* clothes. He will need them next winter." The explanation seemed innocent. Actually, the Gestapo were acting on their own account and my clothes found their way onto the black market in Germany... I was surprised to see the French at Nuremberg so well dressed.

* Roger Bousquet was the pseudonym I had chosen for myself as I carried out my activities in the occupied part of France. I parted my hair on the other side, grew a moustache and travelled around with the false papers (unfortunately unbeknownst to me at the time, false papers of a markedly inferior quality) provided by my uncle.

The furniture in Lalouette's office was austere, in keeping with the monastic atmosphere of the Courts of Law. To the left on entering there was a safe supplied by the Americans; in it, Lalouette kept for his daughters the chocolate and boiled sweets allocated each week at the PX. As he was very shrewd, he suspected that the American secret services possessed a key to the office and the combination to the safe. This would have allowed them, when the building was deserted at night, to read his most secret letters to the Quai d'Orsay. That is why he kept his correspondence in a wooden filing cabinet near the window behind his desk. A rod, a ring and a tin lock served to ensure the inviolability of his archives. I noticed, though, on more than one occasion when Lalouette was away, that the lock had been forced.

Two tables faced the walls, one for de la Gorce on the right and the other for me on the left. To the right, a door, kept locked, led to the office where the assistants to the French judges worked. The window looked out onto a room full of noisy American soldiers in a building on the other side of a narrow alleyway.

At our first meeting Lalouette asked me the question with which he welcomed new visitors, "Did you have a good trip?" He was a stickler for etiquette and had at his disposal a whole arsenal of small talk that he could pull out of his pocket according to the occasion, his face inscrutable. Then, he did with me what French diplomats call a *'tour d'horizon'*. The aim of this was, I soon realised, to elicit an answer to a question that was never directly formulated: "To which social category do you belong?" I was tempted to tell him not to beat about the bush, but just ask me straight out what my father did for a living.

I learned a lot from Lalouette. His conversation was itself as good as a course in diplomatic history for the years preceding the war. He had only to tell the story of his career as a young diplomat in Vienna, Prague and Berlin. He was wonderfully well prepared for the Trial. The various stages in his career meant that he had witnessed first-hand all of the crimes mentioned in the indictment: conspiracy, crimes against peace, war crimes, and crimes against humanity.

When Dollfuss was murdered Lalouette was posted to Vienna. Always alert in critical moments, he followed step by step the unfolding of the failed Putsch. At one point he pushed open a door and found himself in the presence of Dollfuss' corpse, still warm, lying on a sofa, alone in death, forgotten by all at the most tragic moment. Lalouette had fallen in love with Austria, which had become his second native land. He was accepted by Austrian society and was one of a shooting party along with von Papen when the latter was Ambassador to Vienna. Lalouette could now recount how considerate von Papen had been towards him on this occasion.

Seeing Lalouette at the table of the French Prosecution, did von Papen, today in the dock, remember that particular shooting party to which both had been invited? After Vienna, Lalouette went to Prague and soon after to Berlin, then under the iron rule of François-Poncet, still a strong influence over the young diplomats. In certain ways, through Lalouette, the spirit of François-Poncet was present at Nuremberg.

François-Poncet had not merely been a great French ambassador; curiously, he was also very popular with the lower classes in Berlin. They were neither unpleasant nor in the least revanchist, but saw in François-Poncet the archetype of the elegant Frenchman. He was always carefully dressed, always wearing gloves; he was a '*Monsieur*' with a waxed and curled moustache, a reminder of the days of the Kaiser. To his assistants François-Poncet was a severe master; when after the war they talked of him, their admiration was mixed with retrospective fear. Lalouette told me how François-Poncet used to mark out of a possible 20 the draft telegrams or letters submitted by the young diplomats. "Not bad," he would say, "It is worth a 12." Each had to do his homework without fail: at least one long "despatch" and two or three short telegrams every week.

Later, I hear Seydoux, who had also been posted to Berlin, telling how he would arrive at the embassy in Unter den Linden at six o'clock in the morning when it was his turn to write a summary of the daily press. His wife, who drove him, waited in an adjacent street while her husband completed his work. When his report was completed, Seydoux submitted it to the ambassador; he, acting the part of the "*grand seigneur*", received Seydoux while still in bed, reading the Berlin newspapers. Seydoux would then rejoin his wife and joyfully announce: "Today I got a 13!" This was clearly above the pass mark and exactly halfway between "*Assez bien*" and "*Bien*". Since his training under François-Poncet, Lalouette had kept up the habit of sending a letter and two telegrams every week. Those at the Quai d'Orsay told him: "You write too much." "But no!" he said, staring straight at me, "One must write!"

François-Poncet's mission to Berlin ended in failure; he was unable to prevent the outbreak of war between the two countries. Besides, he had left Berlin for Rome soon after the Munich Agreement of

1938. At the time, he thought he could have done more. He began by trying to negotiate with Roehm soon after Hitler rose to power. Later, François-Poncet believed he could play the Goering card – and this took us back to the Nuremberg trial.

François-Poncet discovered that Goering saw himself in the role of Prince of Peace, thus thought it would be clever to play on the vanity of the fat Hermann by inviting him to a grand dinner in his honour, held at the French Embassy, then by lavishing upon him the respect and compliments Goering so craved. The essential piece in this move towards the conquest of Goering was the Assistant to the Air Attaché, Stehlin, a young and brilliant officer and patriot from the Alsace. After the war, a retired colonel, who had been in Berlin at the same time as Stehlin, told me the following story – which deserved to become the subject of an "*image d'Epinal*". One day, Stehlin took off in a small private plane and crash-landed deliberately on a German military airfield "in order to see what was going on"; the Germans were suspected of experimenting with a new weapon. Stehlin broke both legs. François-Poncet visited him in hospital to pin on his chest the Cross of the Legion of Honour; he wished to add a few words of commiseration, but Stehlin interrupted him: "*Monsieur l'Ambassadeur*, it is nothing ... it is for France."

François-Poncet was succeeded in Berlin by Coulondre, who gave a little more background information in his memoirs. Stehlin was "as handsome as he was intelligent" and succeeded in attracting the attention of General Bodenschatz, A.D.C. to Goering. Stehlin himself recounted the story much later: conversations between him and Bodenschatz mentioned avoiding a war between

France and Germany. Goering let it be known through Stehlin to the French embassy that he approved of these contacts and talks. French diplomats thus pulled off a subtle coup, bypassing official diplomacy and negotiating directly with the Number Two of the regime, a man radiating human warmth, whereas Ribbentrop or Hitler were a different story.

During the Trial, Lalouette asked to see Goering and was allowed to visit him in his cell. Why? Lalouette never breathed a word about it. I wondered sometimes whether François-Poncet had offered through Lalouette to attend the trial and somehow to testify to Goering's efforts at peace. I believe, though, that François-Poncet underestimated Goering, whose character was dominated not merely by vanity; he was also very cunning. No doubt Goering indeed wanted peace, as did almost everybody else, but when he sought peace with France it was probably so as to prevent interference in Germany's attack on Poland.

Who had been duped in the Stehlin affair? Stehlin believed that both Bodenschatz and Goering confided in him, revealed re-armament secrets about the Luftwaffe, because they sincerely wanted peace –

and to thwart Hitler's plans – with Bodenschatz unwittingly telling him more than he should have.[2]

Lalouette favoured two topics of conversation: the last day of peace, and his appointment to Daladier's private office once war was declared. He told how, on the eve of the war, the Berlin Embassy advised Daladier to stand firm. Hitler was bluffing. This culminated in Coulondre's famous letter to Daladier: "You are, I believe, an angler, *Monsieur le Président* ... stand firm, the fish have been nibbling." This letter was unfortunate less because of its content than of the method of transmission. It was carried to Paris by a special and extraordinary messenger, the French consul at Frankfurt, who happened to be going to France at that very moment. If only Coulondre had sent the usual coded telegram, it would have been intercepted and deciphered by the German Secret Service (the *Forschungsamt* of which Goering was nominally the head) and given the Germans food for thought: was France actually planning not to submit?

After the war, Lalouette considered that the Berlin Embassy had been right to advocate resisting Hitler in 1939. The Embassy was also in 1939 trying

---

[2] *There might have been on Goering's part a clear effort to mislead the French, with the help of Bodenschatz; instead of letting French intelligence services accumulate pieces of second-hand information, he supplied them directly with data from the best sources, perfectly authentic. The aim was to prove to the French that they did not stand a chance in a war with Germany. In the same spirit, General Vuillemin was in 1938 invited to Germany, where he was shown all that Germany possessed as far as the air force and aircraft industry were concerned. The psychological aim was achieved. The French High Command not only appreciated the importance of German re-armament; they tended to overestimate it. This was one of the main causes of the Munich capitulation and of the inactivity during the Phoney War. See in this connection Wilhelm Von Schramm, Geheimdienst in Zweiten Weltkrieg, Munich, 1974, pp. 46-53.*

to win another skirmish in the diplomatic battle lost in Munich in the preceding year. However, it is possible that Coulondre's letter might not have been fully understood; where it said "Stand firm, *Monsieur le Président*", Coulondre could have meant: "*Monsieur le Président*, we know that you are a lucid man, but also that you are weak. You make vigorous speeches, yet at the first opportunity you give way. This time, *Monsieur le Président*, one must not submit." Who knows? Perhaps Coulondre intended to say, "We know that you want to avoid war at any price. Stand firm. Refuse even to entertain the idea! Hitler is bluffing; he does not want war either. Stay out of it!"

There was indeed some wavering at the French Embassy in the very last days until war broke out. It is hardly possible to know everything about the most secret interventions that might have been taking place at the eleventh hour. Lalouette talked freely only about one curious incident, of which he was the hero. When France and Germany found themselves formally in a state of phoney war, the telephone of the Embassy was cut off; Lalouette, as cleverly as ever, crossed Unter den Linden and went to the Adlon Hotel, from where he telephoned the Quai d'Orsay as if nothing were amiss. He kept this up the whole afternoon. What he actually said is unknown.

In the following weeks, Lalouette found himself attached to the private office of the '*Président*' – by whom Lalouette meant Daladier. The significance of the appointment should have been clear. The press, however, chose to see in the presence in Daladier's cabinet of one or more diplomats from Berlin proof that the French government wanted to wage war against Germany, with France acquiring full knowledge of the circumstances and calling on the advice of experts. It appears to me today that the real significance of the diplomats was quite obvious: during what had become the Phoney War, the issue was rather to negotiate than to fight with the Germans. Faithful to himself and consistent in his behaviour Daladier, who had taken the huge decision of declaring war, had but one aim: to rescind it through diplomatic negotiation.

This war was hardly a fortnight old when the Quai d'Orsay sent a secret emissary to Luxembourg. He went to meet the German minister, Radowitz. The Quai d'Orsay chose Henri Blanche; he was the son of a diplomat and was married to the daughter of a German diplomat, Count Podewills; Blanche had known Radowitz before the war. They asked him whether, through his family connections, he could contact the head of a German diplomatic mission abroad. Blanche mentioned Radowitz in Luxembourg then was instructed not to breathe a word of his trip to Cambon, France's own minister in Luxembourg. Blanche set off, his passport stamped with the visa of a diplomatic courier, and appeared at Radowitz's house on 17 September 1939.

Blanche's message could not directly quote Daladier. According to Radowitz, Blanche declared that "many people in France thought that England had drawn France into the war and that those people were beginning to exert some pressure on the Quai d'Orsay" – although the identity of those powerful enough to influence the Quai d'Orsay was not specified. "They" wanted France honourably out of the situation, viewing the prospect of an intensification of the war between France and Germany as a catastrophe.

At this very moment, the German armies were crushing Poland, which France had promised to help defend with all of its forces. Warsaw fell ten days later, on 27 September. Of course, added Blanche, the Quai d'Orsay was most anxious for such views not to be expressed publicly and for his mission to remain strictly confidential.[3]

In Daladier's office, Lalouette was exposed to the flavour of high society and of policy at the highest level. He reflected the President's personality in many anecdotes which, taken up by the press at the time, must have helped to create an image of Daladier as the organiser of victory, the "Lazare Carnot" of the Second World War. One anecdote has remained unpublished. Daladier was once invited to dinner by the US Ambassador, who told him that the US President was on the telephone and asked whether Daladier would like to speak to him. Daladier took the receiver, but was struck dumb by the notion of conversing with Roosevelt across the Atlantic.

Lalouette, through his pre-war postings, was better prepared than anyone within the French delegation to appreciate the import of Counts 1 (conspiring against peace) and 2 (preparing a war of aggression) of the indictment. From his career during the war as a member of the Scapini mission[4] Counts 3 (committing war crimes) and 4 (committing crimes against humanity) should have become obvious, but

---

[3] *From Radowitz's memo of 17 September 1939. That same evening the German diplomat sent to Berlin a letter that formulated, probably in more precise terms, the message from the Quai d'Orsay. (Microfilm 115/117, 942-3, Document no. 87 in the official publication of the German diplomatic documents of the period, Series D, Vol. VIII. Documents on German Foreign Policy.)*

[4] *Scapini, a member of the French Parliament between the two wars, had lost his eyesight during World War 1. Within the framework of the policy of Collaboration, he was sent to Germany during World War II with the rank of Ambassador and was given the task of looking after the interests of the French prisoners of war.*

Lalouette preferred not to talk about this period. He may well have taken an interest in deer hunting, an aristocratic pastime, in the company of von Papen, but seemed unable to bear the thought of brutality between men, which was bad taste and, in the final analysis, vulgar. He made only one allusion to me about his past in wartime Germany after the trial: "You are going to Berlin to study German archives. Try and see if I am mentioned in them. I know that my name was given to the Gestapo."

To me Lalouette was living proof of the continuity in Franco-German relations. Beyond wars, defeats and victories, there was a certain obsession on the part of the French with Germany, necessarily enemy and partner simultaneously. I could not discover at which point for Lalouette the past and the future met; he was truly conservative, if only to conform to the tradition of his calling. Perhaps, though, it was only a pose demonstrating that he accepted the values of a sophisticated world. He could make you dizzy with his vision of Europe's political future. He drew a fanciful picture of a united Europe, where Germany, Austria and France would obviously dominate; yes, France would be first among the second-rank powers. La Gorce went one better: "Yes, even so, it would be more grandiose than trying to annex Brigue and Tende.[5] When one thinks of all the other powers waiting for France to take world leadership against the United States and Russia!"

---

[5] *Brigue and Tende belonged to an Italian district in the Alps which France wished to annex – and eventually did, in order to straighten the border between the two countries.*

CHAPTER 2

The Schacht Affair

My first task at Nuremberg had been to write a "letter" on Schacht. Lalouette was in the habit of writing a three- or four-page letter on the examination of each of the Accused, and for the past few months his correspondence with the Quai d'Orsay was limited to this. Schacht had just been testifying; Lalouette gave me, as a model, his own letter on von Papen, who had preceded Schacht in the witness box. I remembered one sentence: "The cross-examination was for the former Chancellor a painful ordeal."

A painful ordeal? Maxwell Fyfe had in his cross-examination effectively pulled von Papen to pieces. He called him a liar, an ambitious man preoccupied only with his career, offering shamelessly his services to Hitler the day after the Nazis had murdered his closest assistant. Maxwell Fyfe argued that von Papen was the most guilty of the Accused, in the sense that he had deliberately put Hitler in power and had no scruples about serving the regime until the end, as Ambassador first in Vienna, preparing the *Anschluss*, then in Ankara.

I wanted to find out about Schacht's character. His face had been familiar to newspaper readers for decades. The photographs and caricatures described accurately how he looked: the crewcut, the narrow moustache and mouth, the severe gaze, and the celluloid collar, which seemed to elongate his neck. I remembered that before the war, at Sciences Po, a certain Céré, who was holding a seminar on diplomatic history "to go deeper into questions", spoke many times of Dr. Schacht. However, the only solid piece of information Céré would give us was that Schacht had just married again; his bride was a very young woman, which suggested an undertone of immorality and perhaps the existence of a double life behind the façade of financial respectability that Schacht had for so long displayed to the world.

On the *quais* in Paris, I bought a doctoral thesis on law, rather remarkable for this type of academic exercise, by M. Harblay: "Germany's bankruptcy towards its private creditors". This bankruptcy was one crime among many committed by Germany at the time. The author seemed to write from experience. He gave a short word-portrait of Schacht, also referring to his recent marriage. Whatever any previous significance of Schacht's marriage might have been, it was *a priori* not enough to condemn him to death, let alone to understand his character. Even then I was conscious of my ignorance, but was wrong to worry: reading the text of Schacht's examination told me everything I needed to know.

It was obvious that Schacht presented his "case" very cleverly: he began by informing the Tribunal that, as was his father, he was a freemason. From the outset this would demonstrate that he stood aloof from the world of the Nazis. Schacht explained further and in some detail his long quarrel with Goering: how he had given up all his posts of effective responsibility, including that of President of the Reichsbank, because he wanted to adhere strictly to the rules of monetary orthodoxy, i.e., to repay the Mefo drafts,[6] which had been used to stimulate industrial investments after Hitler came to power. Goering, though, proposed not to repay these, but to take the path of inflation and fraud. To put the final touch to his self-portrait Schacht described how he tried to finance the emigration of the Jews so that their departure would take place under less harrowing conditions. It was a rather neat *tour de force* that Schacht succeeded in presenting himself to the judges as Goering's sworn enemy.

This was all the more impressive as it concerned a difficult period for Schacht – the years before the war when he could have been suspected of having played a part in preparing a war of aggression by financing German rearmament. The rest was easy. Having proved that, long before the war, he had relinquished all of such positions, he had no difficulty in proving that he remained a minister only on paper; the Council of Ministers never met. How could Schacht be accused of war crimes? During the war he had played no part. He would prove, thanks to the witness Gisevius, that he belonged to the Resistance.

Moreover, he had even been incarcerated in a concentration camp towards the end of the war.

This was the image Schacht succeeded in projecting: a banker of rigorous integrity, a direct opponent of Goering, an enemy of Nazism, and a Resistant. My letter to the Quai d'Orsay tried to

---

[6] *Mefo (Metallforschung Gmbh) was a fictitious company. German industrialists were invited to draw bills on the company; these were automatically discounted by the Reichsbank. In this way German industry obtained the funds it needed.*

convey this image objectively and to suggest the impression Schacht could make on the Tribunal. From my remarks it was clear that Schacht would probably be acquitted.

Actually, I was not at all convinced that the image reflected the real Schacht. To help Hitler to come to power, as Schacht had done, then to work with Hitler for several years was at the least a mark of a nationalist mentality. To my mind, Schacht could plead at most that he was mistaken and that, later, his quarrel with Goering had opened his eyes.

Lalouette paid me no compliments, but he was very pleasantly surprised by my draft. This he handed over, in my presence, to his secretary to have it typed. He mentioned that the despatch sent off to the Quai d'Orsay would have my initials in the top left-hand corner. I was, of course, honoured by this mark of esteem... In the days that followed Lalouette and also La Gorce, who aligned himself with his superior, were all smiles. We were accomplices. It was as if I suddenly became one of them – or as if I arrived dressed similarly to Lalouette's chequered suit, green tie, and walking on box-calf shoes with a triple sole. That particular morning, Lalouette was rather busy. He went into and out of his room with bundles of papers, and to the office of the magistrates. He came back to fetch more documents and eventually asked: "So, are you going to the courtroom this morning?"

A few days earlier, on my way to the courtroom, I pushed open a glass door and found myself face to face with one of the American civil employees. She wore the olive green forage cap of the military although it had only the US initials as a badge. She was a mature woman, of an age I could not determine as I was then rather young and all women older than myself seemed elderly. We stood a short while without moving until she suddenly looked shocked, clutching her two large, rounded breasts. She did not look very American: those at Nuremberg were slim, smiling, and provocative, girls rather than women. But in front of me stood a lady, middle class, her black hair pulled back with no concession to youthful fashion. She exclaimed in French: "*Mon Dieu! Où vous ai-je déja rencontré?*" ("My God! Where have I met you before?") Then I recognised her – Frau Pick!

It was something of a nightmare to meet at Nuremberg a member of the Toulouse Gestapo or one of their acolytes, just like that, free, and in American uniform! Frau Pick did not belong formally to the Gestapo; she was in principle an internee like the rest of us, although for longer. In the eyes of the Germans, the time already spent in Caffarelli conferred upon her the right to an exceptional status, as the length of time in prison was the only means to promotion they recognised. After less than three weeks I had become one of the elders there, soon after a convoy for Germany had virtually emptied our prison. All that was left was a sort of "command team". This was made up of the true elders on the Jewish side, headed by Zarine, an operetta singer of Romanian origin[7], and of seven or eight recent arrivals like myself; we were headed by a Pole, Adamozack, who somehow acquired there the title of Sergeant. In civilian life he was the director of the

---

[7] *Zarine was described in a study on the Toulouse Gestapo published by Historia (No Hors Série 27, Paris, 1972, p. 88) as an agent of Soviet origin. Zarine probably came from Bessarabia and could be considered either as Soviet or as Romanian, depending on which country currently annexed Bessarabia. However, in Caffarelli he was always said to be Romanian.*

casino of Amélie-les-Bains or another spa in the Pyrenees.

The old hands were put in positions of trust. Frau Pick was the secretary who typed the confessions of the prisoners; she was so skilled that she could do so directly into German. This was why, to my mind. Frau Pick was part of the Gestapo. She was there, directly involved, when the Jews who had just been arrested were beaten in order to force out of them the information of where their mothers, their wives, their children or their grandparents were hiding.

War literature, the cinema and television have frequently shown very long, dramatic sessions from which the victim emerged unconscious. In Caffarelli there were only short sessions, lasting only ten minutes, half an hour at the most. The Jews arrived in the courtyard in a black Citroën. They climbed the staircase, hustled by the Gestapo and groaning softly. The examination could be heard through the open windows in the fierce heat of July. It began rather quietly, the muffled voices of the Gestapo evidently asking questions. There would be a silent interval then a loud, shrill scream, then another, then another... Men screamed in the voices they had as children. The Gestapo had them handcuffed so that they could not defend themselves and hit their faces with a bunch of keys. This usually lasted a few minutes until silence again prevailed. The Gestapo had difficulty in obtaining information about the Resistance, too, or about the lives of its members. One of the arrivals at Caffarelli was someone I had known and admired before the war.

For about a year I used to go to a restaurant, *Le Petit Trou*, when I was underground. It was the cheapest restaurant in Toulouse, not too fussy about coupons. As it bordered on a square where a market was held in the mornings, it enjoyed special sources of supply, being well placed to buy left-over produce at the end of each morning. The best menus were the *bœuf bourguignon* and the lentils in gravy on Wednesday evenings. Even on other days *Le Petit Trou* did not do badly, serving *hors d'œuvres*, including two slices of pork sausage, a tomato and sometimes a sardine in oil. It was not very different from pre-war days.

Monsieur Louis, who before the war no doubt had his own business, lived semi-clandestinely in Toulouse, accepting a modest job far below his capacities. The clientele at *Le Petit Trou* came from the poorest social strata of the town; they barely belonged to regular society, or to society at all. *Le Petit Trou* seemed aptly named. I imagined that the clients who lacked the strength to leave it would fall into the underground world of the soup kitchens, of night shelters at best and as tramps at worst, a frightening world. I believe they felt the chasm opening under their feet. Some of them, I am sure, knew the dangers yet just managed to surface again, however briefly. For the moment they were in high spirits and the atmosphere was cheerful enough.

A couple of old actors, who had known only unemployment since the outbreak of war, kept a certain air about them. The woman wore a small round hat during her meals, a way of retaining something of her middle-class dignity, and a length of fur around her neck. It was a young fox and had only one glass eye. None of the clients had regular work – or if they did, it was dirty or unhealthy.

I usually sat near the entrance and occasionally took my meals in the company of two tarts, one young and the other older, who worked together. How did they manage to be so poor? They had been taken over by pimps of their respective ages, withdrawn characters and not very talkative, who arrived at *Le Petit Trou* together to pick up their cash. The women did not know how to organise their work. They spent their afternoons at cinemas with casual clients. Their rates could not have been very high. Not only were they badly dressed and badly made-up, they were also badly washed. The older one – probably no more than thirty-five – was a brunette, with an urchin haircut. A touch of red took the shape of a heart on her upper lip. She was petite, always dressed in black. By contrast, the younger one was blonde, tall, plump, passive, and without many worries. She would ponder whether I was interested in her. One day, as I was telling her that she was lucky to have so many ration coupons, she asked me, "Why don't you marry a J3 woman?"[8] I interpreted this as an almost serious propositioning.

The restaurant was long and narrow, like a corridor. At the far end, alone at his table and with his back to the other customers, sat a *Milicien* in a black leather jacket. He never mixed, never said a word, and was ignored by everyone. He sat facing M. Louis, who was high in his "pulpit" overseeing the dining room.

M. Louis was the cashier and also responsible for relaying the orders between the waitresses and the kitchen: "M. Louis! One lentil and two green beans for the table of three!" I admired M. Louis. Always calm, he never raised his voice. His competence never failed him. He turned towards the

---

[8] *For the purposes of food rationing, J3 was the category of people aged between 12 and 21.*

waitresses or the kitchen in the way a conductor would address himself to the violins or to the brass. *Le Petit Trou* ran without a hitch. I wondered whether the *Milicien*[1] had denounced M. Louis to the Gestapo, as he must have discovered that M. Louis was Jewish, but was not sure: the *Milice* themselves arrested Jews and handed them over. One Sunday morning we saw about fifty of them arriving at Caffarelli. They were a pitiful sight.

The *Miliciens** had beaten the living daylights out of them – so much so that the Germans of the Gestapo, and the soldiers on guard duty, shook their heads and expressed rather sanctimoniously their disapproval of such meaningless brutality. The group was sent straight to the washroom to clean off the coagulated blood. I can still see one of them, stripped to the waist, a man in his fifties, with a crew cut, a square moustache and a short nose. His back bore long diagonal slashes. His companions did not dare to wash the newly formed scabs for fear of making the blood run again. The Vichy claimed to spare French Jews, yet these Jews seemed French. Possibly, it was a form of patriotism for the *Milice* to flog Jews of Polish or German origin because they were foreigners. I asked M. Louis: "Why did they beat you?" "They wanted to know the address of my sister ... so I gave it to them and they left me alone." He did not look unhappy; his face was at rest, almost smiling. It was the usual reaction after the blows, the feeling that it was finished and that the pain would not come back. "Moreover," he added, "There was time to warn my sister. They will not find her." As he talked, Frau Pick finished typing the account of his interrogation.

The Milice Française (French Militia), generally called the Milice, was a political paramilitary organisation created on January 30, 1943 by the Vichy regime (with German aid) to help fight against the French Resistance during World War II.

And here she was, standing in front of me at Nuremberg, this woman from Berlin, now wearing an American uniform and a forage cap sitting smartly on the side of her head. "Well," I told her, "You knew me in Toulouse, at Caffarelli." She let out a sigh of relief and her large chest lowered. She was reassured. Still, I would very much have liked to know what her first fears were. She obviously associated me with disturbing memories of her recent past. Yes, now she could see me again among the hundreds of faces filing past her on the staircases of Caffarelli, on their way to the concentration camps in Germany. I was one of the few veterans still left. She talked to me about the last days of Caffarelli.

"You know, we were lucky. Three days before the Liberation, the General commanding in Toulouse gave the order to liquidate the prisons. But the Gestapo were afraid of reactions from the population; they decided to shoot only a few, on principle, and to avoid giving the impression they were disobeying an order. About twenty internees from Saint-Michel and then from Caffarelli were executed."

I remembered how after the Liberation I had gone to see one of my former companions at Caffarelli, the only true Resistant among us, a bank clerk in Toulouse. He was examining papers behind the counter, lost in a dream, slightly embarrassed that I should pay him a private visit during working hours. He looked from time to time towards the manager's office. That did not surprise me because I knew that his manager had married his daughter to a distant cousin of mine, a typical *Pétainiste* and collaborator. The chances were that the manager had not been very favourable to the Resistance during the war. My Caffarelli companion, the only one in whom I confided in prison, told me some news of the other internees. Then he talked about Frau Pick: "That one, my friends and I would very much like to find her. We are trying..." He did not tell me why, but in those matters suspicion is almost worse than a direct accusation. I never knew what his grudge was against Frau Pick, and I never saw him again. He was a squat chap of about forty, with steel-rimmed glasses and an obstinate but worried air. He might have been more sensitive than he looked. In prison, he admired an old peasant from the Landes area, whom the Gestapo arrested because his son had joined the *Maquis*, and used to comment, "He has tremendous morale, more than any of us." However, I do not think that the bank clerk was actually well acquainted with the mentality of the peasants, who might show resilience to suffering yet also have their sorrows. The *Landais* told me, "I have been in prison six months. I am almost seventy years old, and it is the first time in my life that I have not watched the leaves grow on the trees in spring."

In Frau Pick's life, a shadowy zone covered the two years between her departure from Caffarelli at the end of August 1944 and our meeting in the corridors of the Tribunal of Nuremberg in July 1946. I should have questioned her more closely as she seemed no longer embarrassed. She continued, "- And do you know, the *Unteroffizier* and the soldiers guarding us were nice with us. They are now near Avignon in a prisoner-of-war camp. They were caught in the Rhône valley. But I see to it that they get their cigarettes, their chocolate, and that they don't lack anything."

Frau Pick was now talking as if she were a German Hausfrau, which sounded strange after her international career of those last few years. Actually, until that moment I did not know what had happened to Muehlhausen and his little gang.

A strange relationship developed between warders and prisoners. In the evenings after dinner, when we were allowed into the courtyard for some fresh air, Muehlhausen chatted with a small group of Jews of German origin. They retained their nostalgia for the Germany of old, the Germany of the Weimar years that remained their country. They talked about those thousand details of daily life, trivialities, no doubt, which revealed their attachment to a bygone world. What were the brands of chocolate? Could one get cigarettes from vending machines? I noticed, too, how the word *'Automat'* could sound comical to French ears. The conversation focused, however, on more serious subjects such as the possible future of the Jewish people – Zionism? The young Jews smiled and were sceptical; they spoke perfect German although they had been educated in France. Even at fifteen or sixteen years of age they tended towards preparing for the *'agrégation'*.

With the passage of time I observed that Muehlhausen had to make an effort to keep the conversation on a courteous footing. After a while, the Jews to whom he was speaking would go away and join in with the other internees in that courtyard, over which darkness slowly crept. Muehlhausen would then turn to me and slip into my ear some offensive remark that allowed his basic anti-Semitism to escape: "*Diese Juden... zu klug...*" ("These Jews, so clever").

Some soldiers took the Jews food, hidden in their gasmask cases. It was mostly ham sandwiches delivered by friends and relations to the guardroom at the entrance to the barracks. Muehlhausen would let it through although he always made some comment, "- And the Mosaic law ... the Torah ... forbidding you to eat pork?"

It also happened that the internees would do a good turn for the soldiers. On a particularly hot afternoon one of the soldiers on duty, posted at the corner of the building, fell asleep on his chair, submachine gun across his knees. One of us went to wake him by tapping him on the shoulder. Actually, the soldiers guarding us were not in the prime of youth and were given very little rest. Once a fortnight they were entitled to half a day in town and a brothel ticket. They went, carrying their rifles.

Matters were less relaxed when there was an air-raid warning. We were then locked up in the building, with all doors closed. The soldiers took up their position in the trenches behind machine guns trained on the doors in case we took it into our heads to get out. The Germans did not want to see a repetition of the Amiens incident, where the RAF bombed the prison walls to allow certain Resistance internees to escape.

Seeing Frau Pick again awakened all sorts of memories. She continued with her story: "As for Karta, the Czech doctor, he is still in prison. What do you expect? He does not want to work... I can do nothing for him."

CHAPTER 3

The Court

The morning sitting of 12 July 1946 had not yet started. A group of barristers were chatting near the door. They were very dissimilar, of all shapes and sizes. Some bore duelling scars on their cheeks. I recognised Seidel, an aggressive and ill-tempered little runt: he was prancing around the group as if he were going to bite. He wanted at all costs to lay before the eyes of the Tribunal the text of the Soviet-German pact of 1939. There was also Kranzbuehler with his small, round head. He wore a discreet navy-blue suit as he had been forbidden to wear his uniform of Judge of the German Admiralty. Another was Laternser, rather theatrical when it was his turn to speak. He was said also to be a comic-opera singer. In the heat of the action, he threw his head back, hurled an arm and forefinger at the witness, and froze in this pose for as long as was needed by a singer of the Capitole in Toulouse to prove that he could 'hold the note'. Usually, everything was down-to-earth in the courtroom; however, Laternser succeeded in creating a dramatic atmosphere in this, the greatest show on earth at the time. He questioned Goering with a certain solemnity, prefacing each question with *"Herr Reichsmarschall!"*

Goering, if wearing a white wig, could have played the part of the Baron von Muenchhausen or that of a chubby good Germanic fairy, waving a marshal's baton gleaming with diamonds instead of a magic wand. Goering had a high, soft voice. Sitting in the dock, holding forth during the interval, a blanket covering his knees, he reminded one of an old biddy pensioned off on the Riviera. During the war, when he reviewed the troops, the soldiers could not help but notice that the *Reischmarschall* wore outrageous make-up. The rows of medals on his chest were displayed as jewels. Old hands at Nuremberg whispered to me that Goering's propensity for femininity was the result of a war wound that deprived him of part of his virility. This seemed a typically French explanation, offered in a tone of commiseration.[9]

Goering was first among the Accused; he sat closest to me. Behind him, in the back row, sat Doenitz, an intense, fanatical old seadog, hiding his rage behind sunglasses. Another admiral, Raeder, who had sailed under several regimes, sat next to Doenitz. Raeder's photograph, as I had seen it, was kept on the desk of William II's yacht during the Kiel regattas before the 1914 war. Then, Raeder sported a wing-collar and black tie, his hair parted in the middle. He was smiling. All his life he had resembled a distinguished butler, someone who had become very tolerant after observing perhaps too closely the foibles and follies of his superiors. I wondered why the two grand admirals were placed in the second row, as if it were a sign that they were considered less guilty.

Next to them were Baloúr von Schirach and Sauckel. The former ended the war as *Gauleiter* in

---

[9] *Actually, Goering had been wounded in the thigh at the 1923 Putsch at Munich.*

Vienna; for the general public, he had been Fuehrer of the national-socialist youth. He had a certain elegance, and wrote poems to youth. He would have liked to obtain permission to speak on the radio, to tell the young Germans that they had been misled. Sauckel was the only one among the Accused to have the rough look of a manual worker, who had worked his way up by pulling on his own bootstraps. A Communist barrister from Paris, Joe Nordmann, whom I had been asked to accompany – as no one in the delegation seemed anxious to meet such dangerous characters – commented one evening: "I still prefer the worker's mug of Sauckel to the fairy's face of Schirach."

Further along was Jodl. Small, insignificant, in a green military tunic, he was always immersed in a dossier. He was the staff officer *par excellence*, from the artillery, and had been Chief of Operations during the whole of the war. We would see what sort of operation he could still prepare. I could hardly see the other Accused in the second row; only intermittently the mop of white hair belonging to von Papen, Neurath's large paunch below his well-groomed moustache and slicked-down hair. Beyond them were the crewcut of the Austrian Seyss-Inquart and the round head of Speer. Finally, there sat Fritsche, a colourless character if ever there was one, difficult to observe from where I sat.

I was in an even worse position to see the front row except, naturally, Goering, whose body obscured the others. From time to time, Rudolf Hess turned his head to look at us and at the public. Was he actually mad and irresponsible? Was he feigning madness? The question had been amply examined at the beginning of the trial and the international experts held him to be technically responsible: if he had now lost his memory, it was because he had chosen to lose it. I thought he looked very much overwrought. During the Third Reich, if newsreels are any indication, he was just as excitable then. Hess was very high in the hierarchy of the party, but did not enter the government. His part was played within the party, of which he had become the 'conscience'. How much responsibility Hess had remains an enigma.

After Hess, also in the front row, came Ribbentrop, a vain man. He held his head high, his complexion turning from grey to green. He was racked by a deep anxiety. After Munich, Hitler had said: "[Ribbentrop] is better than Bismarck!" However, at Nuremberg it was generally acknowledged that Ribbentrop was not intelligent.

From where I sat I could see no further than Ribbentrop, although I glimpsed the other Accused when they entered the courtroom. There was Keitel, pacing back and forth like a tall gander when space allowed. Kaltenbrunner was an Austrian whose face bore an angry slash. This suggested that he had been a student although in his physique, I thought, he resembled a simple policeman of the 'bruiser' type.[10]

Alfred Rosenberg had, thanks to the publication of his *Der Mythus des 20. Jahrhunderts* (*The Myth of the Twentieth Century*), acquired the reputation of a thinker. I had no occasion to form an opinion of him. Then came Frick, former Minister of the Interior, who wore a sports jacket with a small check. He came

---

[10] *It was a curious experience to see him in 1944 in the audience of the film of the trial of the 20 July plotters, where he sat in the first row, smiling and smug. Less than two years later at Nuremberg he sat in the front row of the Accused: a complete reversal of roles. The scar on his face was the result of a car accident and not, as commonly believed, the consequence of a duel.*

from the Bavarian civil service and had helped Hitler during his beginnings in Munich, particularly at the time of the 1923 Putsch. Between Rosenberg and Frick sat Frank, Governor of Occupied Poland and a trained lawyer. Lalouette often talked of Frank, who in prison converted to Catholicism. In the course of Frank's examination he confessed to everything of which he was accused.[11] He was perhaps the only one of the Accused who did not struggle against approaching death. Curiously, there was a certain similarity between Lalouette and Frank: both faces were impassive and thick-lipped. Next to last in the front row was Funk, President of the *Reichsbank*, a cunning man, head leaning to the right and sunk between his shoulders. Schacht's long neck was the last I could identify along that bench.

The Tribunal had indeed enough to keep itself busy, with twenty-one Accused. Originally, there were also Ley, the labour minister, an alcoholic who had committed suicide in prison, and Gustave Krupp, industrialist, who had been excused because of illness. However, some of the highest individuals of the régime were missing, among them Hitler, Goebbels, Himmler, and Borman. The last was judged in his absence.

As a group, stripped of their uniforms, medals and paraphernalia, far from the fanfare of the military parades and mass meetings, these Germans in the dock looked very ordinary. As someone commented, they could have been chosen at random

---

[11] *During the trial Frank wrote memoirs, published after his death. They contained this revelation: Hitler had entrusted him at one time with the task of researching his own family origins. Frank claimed to have discovered that Hitler was part Jewish, a thesis since taken up by certain authors yet which pleases nobody.*

at the exit of a railway station, all having alighted from the same train: farmers, soldiers, sailors, journalists, civil servants, bourgeois, and Bavarians. The suits they wore at the trial – brown, blue, grey – could have been those of any worker in his Sunday best. Goering alone, whose light-grey tunic hung loose around his hips, seemed still to be in disguise. It took some time to perceive in their attitudes and their bearing the ghosts of what they had been.

The French had placed their future in the hands of these same Nazi chiefs, now sitting quietly in two rows in the dock. I thought back to June 1940 when the French believed that the Germans had won the war and thus surrendered to the same Goering, Ribbentrop, Keitel, and Jodl who today looked rather sheepish.

In 1940 the French did not ask themselves what would constitute peace. It was assumed that after the war, things would somehow return to what they had been before, as if the defeat and Occupation were merely parentheses. No one imagined what the final peace would hold in the event of a German victory, yet Germany could well have won the war. Until 1943, the scales failed to tip decisively on the side of the Allies.

Pétain asked in June 1940 not for the conditions of surrender, but for "the peace conditions". The Germans had themselves been surprised at the request. The Spanish ambassador to France, chosen as intermediary, had to ask Baudouin, the new Minister for Foreign Affairs, to confirm the words, for he could not believe his ears. Indeed, Pétain, Laval, and Baudouin wanted to know the *peace* conditions.[12] The French people did not know this, nor did the British Government. It was a betrayal by those who only the day before were Allies.

The collection of hunched shoulders and greying skulls that I contemplated from one side at Nuremberg had proudly paced up and down the diplomatic scene only a few years before, determining arbitrarily the fate of France and the French. I wondered whether we should pity enemies now that they were powerless, or to remember what they planned to do when power was theirs. Did they simply intend to re-annex Alsace and Lorraine, and even perhaps to incorporate Burgundy, as Himmler was supposed to have said? Burgundy? Why Burgundy? Probably only because it lay next to the German border. Did the Germans themselves know what they wanted in the exhilarating days of victory? Who decided? Goering or Ribbentrop? Keitel or Jodl? To what extent was the Armistice a simple military agreement for a limited period? The situation is not yet completely clear, although with the help of captured German archives and of the secret recordings of the Armistice negotiations we may find out whether the Germans gave to Pétain's plenipotentiaries the *peace* conditions under the cover of these being the Armistice conditions. If this were the case, France's profile within a post-war

---

[12] *Several documents from the German diplomatic archives confirm this. See the telegrams nos. 1929 and 1930 from Stohrer, the German ambassador in Madrid (Auswaertiges Amt, Microfilm 121; 119, 599-601, dossier "St.S. Dtsch. – Frz. Bez. Bd.2") and also the official publication of German diplomatic documents, Vol. IX, doc. No. 459. It is now interesting to note that on 18 June Baudouin in fact had made a declaration, the conclusion of which was, "This is why the government presided over by Marshal Pétain had to ask the enemy what his peace conditions would be." (Jean Montigny, Toute la Verité sur un Mois Dramatique de Notre Histoire, Clermont-Ferrand, 1940, p.15). The word 'peace' had previously gone unnoticed.*

German Europe must be clarified. France would have been split into two and "France" reduced to the southern zone, a largely agricultural France turned towards the Mediterranean Sea, as was Italy, separated from direct access to the open seas of the Atlantic. The demarcation line would have become the permanent border between France and Germany, that is, between southern France and the *départements* placed directly under German influence to the north.[13] Ribbentrop, in his memoirs written in the shadow of the scaffold, noted that the Vichy leaders were talking as if they had won the war. They had no idea, he commented, of what was waiting for them after the end of the war.

Listening to the recording of the Armistice negotiations of June 1940 is enough to dispel any sympathy for Keitel or Jodl. At the time of the victory, they made no efforts to conceal their arrogance. Keitel, in particular, was nicknamed "*Lakaitel*" (the lackey) by his colleagues, who all disliked him. He adopted the jerky delivery, the metallic tone, all of the mannerisms of the voice that could emphasise the superiority of a general staff officer in his hour of triumph. Today, Keitel had an expressionless and empty look, his chin held high yet with a vagueness

---

[13] *For several months in 1946 and later, agents of a French intelligence service went through the German diplomatic archives to find a map of France where the "green line" had allegedly been drawn to represent the border between France and Germany in a future peace treaty. They found nothing; I do not know what information drove their search. The archives of the Ministry of the Interior and, in particular, the files of State Secretary Stuckart should have been consulted. However, I did find, in the archives of the First German Army, which had its headquarters in Bordeaux during the Occupation, a one-millionth scale Michelin map on which had been drawn a thick green line. It was the actual demarcation line. Possibly a simple coincidence, yet it reminded me of the green pencil Ribbentrop used on several occasions to trace the new borders of European states when he still had the power to do so.*

in his washed-out blue eyes. Jodl was bent, his head bowed, examining a dossier – he could not stop working.

Keitel began, in Compiègne in 1940, by reading to the French delegates a Hitler declaration that tried to be moderate, almost accommodating. Hitler said: "We want to erase in this very place, in the performing of the Armistice, the 1918 humiliation. However, Germany does not want to give to the Armistice a character that would be humiliating for so brave an adversary as France." Keitel repeatedly described the conditions offered as *"grosszeugig"* (generous); this Schmidt, the obsequious Schmidt, interpreter of Hitler and Ribbentrop on the grand occasions, translated the adjective perhaps inaccurately as "liberal".

Were the 1940 conditions really to be less humiliating than those of the 1918 Armistice? The Germans tried their best to be amiable. They treated General Huntziger with all possible tact. "This is between soldiers!" they said. Huntziger seized on this word eagerly in trying to establish a personal contact with the Germans. Despite this, whenever Huntziger or ambassador Leon Noël asked for further information, the Germans became furious. The conditions were much harder than they had suspected, most of all regarding the demarcation line that split France into two. The French clung on as best they could, asking for explanations and *"éclaircissements"* (clarifications), a word from the diplomatic vocabulary that allowed them to insist without offending the Germans.

The Germans were becoming impatient, dropping their initially very formal courtesy and thus unmasking themselves. When Jodl took Keitel's place in the course of the negotiations, he showed his irritation with all of those requests for further information, as he thought that by querying them the French were trying to quibble in order to obtain better conditions. He added, "I want to discuss with soldiers, not with lawyers." (Leon Noël was a lawyer.) Keitel, having consulted Goering, returned to the session and said, "All of these questions about details will be settled by the Armistice Commission. Now the question is: do you want, yes or no, to stop the fighting? You must take it or leave it."

The Germans did not need to put themselves out. It emerged clearly from the French statements that their hands were tied – they wanted to sign at any price. The one request constantly put forward by Huntziger was that German troops keep away from Bordeaux, as the French government required time for its "*délibérations*". Marshal Pétain had, prior to the negotiations, sent a telegram to Hitler asking him to stop the advance of his troops on Bordeaux. He had received no answer. Keitel said, "Bordeaux will be spared only if you sign today."

It became obvious during the negotiations that the French diplomats would have some cards to play. The French navy and air force were intact, and could have gone to North Africa or to Britain. That was what the Germans feared most. From the outset, though, Huntziger accepted that the navy and air force would stay where they were. He gave up all other concessions provided that the Germans did not take Bordeaux, which would have prevented Pétain from seizing power. Thus the Armistice – more of a capitulation – was concluded among soldiers. Keitel congratulated Huntziger on having defended French interests so well. He also gave himself full marks: "It is honourable for the victor to honour the vanquished." In conclusion, Keitel asked all participants to stand "to honour those who, on both sides, fell for their country."

Huntziger was so deeply moved that he was unable to respond to Keitel's heavy compliments. Words choked in his throat; he was on the verge of tears. He telephoned Weygand: "It is done, *mon Général*... well, you understand me, *mon Général!*" The faint yet very calm voice of Weygand, that of a distinguished old man, could be heard asking Huntziger to come later to "report" to him.

Were the Armistice conditions actually the peace conditions? At first glance, no. Keitel repeated time and again – too often, perhaps – that these were not the peace conditions, and that these Armistice conditions had been dictated only by the necessity of carrying on the war with Britain, which persisted stubbornly in its desire to fight. Huntziger responded by asking whether it was really necessary to occupy Paris and half of France in order to fight the British. The Occupation of Paris seemed to him particularly shocking. He pleaded: "Would you by any chance intend to prolong the occupation of Paris, which is inside the territory? The Parisian population, you know how emotional they are, how chauvinistic they are, I will admit. Do you really believe it is a good thing for you to want to prolong an occupation such as that of Paris?" His words did not change the attitude of the Germans, who suggested in response that the French government should come back to sit in Occupied Paris.

Did the Agreement contain only clauses characteristic of an Armistice? Huntziger put his finger on an ambiguous section: "I have seen, actually, that this was mentioned further on. The

German government intends to reduce to a strict minimum the occupation of the west coast [of France] after the cessation of hostilities with England. It is true. We understand that you require certain guarantees, of course, but we would like just the same to know approximately what 'the strict minimum' means. This is a question I have already asked."

It was a very pertinent question. For how long did the Germans intend to occupy the Atlantic coast *after* the cessation of hostilities with England? If the conditions of the Armistice were dictated solely with the aim of pursuing the fight with Britain, there was no justification for the occupation of the French coast after the end of hostilities with England. Neither Keitel nor Jodl made any response.[14]

A closer look at Hitler's message, read out by Keitel at the beginning of the negotiations, shows that Hitler suggested a link between Armistice and peace. As it was, it mentioned that three motives inspired the German conditions:

To prevent a resumption of hostilities,

To give Germany full security in the war against England, and

To create the conditions necessary for founding a durable peace.

---

[14] *The clause in question does not appear in certain publications of the text of the Armistice; it was the penultimate paragraph of Article 3: "The German Government intends to reduce to the strict minimum the occupation of the west coast after the cessation of hostilities with England." (Auswaertiges Amt. Handakten Schmidt, Microfilm 66/46.471-2.) See also the official text of the Armistice convention published at the time: Jean Montigny, Toute la vérité sur un mois dramatique de notre histoire, p. 112.*

This last motive seemed to herald the conditions for peace. It would be justifiable to think that there was in the Armistice conditions an element of ambiguity, one not widely perceived by the French at the time yet revealing the deeper intentions of the Germans – the same type of ambiguity encountered a few months later at Montoire. There, too, the true intentions went further than the actual declarations.

Montoire might well have envisaged officially "a collaboration with honour", and the conversation between Hitler and Pétain remained relatively innocuous. The true intentions were very different, as stated in the memo of General Warlimont of 2 November 1940:

The conversation between the *Fuehrer* and Pétain aimed, at the military level, at arriving at a collaboration with France going as far as possible into the future conduct of the war with England. However, it is not envisaged for the time being that France declare itself in a state of war with England. Provisionally, France would adopt, rather, the position of a non-belligerent power, which on its territories would tolerate certain measures taken for conducting the war and would support them if necessary by using its own means of defence. Should this attitude result in a state of war with England, France should be ready to accept also this consequence.[15]

Warlimont acknowledged that the Hitler-Pétain conversation had not covered in detail such steps, and added: "It results, however, from the memo handed to us by Laval and Huntziger on 31 October

---

[15] *This document is now held at the Imperial War Museum, London; it was previously at the Cabinet Office.*

that the French have understood our intentions and approve them."

Montoire and the Collaboration policy divided the French during the war even more than did the Armistice, but in this case too they had not been told everything. Back from Montoire, Pétain in his famous declaration to the French announcing the policy of Collaboration said, "The Armistice is not the peace."

The Germans did not formally grant peace to the France of Pétain any more than they did later to the Norway of Quisling, despite the latter's insistent pleas. The signing of the peace with France would have entailed for Hitler the obligation of freeing the prisoners of war, which would have meant the loss of valued hostages. It was preferable to tell the French that there was talk only of an Armistice, and let them hope for advantageous peace terms. It gave the Germans some leverage to demand from the French a closer alliance with Germany.

In this context, the formula used by Pétain ("The Armistice is not the peace") acquires a new dimension. At first sight it is innocuous enough. The ordinary Frenchmen and –women, who did not know that Pétain had applied for *peace* in June 1940, could attach no significance to such a self-evident statement that the Armistice was not the peace.

At Montoire, Hitler took his partners by degrees further than they really wanted to go; he had done so once before in internal German politics. He was practising the art of deception. Really Hitler wanted to bring France back into the war – on the German side. A speechwriter preparing Pétain's statement after Montoire included the words: "Yes, there has been the Armistice, but it is not the peace, as everybody should know, but it is for another reason not the peace, as we are going in fact to re-enter the war – on the side of the Germans, this time."

Over the issue of peace with France, Hitler manipulated those around him and not only Pétain or Laval. Goering and Ribbentrop were in June 1940 ignorant of the ultimate intentions of the Fuehrer. In the days following the Armistice both Goering and Ribbentrop wanted to elaborate the terms of the peace treaty with France, possibly for each to gain more power.

Hitler did not resolve the conflict between the two; he let the discussion continue through intermediaries at the level of State Secretaries and top civil servants. Ribbentrop wanted the following solution to win acceptance:

It is obvious that inasmuch as the state of war is brought to an end by treaties with foreign governments, the drafting of such treaties, even where they concern internal German affairs, remains the exclusive responsibility of the Auswaertiges Amt. The countries occupied by us, the future fate of which is determined not by international treaties but unilaterally by orders of the Fuehrer or by the laws of the German Reich, must be considered already as part of Great Germany, and consequently the setting up of their economic and financial structure is an internal German affair, for which the Auswaertiges Amt is not competent. For which occupied countries is a unilateral German decision to be taken? The question is not yet settled for the time being. That is why it is necessary, even in the case of those countries, that the possibility of an international settlement must be envisaged and become the object of preparatory work within the *Auswaertiges Amt.*[16]

Thus, on 26 June 1940, Ribbentrop did not then know which Occupied countries would be annexed by Germany (or incorporated into Great Germany). What, then, would be the fate of Luxembourg, Holland, Belgium, and Occupied France? As for Occupied France, there was already no doubt that its economy would from now on be in the hands of the military. By contrast, it seemed confirmed that non-Occupied France, which was to become Vichy France, would be recognised as a sovereign country even though its economy would be integrated into the Great Germany financial complex.

For the time being the future of France remained undecided. Only Hitler could have said what it would be. He gave no say in the matter to Goering or Ribbentrop. Rather, he gave his own instructions to Stuckart, a State Secretary in the Ministry of the Interior, who, incidentally, refused to communicate to Ribbentrop the map he was drawing, saying that the *Fuehrer* had told him not to put anything on paper.[17]

Nevertheless, Stuckart in early July sent a memo to Hitler. It proposed the annexation of the Flemish coast down to the Somme, and the incorporation into the territory of the Reich the provinces of Alsace and Lorraine, including Verdun,

---

[16] *Telegram 112 from Ribbentrop (Baumschule) to Weizsaecker of 26 June 1940. (Auswaertiges Amt. Microfilm 1892H; 426.118-9.)*
[17] *Memo by von Rintelen of 1 July 1940 (Auswaertiges Amt. Microfilm 1892H; 426.197.8.)*

as well as an important part of Burgundy.[18] This was almost exactly what the pan-Germanists had claimed during the First World War.

These proposals were not, however, final. Hitler was playing his cards close to his chest, and did not reveal his plans for a peace with France.[19]

Schacht, through his lawyer, was to say at Nuremberg that Hitler promised everything to everybody and deceived everyone concerning of his ultimate intentions. Schacht saw in this use of ambiguity an excuse for himself. The extent to which Goering and Ribbentrop could have invoked the same justification through showing how the responsibilities were allocated under the Nazi regime, how Hitler took decisions without consulting them and against their judgement, may be considered. They could have proved that their individual responsibilities were not as they seemed. Furthermore, these were not as the tasks usually attached to the exalted posts they occupied. Schacht knew how to keep his distance from Hitler, which neither Goering nor Ribbentrop attempted to accomplish during the trial.

---

[18] *We know this from one of the subsequent Nuremberg trials: Affidavit Globke (NG: 3540) and Affidavit Adolf Kas (NG; 3572). According to Globke, a second memorandum was prepared at a later date on the initiative of Stuckart, proposing merely a return to the 1919 borders. The two documents are kept in Goettingen at the Institut fuer Voelkerrecht. See G. Geschke, Die Deutsche Frankreich-politik 1940, Berlin-Frankfurt, 1960, p. 35.*

[19] *My recent reading of the Ministry of the Interior files for that period leaves me with the impression that the territories occupied by the Wehrmacht in July 1940 were destined to become part of the Reich. Also, when the southern part of France was occupied in November 1942, the legal conditions created by the Armistice were not modified. It was still considered that the sovereignty of the French state prevailed east and south of the line of demarcation, while the status of the occupied zone was settled by the Armistice. (War Diary of the Army Group G, 2 August 1944.) This suggests that the line of demarcation was of lasting importance and that the Armistice had created a permanent situation.*

The Accused, who now appeared harmless, were Germans ill intentioned towards France. It must be asked whether they could be accused of this: at one and the same time accused of what actually took place during the war and of what would have taken place if Germany had won the war; whether Goering, Ribbentrop, Keitel, and Jodl could be blamed for the conditions either of the Armistice or the possible peace.

Who was deceiving whom? Who was really responsible? Did Hitler delude everyone, as Schacht maintained? If so, how did he do it? Or did Hitler himself not know which way he would turn, improvising at every step? He was publicly the champion of simple and radical solutions; a closer look behind the scenes reveals his hesitancy. In 1940 he was considering various solutions while pursuing none to its ultimate conclusion. He weighed up how to attack Britain: directly, by crossing the Channel; indirectly, through a Mediterranean war in Africa and the Middle East, or to make France enter the war, capture Gibraltar, and block the entrance to the Mediterranean Sea. Finally, he met Pétain to try – without telling him openly – to bring France back into the war on the side of Germany.

The hearing always began with a resounding "Atten-SHUN!" from the Marshal of the Court. The whole of the courtroom jumped up and stood to attention. Each time, I saw myself in prison in Toulouse, shouting *"Stil-ge-stand-en!"* while Petit-Louis and his pals straightened up.

The Judges entered. They were almost silent characters except Sir Geoffrey Lawrence, the President, who was a real President and not a public prosecutor. The French magistrates present at the trial were astounded by the 'Anglo-Saxon' procedure. Incredible! The investigation took place at a public hearing! The Accused could be witnesses for their own defence! The Prosecutors were required publicly to produce the proof of guilt and had to accept the Accused's seeing every item critically examined by the Defence!

A public hearing in France is rather stagey – everything takes place quickly, to make it more dramatic. Nuremberg was the opposite of melodrama. Proceedings went quietly and calmly. No one raised a voice. Moreover, with the system of simultaneous translations, only one person at a time could speak into the microphone, and most of the listeners heard only the impersonal voices of the interpreters. Entering the room in the middle of a sitting, the absence of 'atmosphere' came as a surprise. Only a very thin voice, which few could hear directly, was perceived. Even those who understood the language being spoken by the Accused wore headphones. Rhetorical effects were ruled out. From time to time, an orange light would come on in front of the speaker. This meant "Speak more slowly; the interpreters cannot keep up with you." If the speaker became carried away by his own eloquence, the red lamp would light: "Stop! The interpreters have lost you!"

Lord Justice Lawrence cared above all about the dignity of the debates the decorum of the whole proceedings. There would be no shouting, no unexpected interventions, no laughter, only perhaps a few smiles. He allowed himself at most a discreetly humorous remark to put a barrister in his place, and to make sure of the smooth application of the order of procedure that the Tribunal had imposed upon itself.

The other Judges passed the time as best they could. Donnedieu de Vabres, the French Judge, Professor at the Faculty of Law in Paris, had for decades represented France at international congresses of 'penology'. When I was a student, I had the other specialist, Hugeney, as Professor of Penal Law. Donnedieu de Vabres had a square face, with horn-rimmed spectacles and a walrus moustache. He scarcely looked at the public or the Accused. He took notes. When he put down his pen for the last time, having taken notes for six hours a day for about nine months, the trial was concluded. There remained only a verdict. Donnedieu de Vabres' eventual substitute was Falco, weasel-faced, and a Judge at the Court of Cassation. Falco did not write; he was a reader, and consulted endlessly the documents submitted to the Tribunal. Curiously, during my enforced leisure in Toulouse during the last year of the Occupation I met his daughter in the public library where I spent my days. She was working towards a degree in English, and occasionally came to Toulouse. She must have been living some distance away in an isolated village, with her family, in hiding.

The French Judges sat on the extreme left of the President. The Soviet Judges sat on the far right. Their principal Judge was Nikitchenko, wearing a general's uniform. He had *pince-nez* and the air of a strict schoolmaster, severe yet fair. 'Jonas Timoferevitch' was Vice-President of the Supreme Council of the USSR. According to the watered-down confidences of Donnedieu de Vabres after the trial, Nikitchenko was "above all a very correct and very distinguished civil servant", while his deputy, the 'colonel' Volchkov, who was at the same time judge and Professor of Penal Law in Moscow, "seemed prompted by the fervent beliefs of the party."

The two American Judges, placed between the French Judges and the President, were in complete contrast to each other. Biddle held himself very erect; he had the fine head of a greyhound. I was not surprised to learn that he had Indian blood. Maybe this explained the dignity of his posture. A former justice minister, he had moved in political circles and was the organiser of the Tribunal. His deputy, Parker, leaning heavily on his elbows, had the quiet and reassuring air of a trustworthy watchdog.

The President, an iron hand in a velvet glove, adopted an air of inefficiency, pretending to be lost in a mountain of paper, looking at barristers and prosecutors over his spectacles to ask them multiple questions over minute and apparently trivial details relating, usually, to the numbers to be allotted to this or that document. At his side, Sir Norman Birkett would jot down a few words from time to time in a small notebook, raising his eyes towards the ceiling as if seeking inspiration. According to certain members of the British delegation, Birkett spent his time during the lengthy sittings composing poems. Less eccentric than he may have seemed, he discovered in his youth that he had an aptitude for words and dialect. Where could he make the best use of his gifts? – in the legal profession, as a barrister, obviously! In the course of his career, very few of his clients ended their existence at the end of a rope. Rumour has it that Birkett was the one who wrote the Nuremberg Judgement.

The Judges appeared to work in harmony. In practice, only the President spoke during the hearings yet there must have been lively discussions in the Council Chamber. Echoes of these were heard when the other Judges intervened publicly to question the witnesses, the barristers, and even the prosecutors. The Soviet Judge let it be known, in an annexe to the Judgement, that he disagreed with the acquittal of Schacht, von Papen and Fritzsche. Donnedieu de Vabres, who himself differed from Falco on many points, suggested that Nikitchenko and Volchkov did not always agree; also, that Biddle, a Democrat with the Roosevelt Administration, was sometimes in conflict with Parker, who belonged to the Republican Party. Only the British, it seemed, took a united stand. Moreover, Donnedieu noted that Birkett possessed "the art of finding at the end of discussions the clever formula that would minimise disagreements." During and after the trial, the Soviets like to publicise the complete harmony prevailing at Nuremberg among wartime Allies, and wished that, as agreed, more trials should follow. However, the Soviets had their own reasons for distinguishing between the French Judges: Falco, for whom they expressed an unqualified admiration, and Donnedieu, whom they would not have minded discrediting. The Soviets took note of the 'relations' of the very aggressive Dr. Seidl, defending the Justice Minister, who told the Tribunal how Donnedieu de Vabres, in the course of his missions abroad before the war, had visited the German Law Academy, of which Frank was President. On that occasion Donnedieu made a speech in which he commented: "The present advantage of a totalitarian regime comes from its energy, its vigour of youth capable of satisfying new needs as they arise."[20]

The Russians also remembered what Donnedieu said during the trial, probably in the Council Chamber: "The law of nations recognises as combatants only men in military uniform. If the

---

[20] See Arkadi Poltork, *Le procès de Nuremberg*, Moscow, 1969.

people rise up in arms, they are acting as outlaws. The enemy is justified in holding such subjects to be rioters and to shoot them without hesitation."[21]

---

[21] *Ibid.*

CHAPTER 4

The Plea for Streicher

On 12 July 1946, Marx, Defence Counsel for Streicher, continued with his speech. In many respects, Streicher passed for an exemplary Nazi. He had been one of the first Party members, *Gauleiter* of Nuremberg, and editor of the *Stuermer*, an anti-clerical yet above all anti-Semitic publication. Obviously, Streicher was indefensible. Anti-Semitism had become a phrase one hardly dared mention; it evoked all of the awful crimes committed against the Jews, as well as others, and immediately caused an embarrassed reaction from non-Jews.

The *Stuermer* was, before the war, regularly quoted in the Western press, week after week, as the paradigm of what was really in Nazi minds. Events proved that the anti-Semitism of the Nazis was not merely a propaganda theme. The Nazis quite simply eliminated the Jews physically. What, then, could Streicher's Counsel for the Defence say? Marx did his best; he tried to prove that Streicher's part had not been as might have been assumed, that Streicher was not prominent in the Nazi regime, and, consequently, that he could not be considered a "Major War Criminal".

Admittedly, said the Counsel, Streicher had been a member of the Party from its beginnings. This cannot be denied. Nevertheless, it cannot be said that the Party pursued criminal aims from the outset. Its programme was not at all secret, and it aimed at taking power only through legal means. It would be undemocratic to reproach Streicher today with having belonged to a Party recognised and accepted by the Weimar Republic. Streicher may be criticised for supporting Hitler's rise to power, yet it is surely the aim of all political parties to come to power.

The whole of Marx's pleadings in favour of Streicher were unpleasant. It was tempting to counter every single one of the arguments he put forward, and instead to say that the Nazi party was indeed not like the others, that it was undemocratic, and that it proposed nothing less than the suppression of all other parties. Unfortunately, the Prosecution laid itself open to criticism, as it had formulated a general charge of conspiracy against all of the Accused. The conspiracy implied that there was a direct link between, firstly, the agitation of Hitler and the Nazis in Munich at the time of the 1923 *Putsch* and, secondly, everything that took place later, including the concentration camps. This thesis could have been upheld by an historian, although it may not have been sufficient to justify a condemnation. The personal responsibility of Streicher had to be proved.

His Counsel demonstrated that Streicher could not have played a part in the wars of aggression. After the Nazi Party came to power, Streicher was not close to Hitler. In any case, after 1938 Streicher had no personal contact with the Party leaders, Hitler, Goering, Goebbels, Himmler or Bormann. Hitler did not involve Streicher in the drawing up of military plans.

There remained, however, the problem of disposing of the accusation of anti-Semitism, which could not be denied. Marx proposed a rather radical and unexpected thesis, which made the issue disappear as if by magic. One cannot, he claimed, reproach Streicher with having converted the Germans to anti-Semitism. It was a fact that there was no hatred for the Jews in the hearts or minds of the German people or of the German youth. The persecution of the Jews had been the work not of the people, but of the government. The latter had to make laws to exclude the Jews from the national community. The pogroms such as *Kristallnacht* were organised by the Nazi leaders – and were not a spontaneous reaction of the people to the murder of von Rath, the diplomat at the German Embassy in Paris. It could not be claimed that the *Stuermer* had implanted or fostered anti-Semitism in Germany.

The Germans were not anti-Semitic, after all. I was not the only one to find this hard to believe, especially given the feelings of the French in this respect. Perhaps the Germans' anti-Semitism was of a different quality. While the *Stuermer* stood out for its vulgarity, *l'Action Française* – equally anti-Semitic – was written in an elegant style by authors such as Charles Maurras, and did not address itself to the lower classes. In my native Vendée it was read, rather, by country squires and was to be found more often in châteaux than in thatched cottages.

I did not have to look very far afield to find evidence of the existence of anti-Semitism in France. I had only to evoke the family atmosphere I had found in Montpellier in 1941, when I was demobilised and when, instead of going back to Paris, I took refuge in my maternal grandfather's home. My grandfather was a genuine anti-Dreyfusard; his dinner-table conversation since the Affair had not ceased, in the course of several generations, to denounce the Jews. In 1941 he saw a direct consequence of the Blum ministry of 1936 in the then current misfortunes of France. At his side, my uncle was no less extreme and fanatical in his political views. He was more racist than anti-Semitic (he did not read the Drumont of *La France Juive*). My uncle was a patriot and war veteran of 1914-18; his mentality was not very different from that of the average Nazi in Germany. He had, since 1934, been a militant with the *Volontaires Nationaux*, led by Colonel de la Rocque.

My uncle told me in 1941 of the almost conspiratorial political activities before the war: the nighttime rides, the mass meetings in the depths of the countryside, all carried out with military precision. Then came the sudden appearance of the Chief, revealed in spotlights and car headlamps. Here was de la Rocque himself, come to harangue the faithful. It was adventure with a scent of illegality.

The aims of the militants could have been to seize power by driving the Deputies out of the Chamber, thus to impose a strong regime and to save France from its perils. Hitler's Germany threatened. The Communists were talking in loud voices, brandishing the spectre of the workers' seizing power and no doubt preparing for the great upheaval. At the same time, as *l'Action Française* repeatedly maintained, the Christian Democrats were dragging Brittany away from the traditional ideas in order to hand it over to "the Commies".

De la Rocque was carried as if on a wave, but my uncle felt that he was not a man of action. "Action" would have meant destroying everything, creating a *Putsch* in Paris and settling accounts at village level with a Radical Mayor and a Socialist schoolteacher. Alas, de la Rocque was a "wet". He was someone who could push an opponent. At those meetings in the dead of night de la Rocque talked of social problems: he had himself seen, he said, in the Paris suburbs, young mothers who did not even have teats to bottle-feed their babies! For the fanatic faithful, ready to leap to the attack of anything, the story of the teats was not enough to stir their spirit.

Listening to these tales, I dared not smile, for my uncle was a giant. He saw no humour in such matters and was quick to use a blow to enforce an argument. I saw in his talk, however, a contradiction I was also to perceive among the Nazis: my uncle was in favour of law and order, of traditional ideas, of maintaining society as it was, yet at the same time he was against all institutions, against the politicians (they were all corrupt), against the bureaucrats (all loafers), against the generals (if they were Republicans), and even against the clergy (if they meddled in politics). I was confronted with the actual problem of 'revolutionary conservatism'. Goebbels, for Germany, had thought it necessary to explain himself on this topic by pondering aloud whether the National Socialist Party was revolutionary. His answer was obscure – hardly surprising, as the Nazis were better at playing on emotions than at manipulating ideas. Moreover, when he examined this question, Goebbels was already in power. He could not too clearly define himself as a 'revolutionary' and thus alarm the major industrialists and right-thinking middle classes, whose support was necessary to the Nazis.[22]

The attempt by Streicher's Counsel to 'whitewash' the German people in the context of anti-Semitism seemed to me rather blatant trickery. The issue now arose as to how to give an account of such a plea without giving in any way the impression that I accepted its validity. A nice chore for my first day in the courtroom!

Thinking back to Caffarelli two years earlier, I asked myself what my Jewish companions there, mostly of German origin, would have said if they had heard the speech by Streicher's Counsel. I was fairly close to them, and sought their company during the evening "breaks", which we took all together: men and women, Jews and "Aryans". I listened to their conversation in German with the *Unteroffizier* and the other guards. They talked of the Germany they had known, with lingering nostalgia. They wondered why the Gestapo hunted those Germans down as far as the south of France, Germans who had done everything possible to leave a Germany that did not want them.

---

[22] *To understand that the question could have been asked, it is useful to know the intellectual context, studied before the war by Vermeil in Doctrinaires de la Revolution Allemande 1918-1938 (Paris, 1938). These doctrinaires of the German (i.e., nationalist) Revolution include among their ranks names that it today seems surprising to place side by side: Walter Tathenau, Keyserling, Thomas Mann, Oswald Spengler, Moeller van den Bruck, the group of the "Tat", as well as Hitler, Rosenberg, Darre, Ley and Goebbels, to whom Nietzsche should be added. More recently, an American scholar has written a thesis on the theorists of the "conservative revolution" under the Weimar Republic (Jeffrey Charles Herf, Reactionary Modernism: Reconciliation of technics and unreason in Weimar Germany and the Third Reich, Brandeis University, 1981). He quotes the names of Hans Freyer, Ernst Juenger, Carl Schmitt, Werner Sombart and Oswald Spengler.*

In Caffarelli, the atmosphere in the Jewish quarters was very different from that among the "Aryans". First of all, there was a social difference. The Jews had respectable professions, such as businessmen and barristers. A few had become farmers because of the war. Among the Aryans we were rather on the fringes of society. The Jews of Caffarelli still believed in the innate goodness of humanity and in the virtues of society.

The Aryans, for their part, at least knew why they were there. I was a *"refractaire"* to the *Service du Travail Obligatoire* (the STO; National Service), in other words, a draft dodger,[23] and when arrested was carrying false papers. This latter crime was punishable by the death penalty during the last days of the Occupation, according to a decision taken by the General commanding in Toulouse. I should have been worried when this was published in the *Dépêche de Toulouse*, which we were getting every day through the little hunchback from the market of the Capitole square; it was hidden at the bottom of crates of courgettes.

For the other Aryans, prison constituted a normal risk of the life they were leading – an occupational hazard. They, at least, lingered no longer under the respectful illusions held by the Jews. The Aryans sniggered about the words of the *Maréchal*: "Frenchmen, you have been deceived ... I keep my promises and even those made by others!" They hummed derisively: "*Maréchal*, here we are! You have given us hope..." They laughed when one of the Petit-Louis gang gave the address of a judge at the

---

[23] *I evaded the S.T.O., the official description under the Occupation of what became known after the war and at Nuremberg as "slave labour".*

Court of Appeal for some small toilet article to be collected. (Very obligingly, the Gestapo had offered to go on such errands so as to allow the internees to keep themselves clean and to shave every day.) On the Aryan side, everything 'respectable' was held up to ridicule and inmates felt freer to express themselves than they did outside prison.

In the evenings in the courtyard, while dusk fell a little earlier each day, it was felt that the Jews were becoming progressively disheartened even if they kept their faith in the future. A blonde woman with a matte complexion and a Slavonic charm told me, "I am fed up. The first thing I shall do when I leave this place will be to have my children baptised. I am fed up. It has lasted too long." The men expressed themselves more crudely: "*Ich habe die Kanale voll!*" ("My 'canal' is full, i.e., I've had enough.")

The most moving moment at Caffarelli took place on the day before the departure of the 30 July convoy. There was great agitation in the Jewish quarters. The Parisian barrister I had often seen before the war in the hall of the law courts had a handsome leonine head with a ginger mane. He lifted his chin, adopting the pose of a tribune, and roared. He was attempting to dominate the crowd and to calm the panic spreading through the quarters, especially through groups of women surrounded by a crowd of young children, many between eight months and two years old. On the staircase, a few men would grab hold of a visitor who was leaving. "Tell my wife I am very courageous," said one of them, still wearing a well-cut checked suit and suède shoes. These past few years he had made a good living growing strawberries a few miles outside Toulouse. Another, who might have been about twenty years old and was powerfully built, stiffened as if to attention to tell that visitor, his last link with the outside world, with his family, and with his past life: "Make sure to tell them that I am leaving with courage and that the youth of France will know how to do their duty." He was probably conscripted into the *Chantiers de Jeunesse* and had retained a *Jeune du Maréchal* style. He believed utterly that he was French – until the Germans discovered that he was a Jew.

The following day, when the convoy was forming, Muehlhausen, the *Unteroffizier*, was getting worried. He feared turmoil and panic. The Jews could attempt a mass escape he would not be able to control. If the Jews had known what Muehlhausen knew about their ultimate destination, they might have made a desperate gesture – anything rather than leave. Muehlhausen went from one group to another, saying: "*Machen Sie keine Gedanken ... Sie worden einem Arbeitsplatz kriegen!*" ("Don't worry – you'll be given a job" [once in Germany]).

Then it was eight o'clock in the morning, the time of departure. The Gestapo were there. Those departing formed two square groups: the Jews, and the Aryans. Even now the Gestapo insisted that they should not mix. They were counted and re-counted. There were about two hundred. We who were staying behind made ourselves as invisible as possible. If the numbers failed to tally, one or two of us would be taken to make the squares perfect. The groups waited for more than an hour, carefully drawn up in lines, a small bundle in front of each one. Among the Aryans there were Petit-Louis and some of the more noteworthy of his group, in particular the Belgian owner of No. 4, the brothel that employed without doubt the most beautiful girls in Toulouse. The issue remained as to how to make a choice among the companions of Petit-Louis. Preference was given to the "heads", those responsible for running the organisation. I think the Gestapo wanted to get rid of the richer among them, for the arrest of the Petit-Louis gang had been a financial operation. The Toulouse Gestapo was short of funds. Its aim was to get their hands on the money lying on the gambling tables of the dive. Once the richer ones were gone, it would be easier to confiscate their wealth at leisure.

Our companions left. They were not seen again. Nobody at that time knew what happened to them. I enquired about it in Toulouse after the Liberation, but their destination was still a mystery. I am not aware that anything further is known today. The fact was that after 30 July, rail travel became difficult. Our companions from Caffarelli, I was told, spent about ten days in Toulouse station, the doors of their cattle trucks standing open. They cooked on the platform. The train eventually left. No news came afterwards. I knew that Petit-Louis was planning to escape on the way. He had hidden a saw in his bundle and expected to be able to cut a section out of the floor of his truck. He deserved to save his neck.

I do not believe that the Jews I saw leaving knew what awaited them. They had heard of Drancy, the first stop in their exodus. Drancy was still France. They did not know they were destined to die. *Unteroffizier* Muehlhausen and the soldiers and warders must have known much more. If not, why the reassurances when they were leaving? Some staff accompanied former convoys to their final destinations in Germany.

Now, in Nuremberg, I imagined myself telling the Jews on the day before they left what Streicher's lawyer was saying: "You know, deep down, the Germans are not really anti-Semitic. – And Streicher, whom you knew at least by repute, is merely a journalist who expresses his personal opinion, as he is fully entitled to do."

Was the publication of the *Stuermer* evidence of the existence of latent anti-Semitism among the Germans? After all, if there is a market for a product, it is because there is a demand. Streicher's Counsel described the diverse fortunes of the magazine. Originally a rag printing 3,000 copies in 1923, the *Stuermer*'s circulation reached 10,000 copies in 1933, and 20,000 the day before the Nazis seized power. In any case, the *Stuermer* was a private publication, not an official one of the Party. Its success was due in large part to the fact that the professional businessman, Fink, had been appointed Managing Director. He knew his way around business matters. Also, he had persuaded Dr. Ley, chief of the Labour Front, to launch an appeal in favour of the *Stuermer*. Another factor was that a certain number of Germans thought that by subscribing to the *Stuermer* they were proving their loyalty towards the new regime and thus preparing their entry into the Party.

If such an explanation were accepted, the Germans under Hitler were not really anti-Semites. At most they pretended to be in order to gain admittance to the Party. This is a perfect definition of opportunism. The explanation is, however, less credible in the case of the *SA* or the *SS*.

While his Counsel made his plea, Streicher remained impassive. He calmly chewed his gum, apparently unperturbed by the occasion. He considered the Tribunal a Jewish machination, he confided to Dr. Gilbert, the officially appointed psychologist. To tell the truth Streicher, an ugly man, had little chance of avoiding the death penalty.[24]

After Counsel's speech for Streicher I began to feel nauseous. This would haunt me in the days and weeks to come. It would make me lose my taste for the task at hand, although I had begun willingly enough when studying the Schacht case. Lalouette realised that my mood had changed. He liked less and less my drafts of "letters" or "telegrams". He was to say: "Well, then, you are no longer interested in the trial."

Why this nausea? It reminded me of the smell that hit you in the face when you entered a railway carriage or a tram packed with Germans, badly dressed and haggard, wrapped in oversized overcoats, emaciated bodies wearing mountain-infantry peaked caps from which the badges had been stripped, a smell perhaps of cold cigars or of badly digested cabbage, the reek of a routed army and of decay.

---

[24] *A member of the US prosecution team, Robert Kempner, made Hoegner the following proposition to the Bavarian Prime Minister: "Don't you want to have Streicher? After all, he is Bavarian. We don't know if he falls under the London Statute. Was he really one of the Main War Criminals, or was he involved only at the ideological level?" Hoegner replied: "Don't do that to me. We wouldn't know what to do with him." (Kempner, Anklaeger einer Epoche, p. 278.)*

CHAPTER 5

The *Fuehrerprinzip*

The morning of 12 July saw the end of the pleas for Streicher. I had some difficulty in putting my reactions into some form of order. The next Counsel was already hard at it, declaring that his client, Funk, was truly a person of no importance, a man without responsibilities. Funk had never held a post within the Party; he had never been in either the *SS* or the *SA*. Admittedly, he had been a member of the *Reichskabinett*, but this organisation had never met after he was appointed Minister for the Economy in 1937. He never had dealings with Hitler, except for the period between February 1933 and August 1934, when he had been Press Chief. This was in fact a time when Hindenburg was still President of the *Reich*, so it will be understood that, given a person of such respectability as Head of State, how can a mere spokesman be reproached for doing what he was told?

Excuses showered thick and fast, seemingly irrefutable. I could see a time when I would content myself with simply noting them down as they emerged, just to see how they would look on paper.

When the morning sitting came to an end, I made for Lalouette's office, next to that of the French judges. The crowd from the court spilled out into the corridors. Counsel, journalists, and visitors disported themselves like schoolchildren who had waited too long for break. The two Soviet Judges in uniform had been the first to leave; they flanked a bald, stocky man in plain clothes, "the man from the *Guepeou*" [the Soviet State police] as Dubost, who pretended to be well informed, described him. The three exchanged enormous jokes; their laughter reverberated throughout the corridors. They rushed and disappeared into their second-floor quarters, the most sinister in the building because no one else ever went there.

Lalouette's office was empty. It was a hot day. The window was open. Opposite, American soldiers from the unit in charge of security were playing the guitar. Reflected in the windowpanes of their room was a view of what was going on in the office of the French judges' staff next door to me. I sat at my small table. Some papers were spread out on Lalouette's desk. They included the transcript of yesterday's court proceedings and a memo from the Quai d'Orsay, which began: "My dear Roger, I went down yesterday to the *Secrétariat des Conférences* and I saw that you were on the list of the next delegation to the UN in New York..."

The door opened. Lalouette, La Gorce, and Gerthoffer were finishing a conversation. Gerthoffer slid into Lalouette's office, angling his shoulder to enter easily, slipping into the room like an eel – and like an eel he had a shiny head. He wanted to show himself as amiable and charming. How pleasant it must be, as a top civil servant surrounded by top civil servants, all so cultured, so witty, and so charming. Gerthoffer was winding up: "–And moreover, the same ratio was to be found on the ground in 1940, when the Germans lined up ten armoured divisions against one French one...". Gerthoffer was doubtless an enlightened Alsatian, with no trace of a German accent. He spoke in a calm, relaxed voice with smooth diction; his monotone blunted the sharper edges of arguments.

The faces of Lalouette and La Gorce remained impassive, yet as soon as Gerthoffer left the room they relaxed and began to comment. La Gorce allowed himself to chuckle, a sign that, sure of his partner's agreement, he thought he could speak freely. Gerthoffer held Schacht responsible for German re-armament, and also for the French defeat. Noticing I was there, Lalouette asked, "Well! What have to tell us about the goings on in the courtroom?"

"This morning," I answered, "Streicher's Counsel concluded his speech."

"What arguments could he use?"

"He said that Streicher was a journalist who had certain ideas about the Jewish problem and that it would be anti-democratic to blame him for expressing himself freely on this subject. He also said that the Germans were not anti-Semitic."

I noticed straight away that this was a version of Streicher's case that Lalouette did not like very much. He cast a nasty glance at me when I reported that the Germans were not anti-Semitic. He sensed that I could be a potential troublemaker or, as the Jesuits say, *un mauvais esprit*. But it was only a temporary cloud, quickly dispersed. What difference did it make, anyhow? Lalouette invited his two 'confidants', La Gorce and me, to lunch, each paying his share – moreover, in Occupation marks. Lalouette was afraid of gaining weight so he filled only three of the twelve sections of the giant American army tray. Foolishly, I let the cooks fill all of them on mine.

Dinner-table conversation among diplomats is often brilliant. Each has a stock of good stories carefully selected to ensure the raconteur's success. Lalouette's stories always unfolded against a dramatic background. It was a fact that his early years in the diplomatic corps coincided with a dangerous period on the international scene. Today, he told the story of Dollfuss' assassination, although this time with a variation. After having recounted how, as ever on the look-out for something to happen, he found himself alone in the presence of the still warm corpse of the little Chancellor of Austria stretched on a divan, he added – and this was the variation: "I rang the Quai d'Orsay, where they were beginning to panic. They were saying, '–But tell us what is going on! Is it war?' I replied, 'Wait! We are in the process of enciphering a long telegram about the events!' When the *Putsch* failed, the German Ambassador let himself become involved in negotiating in favour of the Nazis. An unforgivable gaffe! His successor von Papen had a different style."

This was the point where Lalouette introduced his tale about von Papen: both had been invited to the same shooting party. Lalouette made representations to his host about the advisability of this, but von Papen had shown an almost excessive courtesy towards him, beckoning his chauffeur to drive them even when they had only a few hundred yards to walk.

Several stories alluded, with a touch of respect, to President Daladier. We heard again the story of Roosevelt's telephone call when Daladier was dining at the US Embassy. Roosevelt greeted him with "Hello, Ed!" Daladier did not know how to respond.

I always thought, though, that beneath the veneer of a brilliant diplomat there was in Lalouette a simple fellow who might actually have preferred the years spent in the army to those spent in the embassies. His favourite anecdote was that of a soldier who had been punished on the following grounds: "Left the barracks walking backwards pretending that he was entering." He was so amused by this that he must have seen in it a deeper meaning – that in difficult situations, diplomats try to give the impression of moving forwards while in reality they are retreating.

La Gorce remained pensive. He was discreet about his military life in 1939-40, yet attached great importance to his enlistment in de Lattre's army after the Liberation. He had become a consular attaché under Vichy, and seemed sure of one day entering upon *"la grande carrière"* thanks to his personal connections. La Gorce still looked at the diplomats from the outside, observing them very closely to copy their attitudes and their mannerisms. When I knew him, at the time of the Nuremberg Trial, he had mixed at and frequented the Quai d'Orsay sufficiently to adopt a disenchanted stance. It was as if La Gorce summed up his years of experience in the formula: "To be a good diplomat, one must not be too intelligent." Sometimes, he gave way to an excessive pessimism, quoting to himself the example of the truly great diplomats such as Talleyrand, who had been great because, in the end, he believed in nothing. However, deep down La Gorce was a nice young man still apprehensive about his future as he was thinking of getting married.

Gerthoffer came over to our table, putting on airs and graces, before leaving the canteen. Tolstoi, the Russian interpreter, threw out in passing the information that he had just been offered a post of interpreter at the UN. I commented to Lalouette, "Then the UN seems to be the natural follow-up to Nuremberg." He stared at me fixedly without saying anything, maybe with the intention of embarrassing me. I added, as if to excuse myself, "Yes. He is the third interpreter to be recruited here for the next session of the UN."

Lalouette calmed down. While I was offering him this explanation, I suddenly realised what was going on in his mind and remembered the letter left on his desk, which mentioned his next posting to the UN. Lalouette possibly thought that I had been going through his correspondence and discovered this news. He wanted to be clear about it in his own mind. A few days later, after the morning sitting, he said: "You are staying a little while in the office, are you not? I have a conference that will keep me busy until lunchtime."

I noticed that there were many papers scattered on his desk, and smelled a trap. The window was open; from the next room, that of the French judges and their assistants, all of my moves were reflected in the windows of the building opposite. Thus, I remained quietly at my desk without moving from it that whole hour. Lalouette came back with a broad smile on his face, maybe intended to assure me of his renewed confidence.

In the afternoon, Funk's Counsel resumed his speech: his client was, after all, merely a civil servant and as such simply did his duty. It was true that Funk looked rather colourless. Technically, he was not one of Hitler's old comrades-in-arms (*die alten Kaempfer*) as he became a Nazi only after 1936. Nevertheless, Funk fitted well into the front rank of the group along with Rosenberg and Streicher, and including Frick and Frank, who had been militants almost from the start and had participated in the Munich *Putsch* of 1923. This group, whom I could not see very well from my seat, adopted the rather passive attitude of the Accused who realise that they will have to pay for their misdeeds.

Funk was stooped, his head sunk between his shoulders, yet his voice held a fairly deep and almost ironic resonance. He could have been a storyteller specialising, probably, in racy tales. He had been both civil servant and Minister of the Economy, head of the *Reichsbank*, admittedly lacking the authority to take initiatives since he was placed below Goering. He could possibly be held responsible for crimes against humanity because gold teeth and gold spectacle frames belonging to exterminated Jews were deposited in the vaults of the *Reichsbank*. The Finance Minister, Count Schwerin von Krosigk, had also been involved in the administration of Jewish property. The Counsel thus wanted to know why he was not present at Nuremberg.

In the course of the long speeches for the Defence, I became thoroughly bored and fought with difficulty against dozing off, especially in the afternoon after those much too heavy lunches in the canteen. I saw in my mind's eye the immense tray, each compartment filled by the army cooks as I passed along the counter: a piece of meat, then another, two or three vegetables on top of a corn cob in the corner, and at least two desserts, one a piece of dry cake, the other in the category known by the British as pudding. I ate the lot. Having been hungry for four years, what a dream – or what a nightmare! It was *"la douceur de vivre"* [the sweetness of living] regained. It was paradoxical that under these conditions I was required to evoke the sufferings and deaths of others.

There had previously been a few afternoons of greater interest. Suddenly, an unexpected witness was called. Kempka had been Hitler's former chauffeur, a lout, broad-shouldered and well fed for many years, not very talkative, and then in a flat voice. Bormann's Counsel had him summoned to testify on his patron's death. Kempka was barely intelligible. The President interrupted him several times, saying: "You are speaking too fast! What did he ask you? ... You are still speaking too fast. The last thing I heard was that Bormann was walking in the middle of the line [of people]. Is this correct?" Dodd, the deputy of the American Prosecutor, Jackson, got involved: "You are the only person who can state that Hitler and Bormann are dead."

At the time, Kempka seemed unconvincing as a witness, although all of his assertions were confirmed in later years. What he had to say was fairly precise: on the night of the first to the second of May, he met Bormann near the railway station of the Friedrichstrasse, near a bridge over the Spree known as the Weidendammbruecke. "What was going on at the Friedrichstrasse station?" Bormann asked. "Almost impossible to get through!" Kempka answered. "But with tanks?" asked Bormann. As it happened, tanks and armoured vehicles arrived at this moment. Walking on the left of the convoy Bormann moved forward close to the first tank, which he used as a shield. The column of tanks approached an anti-tank roadblock. After the first tank had gone 40 or 50 metres beyond it, Kempka saw a column of flames. The tank reared into the air, hit precisely on the side where Borman was walking. It was probably the work of a *Panzerfaust* shot from a window. Kempka himself was thrown to one side, unconscious, by the explosion. He did not see what happened to Bormann, whom he called the *Reichsleiter*.

In answer to precise questioning, Kempka said that Bormann was wearing a leather coat, the cap of an SS officer, and the badges of an *Obergruppenfuehrer*. He had met Bormann by chance on the bridge and took cover himself, three or four metres behind Bormann's tank. Kempka had left the Chancellory shelter at about nine o'clock in the evening.

And Hitler? "I can say that Hitler is dead and that he died on 30 April in the afternoon."

Dodd: "I know, but did you see him dying?"

Kempka: "No, I did not see him dying."

He had carried Hitler's corpse outside the shelter, then Eva Braun's. He set fire to them.

Dodd: "Did you actually see Hitler?"

Kempka: "I did not see him himself. The blanket in which he was wrapped was a bit too short and I saw only his legs hanging."

Why was Kempka not believed? Hitler and Bormann had become mythological figures, and myths do not die that easily. Also, the existence of any precise event is in doubt so long as there is no decisive proof. Historians well know that all too often the definitive proof is within touching distance, but the eyewitness needed for confirmation remains elusive. Only probabilities remain.

I did not realise it then, but there was a political significance to the question as to whether or not Hitler was dead. According to Trevor-Roper, the Russians were spreading the rumour that Hitler was alive and had taken refuge in the British Zone of Occupation with the complicity of the authorities. Trevor-Roper's enquiry held the reader spellbound better than any thriller. *The Last Days of Hitler* provided no final proof of Hitler's death yet the work succeeded in re-creating the fantastic atmosphere of Hitler's end. The author made generous use of the diary of "this silly man" Schwerin von Krosigk (a Rhodes scholar), who had stayed in the bunker with Hitler almost until the end.

For me, the most important afternoon was that when an older university Professor came to the lectern and the microphone. He was bent, his face emaciated, with wrinkles so deep they could have been engraved with the calamities of war; he was wrapped in his thick academic gown. He appeared very sensitive to the cold, but when he started to talk he hammered out his words in the diction of a man accustomed to dominating large audiences of students. The name of Professor Jahrreiss was not unknown to me; it was a name encountered frequently in the footnotes of textbooks on public law. What he said was of extraordinary clarity. He inaugurated a phase in the speeches for the Defence by giving a legal opinion of benefit to all of the Accused. He did not fail in his task. As with one stroke of the magic word he proved every single one innocent. Hitler alone, he said, could be guilty. This was the unavoidable consequence of the *Fuehrerprinzip*. But Hitler was not here.

Having caught this vital point in his argument, I escaped in my memory from the four walls of the courtroom. I relived the hot afternoons of Toulouse at Caffarelli two years earlier, in August 1944. The last convoy had left. The few who remained, Jews or Aryans, had a privileged status. They were already veterans, and when the prison filled up again in the course of the coming weeks would be entrusted with administrative tasks of one type or another, which would give them some small benefits. I had become assistant cook, which entitled me to walk around the building and the courtyard freely, instead of being locked up in one room. I had the relative liberty of going from one floor to another, of entering the courtyard, of sawing wood and fuelling the field kitchen where we would re-heat the courgette soup sent by the *Secours National.*

In the courtyard I walked around, back and forth, passing the only four Aryan ladies of Caffarelli; they, too, enjoyed privileges. Rather than being locked up, as were their Jewish counterparts with their children, they had the right to sunbathe out of doors. Another assistant cook noticed my frequent comings and goings near the four women. He whispered in my ear: "One can see that you too are a Parisian; you can't help looking at them." Actually, they returned my smiles, confident and defenceless. They were of very diverse origins. There was the young Comtesse de M., 26 years old, a brunette with a matte complexion. Her husband, a regular army officer, was fighting in the Gaullist ranks. Three tons of arms had been found in her château in the Gers, and she was unlikely to be released any time soon. I rarely had occasion to talk to her. She was worried about her figure: "My husband has known me slim; I shall have to lose weight before he sees me again." In contrast, it was easier to enter into conversation with Lysette. She was older, almost motherly in her attitude towards men. Lysette was blonde; I knew her by sight before my arrest. She wore the same red dress she had on when she spent her evenings at the "American bar" of a fairly posh café behind the *Grand Marché*. On warm evenings, the windows were wide open, and Lysette could be seen smoking blonde cigarettes and posing as a *femme fatale*. "Why is she here?" I asked one day. "She was a prostitute and one evening she refused to sleep with one of the *Gestapists*. The same evening she found herself in prison." He was in fact a French *Gestapist* of Italian origin, puny and greedy.

Lysette once showed me a photograph of her eight-year-old daughter, who was very pretty in her short skirt. Her daughter came every evening with her fiancé. They stood behind the barracks and signalled over the wall to her mother, who was standing at a window on the second floor. When I looked at the picture, Lysette told me to "Look here! Look at her legs! Hey?"

One day, one of the French *Gestapists*, who must have belonged formerly to the Toulouse underworld, came to our room for a friendly visit. This was before the departure of the 30 July convoy. He pretended not to recognise his former pals despite the fact that each asked him, "And me? Will I get out soon?" He answered with a certain unction, in a deep, calm voice, rolling his 'r's, playing the part of a priest-confessor who of course wanted to be understanding but remained somehow threatening: "Ah, you, what a mess you've got yourself into."

He was impeccably dressed in a dark striped suit, his houndstooth tie bulging just enough to be held back by a precious stone mounted on the tie-pin. When it was Lysette's turn to ask, "And me? Will I get out soon?" he answered with a smile, "Why? Don't you like it here?" Lysette said, "But it is my daughter I am worried about. She is eighteen, and I would like to be able to keep an eye on her." This man had, it seemed, been a tailor before he joined the Gestapo; when he was gone, one of his old pals started to say, "When I see this poor Fernand...". Petit-Louis interrupted him abruptly. "Shut your mouth! Wait until we are outside."

A few weeks after the Liberation, I bumped into the third of the four Aryans in Toulouse. She immediately kissed me on both cheeks, moved, probably, by the memory of the ordeals we had shared a month earlier. I remembered she was quite a talker; she would tell the other women in the greatest detail about the problems of her past life. I had caught, passing by, bits of sentences such as, "Then I told my husband, if you do not buy me a car, I shall divorce you." She was tall, brunette, broad-shouldered, and impulsive. I noticed that every evening at exercise break a cluster of men gathered anxiously outside a room next to ours, reserved in the old days for the NCOs. That room was unoccupied during the day. Inside, on the left, there was straw for five or six people; the right-hand side had been carefully swept. It was grey with a layer of dust, but there was not one wisp of straw – exactly as *Unteroffizier* Muehlhausen wanted. I learned that it was reserved for Jewish couples who were separated during the daytime and wished to enjoy a brief embrace in the evening. In defiance of the rules, at least of their spirit, this third Aryan went to the room intended for NCOs in the company of a Jew, about thirty years old, rather dark skinned and as handsome as a film star. He managed to remain elegantly dressed in spite of the rudimentary living conditions at Caffarelli. Later, going down the staircase, where a crowd of young men going nowhere were hurrying, she would say, pretending to be ashamed of herself, "What will these young men think of me?" One of them would answer: "Enjoy yourself while you are young!" I knew very little of the fourth Aryan, who seemed to me rather snobbish. She insisted on addressing me as "*Mon cher baron!*" I never understood why.

Every morning, the four women were taken by a Gestapo service car to the Saint-Michel prison, the Toulouse civilian prison, a wing of which had been taken over by the Germans. They served as chambermaids to some privileged detainees recently arrested, among them the Bishop of Montauban.

In this way, I discovered that the Bishop of Montauban had been active in the Resistance with the support of the priests in his diocese. I talked once with an Italian Jew who had recently been arrested. He seemed perfectly relaxed and not at all anxious. "I do not have to worry," he told me. "In three days I shall get out of here. The Gestapo told me, if you are not a Jew, supply us either with a medical certificate or with a certificate of baptism. So I wrote to the Bishop of Montauban, mentioning the parish where I was baptised and the date, and I shall receive a certificate of baptism." Actually, three days later, he left prison. It was interesting to note that in an individual case the priests of the diocese of Montauban could act courageously.

To my knowledge, there had been only one public gesture of protest from the Church. One day, I was given in great secret a typed strip of paper quoting three lines published in a parish bulletin by Monseigneur Saliège, Archbishop of Toulouse, which began: "Why must the Jews and their families..." But certain priests were trying to play down the significance of this gesture, saying, "Mgr. Saliège is old; he is more than eighty years old. He does not understand what is going on. He is almost blind."

The four Aryan ladies were placed fairly high in the hierarchy of Caffarelli, although it had originally been a camp re-grouping foreign Jews prior to their deportation to Germany. These detainees were due to stay only a few weeks – time enough to arrest the requisite number of Jews to make up a worthwhile convoy for the German camps. For practical purposes, the Gestapo set up a Jewish administrative organisation headed by Zarine, the Bessarabian operetta singer, and including Frau Pick, the secretary from Berlin, and Karta, the Czech doctor. These three were veterans of a Vichy camp that fell into the hands of the Germans in November 1942 when the free zone was occupied. They were the only ones permanently in the camp, and this fact saved their lives. For example, Zarine and Karta were able to keep their mistresses and the mothers of their mistresses near them. Later, Caffarelli included an Aryan section, an overflow from the Saint-Michel prison where the Aryans were also waiting for a convoy to be formed ready for their departure for Germany.

I never knew exactly whether in all cases the deportation to Germany took place directly or if there was an intermediate stage near Paris, such as Drancy for the Jews and Compiègne for the Aryans. The Jews were better informed. They taught me of the existence of Drancy; they talked also with horror of the Jewish Gestapo in Paris, but all this they had learned before their internment. In Caffarelli itself, everything was done to keep them in ignorance of their future fate.

Hence, on the administrative level, the Aryans led a sort of parasitic existence. They were controlled to a certain extent by the Jewish hierarchy, which, oddly, was sanctioned by the Gestapo. It was aimed at separating the Aryans from the Jews "in your interests", *Unteroffizier* Muehlhausen always added, for it now seems obvious to me that he was fully aware of the final destination of the Jews in Germany. Eventually, the four Aryan French ladies enjoyed a vague, non-categorised status, with more pleasant quarters and not being locked up during the day. The *Unteroffizier* and the soldiers treated them with benevolence and the *Gestapists* themselves did not scorn their company. The *Gestapo* came sometimes, three or four at a time, to pay them a visit on Saturday nights, bringing roast chicken, champagne and sweets, feasting with them until late into the night, treating them chivalrously, and not permitting themselves the slightest familiarity.

On the same nights the soldiers received special rations of *Schnapps*. As the feasting came to an end the soldiers could be heard stumbling through the courtyard, while the lugubrious singing of drunken men broke the silence of the night: "*Es geht alles vorueber, es geht alles vorbei... Nach jedem Dezember kommt wieder ... ein Mai...*" ["Everything passes... After every December there'll always be ... a May"]. It kept hope alive.

My mind returned to Professor Jarreiss, who carried on relentlessly with his presentation. The *Fuehrerprinzip* was of an almost unbearable clarity. According to the Constitution of the Third Reich, one man only held all powers; one man only could be responsible, and that was Adolf Hitler. Hence, it was impossible to condemn the "leaders" of the Third Reich. It was an expansion into the civilian hierarchy of the excuse of the military: that of obeying orders. In my days, French military regulations laid down that obedience must be unconditional; that a soldier must obey first and complain later. But who would be so foolish as to complain after the event? To the French, conscious of the power of the State, Jarreiss' argument should have carried a certain weight. I mentioned this to Lalouette, but he attached no importance to it. However, Lalouette's inclinations were more literary than legal.

The argument of the *Fuehrerprinzip* had far-reaching consequences. Indeed, it was of universal importance – and this constituted its weakness. It was so extreme that one had to take it or leave it. As there was little chance that it would be accepted, it was obvious to me that it would be rejected outright. Nevertheless, Jarreiss did some useful work on the question of the war of aggression. Was the war of aggression a crime? Or, more simply, was war a crime? The Prosecution at Nuremberg set great store by the Briand-Kellogg pact, which had "outlawed" war. Until now, no one had taken the Briand-Kellogg pact very seriously.

Jarreiss began his speech – rather, his lecture – in a solemn tone: "My Lord, Your Honours. The great legal question, the fundamental question in this trial, concerns the banning of war by the law of nations, the violation of peace considered as high treason against world order." Jarreiss did not try to convince the judges through pandering to their prejudices or their idiosyncrasies. He did not try to excuse the crimes or the criminals. He looked at matters from an abstract perspective that was at one and the same time both satisfying and disquieting, for after all what sort of reality could be found behind those reasonings that could justify all of the crimes? What, then, was a possible reply to his claim that the violation of peace was a matter for states, a matter of public law? If war were a matter for states, how could "individuals" be condemned?

All of this was simple enough. It was obvious – too obvious. There was nevertheless an obstacle in Jarreiss' way: the Statute of the Tribunal, which defined the crimes of those who were already Major War Criminals. The Professor's argumentation was long and complicated, but the principle remained simple. He trapped the Judges in the following dilemma: either the Statute expressed the law in force, or it expressed the new and consequently "retro-active" law, which was unthinkable. Jarreiss' efforts focused on proving that the Statute failed to express the law in force at the time when the so-called crimes had been committed.

Donnedieu, as usual, took notes ceaselessly. What did he think of the thesis of his colleague, the Professor of Law?

CHAPTER 6

The Collection of Strasbourg University

Before my arrival in Nuremberg, it had been possible to listen to Schacht or von Papen in person, to study their faces and watch their reactions when posed a difficult question. A clumsy reply or poorly controlled reaction would be enough for them to condemn themselves. They were gambling their freedom for years or for life. It was a compelling show, more like a circus, yet the atmosphere was muffled, the scenery discreet, the faces impassive, and the voices deadened. It was voyeurism. The Accused, once respected and fêted, had to strip themselves bare.

On 8 August, though, I had the opportunity to witness a game of poker that reminded me of the cross-examinations of the more stirring episode of the Trials. This took place during the trial of the *SS* as a criminal organisation, for at Nuremberg organisations as well as individuals were judged; the accusation concerned concentration camps. The language of the speeches for the Defence was in no way dramatic. A factor that could explain why there were so few spectators in the courtroom. And interest in the subject was already beginning to wane among the public. This was despite films having been shown, that had been taken by the Americans and the British, of when the camps were liberated: of corpses simply lying around, the walking skeletons of the survivors, the emaciated faces, the bulging eyes, and the striped uniforms and caps that resembled pyjamas. The shock and the horror of the images could not be superseded; nothing worse could lie beyond them. The films showed only a short moment in the life of the inmates, when they were finally leaving hell.

A witness was introduced who in no way corresponded to the commonly held idea of a Nazi or a member of the *SS*. He was bald, with a long black beard, and had an air of gravity that seemed slightly old-fashioned. He could have stepped out of a nineteenth-century painting such as those found in many a French bourgeois family, a portrait of an ancestor who had been a physician and was represented with his elbow resting on a table covered with a cloth of red velvet on which were arranged a few symbolic objects: a lancet, a set of testtubes, or even a microscope, depending on the period.

The witness' name was Wolfram Sievers, and he could certainly have passed for a physician.[25] Popular imagery and Nazi propaganda presented the *SS* as tall, blond, Nordic, muscular, and square-jawed; keen on outdoor pursuits and close to nature. Sievers was just the opposite. He was small, rather puny, had little twinkling eyes, and looked as if he were floating within the dark suit that was too large for his fragile frame. He expressed himself with the accuracy of a man trained in scientific discipline and also as someone who had a feeling for nuances. Sievers was thus intent on dispelling any misunderstandings that could arise from the

---

[25] *Sievers had actually been a commercial agent; as an SS bureaucrat, he had experience in administrative distinctions.*

intemperate use of a given and potentially tendentious word.

He was very much at his ease. He smiled when replying to questions, moving slightly in his chair, winking from time to time in the direction of Goering. Sievers had every reason to be at his ease. He had been examined and cross-examined at length some weeks earlier by the Prosecution and the Defence when appearing before the committee responsible for the selection of possible witnesses. Simple observers such as myself knew little about this committee. I was told that it was a sort of meeting place where Prosecutors and Counsels for the Defence concluded such deals as, "I'll let you have *this* witness, provided that you let me have *that* one." As the trial could not proceed indefinitely, the number of witnesses was necessarily limited. Anyhow, Pelckmann, Counsel for the SS, did not object to Sievers' being called as a witness.[26]

Sievers was not very dangerous. The *Ahnenerbe*, the Institute he had been managing, was an SS organisation in which Himmler had taken a deeply personal interest, and which had undertaken some experimental "biological research" on certain inmates of the concentration camps. Sievers was merely a bureaucrat who forwarded papers from one organisation to another, a sort of "postman", as was to be said a little later.

---

[26] *Airey Neave, a member of the British delegation, had the task of sifting applications from members of the criminal organisations who wished to speak in their favour. Earlier in the trial, he had been appointed by the Tribunal to approach the Defendants and help them to choose Counsel. See Airey Neave, Nuremberg, London, 1978.*

The Prosecutor who examined Sievers was British, Major Elwyn Jones. The Major looked not at all military. He was dressed as British barristers may be when not in court, as he had no gown or wig: a black jacket, striped trousers, a white shirt, and a grey silk tie. It was a uniform for civilians that deeply impressed Gerthoffer who, as a good Alsatian, had a weakness for anything that reminded him of the military. Elwyn Jones was young, elegant, and catlike. His supple body leaned nonchalantly on the lectern. His voice was soft.

Elwyn Jones was Welsh and his style admirably suited the conditions of Nuremberg. Visitors were always surprised by the atmosphere in the courtroom. There were no dramatic gestures as there would have been in France, no shouting, and no echo. When a defendant is speaking into a microphone and looking at an audience wearing headphones, it is a waste of time to yell and difficult to synchronise gestures with the various translations of the interpreters that arrive seconds afterwards.

With a few quick passes Elwyn Jones brought Sievers to the ground he had chosen. Before the committee on 27 June, Sievers stated that he had no direct and personal knowledge of the scientific experiments sponsored by *Ahnenerbe*. He must now, on 8 August, after weeks of silence, have assumed the matter was closed for good. But Elwyn Jones asked another question: "Have you heard of Professor Hirt's collection of skeletons?" At the name "Hirt" Sievers turned pale. In the following minutes I watched the apparently pleasant old man stiffening. His face became fixed, his lips pursed, his delivery was halting and his eyes sunken. I watched his face crumple up and his expression change dramatically, as if I was watching a speeded-up film, as if he had suddenly been confronted by the Angel of Death. It was unexpected, and it was horrible.

The story that followed, outlined against the background of questions and answers, was indeed horrific. Apparently, Hirt was Professor at Strasbourg University, which had become a German University because Alsace, as a consequence of the French defeat in 1940, was to become German again. Hirt was in charge of the anatomy department at the University and set out to build up a collection of skeletons. He also headed one of the scientific institutes of *Ahnenerbe*. Throughout his examination Sievers pretended that he had only a vague knowledge of what Professor Hirt was doing; in any case, *Ahnenerbe* dealt only with scientific matters. Hirt was in direct contact with Himmler and if he, Sievers, had played a part, it was only as messenger or mailbox. Moreover, Sievers had originally been called to testify for the Defence in order to prove that *Ahnenerbe* had nothing to do with the biological experiments undertaken by a certain Dr. Rascher on the inmates of the concentration camps.

Elwyn Jones skilfully made Sievers repeat over and over his denials. He begged him to tell the truth and to keep the oath he had taken as a witness. At the same time, he encouraged Sievers to protest anew his ignorance and innocence. Then, Elwyn Jones laid down his cards one at a time, slowly, each time begging Sievers to tell the truth, to tell all he knew. Elwyn Jones kept up the tension in the courtroom with each document he produced. Sievers' face was white with fear.

The first document was a letter of 6 November 1942 from Brandt, a personal aide of Himmler, to the RSHA, the central organisation in Nazi Germany for security police and repression. It also dealt with intelligence, prisons, and concentration camps. This letter made it known that Himmler gave the order for every assistance to be given to Professor Hirt from Strasbourg in building up his collection of skeletons for the purpose of scientific research, and that Sievers would contact the RSHA to confirm the details.

Elwyn Jones asked, "It was research of a purely academic character, was it not?" Sievers, not suspecting that the question could be ironic, answered, "Of course." Then Elwyn Jones asked, "-And from where would you get the skeletons?" Sievers was again evasive; the question was repeated and Sievers, now as white as a corpse, answered curtly and stiffly: "From Auschwitz."

The story unfolded step by step through the documents: the aim was to collect the skulls of Jewish Bolshevik Commissars, those typical specimens of sub-humanity, particularly repugnant to any good Nazi. As it happened, Strasbourg University, in spite of its treasures, was still too poor in Jewish skulls to be able to draw sound conclusions from its studies. In the interests of science, it had to be ascertained that the skulls were delivered in good condition. Instructions had been given to the *Wehrmacht* to the effect that in the future, Jewish Bolshevik Commissars should be handed over alive to the Military Police, who would be instructed to regroup them and look after them carefully until the arrival of a specialist. The latter would be either a young army medical officer or even a medical student; he would take measurements and photographs, and record a number of facts on the origin and age of this 'material'. After the death of the Jews was accomplished without damaging the head, the specialist would separate the head from the trunk before sending it in a watertight receptacle containing formaldehyde, to ensure preservation. Scientists could devote themselves to studies of comparative anatomy, specifically that of racial differences.

However, there was difficulty in executing this plan, as appeared in a letter of 21 June 1943 from Sievers to an important person not very well known at the time of the Nuremberg trial: the head of Section IV B4 of the *RSHA*, *SS-Oberstuermbahnfuehrer* Eichmann. Sievers indicated that the representative of Ahnenerbe on a special mission at Auschwitz regarding the collection of skeletons had brought his work to an end because of "the danger of contagion". Altogether, 115 people were involved: 79 Jews, two Poles, four Aryans from Central Asia, and 30 Jewish women. They were in quarantine in a barracks for the sick at Auschwitz. They were to be transferred immediately to the Natzweiler. To prevent the contagion from spreading there, they should receive the sterilised clothes of inmates before their transfer.

What had happened? Sievers did not want to say so, but it is likely that before killing those 115 people scientists wished to carry out some experiments on them. At any rate, we know the end of the story. When in 1944 the Americans were nearing Strasbourg, Sievers was worried about concealing the corpses, while deploring their possible loss to science. In order not to lose everything he proposed to strip the bones of the corpses to make them unrecognisable. The flesh would be incinerated, and it would be claimed that they were specimens provided by the French to the anatomy department. Finally, in October 1944, Sievers was in a position to tell Himmler that the whole of the collection had been destroyed.

That was not all. Elwyn Jones intended Sievers to admit that he had played a part in the experiments performed on inmates at Dachau. Sievers struggled as if he were drowning, but Elwyn Jones had irrefutable documents revealing the multiple medical researches taking place in the concentration camps under the aegis of several professors at Strasbourg University, Hirt among them. A noxious gas was mentioned; *Lost* was a poison gas for use in warfare. Hirt was experimenting on the inmates with an antidote. There were also experiments, for the benefit of the Army, on the consequences of freezing – not to be confused, added Sievers, with the experiments on cooling also at Dachau for the benefit of the *Luftwaffe*. Professor Schilling's experiments into malaria were also happening at Dachau. Professor Hirt worked on cancer, too; he had succeeded in isolating live cancerous cells and had demonstrated that the colouring "Tripaflavin" penetrated the nucleus of those cells to destroy them.

As guinea pigs in experiments to make seawater potable, they had used the gypsies. University clinics of Innsbrueck and Vienna, under the direction of the eminent Professors Breitner and Dent respectively, were busy trying to find a coagulant (Polygol). To make the conditions of the experimentation more realistic, Dr. Rauscher fired bullets at selected inmates. The SS medical officers also tried to find the causes of contagious heptatitis. It was not, as had previously been thought, caused by a bacterium but by a virus. The medical officers requested the "right" type of internees: as young as possible, having been condemned to death, and on whom experiments could be carried out at the

Sachsenhausen concentration camp. Himmler granted the request and specified that they should be Jews from Auschwitz, condemned to death, who had belonged to the Polish Resistance.

For his part, Professor Hagen from Strasbourg needed between 100 and 200 inmates to try out his vaccine against typhus. It was also briefly mentioned in the documents that a doctor proposed to Himmler three different methods of sterilising three million Bolshevik prisoners. The bureaucracy made a study of the methods. What was Sievers saying? Admittedly, he had been at Dachau, but never at the same time as Himmler. However, a witness maintained that Sievers had always been there when Himmler attended experiments.

It seemed impossible to enter the intellectual universe of Sievers; he was no doubt a bureaucrat guided by formal rules. He could not be expected to be anything other. Were there moments when he doubted the experiments? At the end of his examination, he said that he had had crises of conscience and that he had even been one of the leading members of a secret Resistance organisation within the Party and the SS. I was not the only one in the courtroom to be sceptical. If it indeed existed, of what could this Resistance movement have consisted?

Sievers claimed he had protested several times against these experiments. As a consequence, Himmler let him know that it would be treason to oppose this scientific work. Himmler told Sievers that he, Himmler, took upon himself the responsibility for these experiments and that nobody was asking Sievers to carry out research himself. Sievers then submitted his case of conscience to the head of his

Resistance organisation. Together, they reached the conclusion that by persisting in his refusal, Sievers would risk only his own neck, to no advantage for the inmates subjected to the experiments.

I wondered whether the most prominent Germans would not in the future try to excuse themselves by invoking activities in the Resistance. Actually, the Germans I met later did not attempt to pretend they had played a double game. Many, though, maintained that they had entertained doubts about Hitler and the Nazis, and that they had told their closest friends about them. I noticed that Schacht, who also presented himself as a Resistant, had reproached foreigners, the British in particular, with not playing the game of German Resistance. I lost count of the times I heard the Germans using the following argument: as foreigners from the world over had come to Hitler's Olympic Games, how could it be expected that the Germans would turn against Hitler?

One Sunday shortly after Sievers' examination I went to Dachau. In Munich I boarded an antiquated train, with wooden benches and open-air platforms at each end of the carriage. Dachau is only one hour from Munich. It is a pretty town, a traditional favourite Sunday excursion. On that day, arriving early in the afternoon, the train was almost empty, as was the square in front of the station. I drank a cup of bad coffee in the *Gaststaette* opposite the station: wooden benches again, and moralising pictures on the walls. I asked the way to the camp. "Camp? What camp? Don't know." I remembered a conversation with a friend of mine who had been deported with his whole village from Alsace. This happened in 1944 when, in the ebb and flow of military operations, his village had been liberated by the Americans then later recaptured by the Germans. He had told me: "There was a railway line leading to the camp, but we had to alight at Dachau station and walk along the railway line." I did the same; I followed the railway line. I came to a relatively low wall, which must have been the outer enclosure of the camp. It surrounded a park. It was possible to peep through a gap in the wall barred by a wrought-iron gate. As in a well-arranged production, the gate was foreground and frame to a fountain, a scene creating an atmosphere of calm and rest. The water gently sprinkled and dropped into the basin. Further along there was a goods train on a siding. The cattle trucks were occupied by "displaced persons". There were entire families, mainly of women and children. The washing was drying in the trees. It looked like a semi-permanent community.

The entrance to the camp was closed on this side. I went around to reach the main entrance. The square in front of it included two administrative buildings to the right and left – one was, I believe, a library. A double wooden gate sealed the main entrance. The architecture was grey and dour, but rather less alarming than a prison entrance. There were no high walls. Above the gate stood a bas-relief eagle with a cruel eye. "Take your hats off in front of the German eagle!" my friend and his companions had been instructed when they first entered. Below was the motto: "*Arbeit macht frei*" ["Work liberates"]. Of course, I knew that it would be there, but to see it intact in Gothic characters gave me a physical shock. The motto was doubly familiar. It belonged to the treasury of German popular wisdom and also my father had, during my youth, told me repeatedly, "*Le travail, c'est la liberté!*" ["Work is freedom!"]. Did he feel that he had a lazy son? My maternal grandmother had instilled it into him in his own youth. This was long before Hitler, long before the Weimar Republic, and long before the First World War. My grandmother came from Heidelberg; she had travelled before 1870 to Paris, where there was in those days a flourishing German colony. She had lived through the painful months of the siege by the Prussians. I have retained the memory of a woman of great kindness, whom I saw three times a year and who corrected my pronunciation when I was learning my first German words. My father tried to bring me up according to the principle that work was an excellent thing, a principle that the Nazis perversely proclaimed at the entrance to Dachau.

I visited Dachau again several years later. The camp was still more or less intact; the trees of the central alley that led to the square, where roll call took place every morning, were considerably taller. All of the huts were occupied by refugees, perhaps those I had seen in the siding near one of the gates. The camp kept its atmosphere of poverty, a forceful reminder of the miseries of war. At the time of my most recent visit, the camp had almost disappeared. All of the huts had been demolished except one, absolutely new, a showpiece. It was the first on the right in the central alley... The hut where the medical experiments took place had disappeared.

Even at the time of the trial, the memory of Dachau was beginning to fade. "This could have happened to me, a year, two years ago..." was never uttered. Yet during the trial for a brief moment there was the feeling of perceiving the immediate reality beyond the veil of history. This was when Elwyn Jones read aloud the testimony of a certain Dr. Pacholegg, whom Sievers had known well. He was a doctor and an inmate; the SS experimenters used his services for their medical research in Dachau.

Consequently, Pacholegg had been given a certain freedom of movement, of which he took advantage to escape towards the end of the war, causing Sievers to fear that he would be held responsible for the disappearance. After the war, Pacholegg, with himself nothing to fear, could speak freely. For example, this is what he said about the experiments made with the use of a decompression chamber on behalf of the Luftwaffe:

I have personally looked with others through the observation window, onto where a prisoner would be held in a vacuum until his lungs burst. A few experiments would cause such a pressure inside the head that the men became mad and would tear their hair out in an effort to alleviate the pressure. They would tear the skin on their heads and their faces with their hands and their nails, trying in their desperation to wound themselves. They would throw themselves head first against the walls, and scream, trying in this way to reduce the pressure on the eardrum. The cases of complete vacuum ended generally in the death of the subject of the experiment. It was so certain that a complete vacuum in the course of an experiment would cause death that in many cases the chamber was used as a method of execution rather than experiment. I had knowledge of the experiments by Rascher[27] where prisoners were submitted for 30 minutes to a vacuum or to a very high pressure, or to a mixture of the two. The experiments were divided into two categories: some were called 'living experiments' and the others simply 'experiments', which meant execution experiments.

---

[27] *Until towards the end of the war, Rascher was the main SS experimenter at Dachau. He was arrested by the Germans themselves. By the time of the trial Rascher was dead and, as Elwyn Jones remarked, Sievers was trying to shift the blame for all responsibilities onto him. Rascher had a close relationship with Himmler.*

Sievers denied being present at these experiments. Pacholegg maintained that Himmler and his assistants usually attended the important experiments and the new ones, and that Sievers was always present at the same time as Himmler. Sievers finally admitted that he had indeed been present at two experiments: one that he had seen "in part" with Professor Hirt, and the other with the decompression chamber.

After such testimonies, it was tempting indeed to think that all of these eminent physicians and professors had succumbed to a tendency to bestiality. However, there had been orders from Himmler and Hitler to cover them and to forbid them to experiment on themselves. Were they fascinated by science as a means to power? The question as to whether such experiments were necessary or even useful arises, as does the element of voyeurism.

Curiously, in the winter of 1946-47 in Berlin, there came an echo of Sievers' declaration at Nuremberg. I frequented a mess in the French sector. One day, a French medical officer came and said, "As you have been at Nuremberg, would you like to come and see General Vincent? He would like to talk to you."

For a brief moment I thought I recognised General Vincent, who belonged to the Army Medical Corps. He was a small chap with a goatee, lost in a khaki coat much too big for him. He had a sharp eye and made peremptory gestures. I was reminded of Sievers at the beginning of his examination. Vincent did not beat about the bush: "The Germans engaged in medical experiments in concentration camps. It would be important for us to know what results they obtained, and which discoveries they have made.

Could you tell me where I could find more documentation?" I thought he was going to add a formulation that I had heard during my recruit training, "... in order to be able to give to the command the information it needs." The words sound all the better in French, where the first syllable of verbs and nouns receives the main emphasis.

I was almost glad to have no information to give Vincent. I referred him to the transcript of the debates at the trial and to the documents introduced by Elwyn Jones. One year later I read in *Le Monde* that General Vincent had been promoted to the dignity of Commander of the Order of the Legion of Honour for a "special mission" to Germany. My first reaction was to assume that General Vincent had succeeded in bringing back a rich harvest of important medical discoveries. On the other hand, it could be that he wrote a purely negative report saying that the medical experiments in the concentration camps had no scientific meaning. Who knows?

Perhaps after all we should be grateful today to the gypsies who were forced to drink seawater, to the eight Polish Jews from the Resistance who had been given viral hepatitis, and to the Dachau inmates dipped in freezing water and warmed up by the embraces of prostitutes from the camp.

CHAPTER 7

Gerthoffer's Legion of Honour

That evening at the Grand Hotel in Nuremberg, Gerthoffer celebrated his Legion of Honour. Obviously, I was not invited. Perched on one of the bar stools, I observed through the slits in the curtains the crowd of uniforms squeezed into the reserved room. La Gorce insisted that I have a cocktail, recommending a White Lady. It did not cost much, only two marks, while a pack of American cigarettes was worth 50 marks. The barman kept shaking the cocktails. With his half-shaven head, he did not seem like a professional; he looked more of a military type. La Gorce called him "John", trying out his English on him, seemingly pretending that Nuremberg was like Geneva, an international centre where the barman, obviously English, was on first-name terms with all of the stars of the political world. La Gorce left me rather hurriedly and disappeared for the rest of the evening. I was beginning to know him well enough to guess that he wanted me to believe that he had been invited to the Gerthoffer reception – or was the fact that he was *not* invited so unbearable that he could stay no longer?

I felt no shame in playing the part of the onlooker who, kept at a distance, contemplates with fascination the graceful evolutions of high society. Actually, there were so many guests and the crowd was so dense that there was very little movement. The same Americans, in dark khaki, standing to attention, glass in hand, were present. I caught a glimpse, though, of Gerthoffer pinned against the entrance door. He was not really a man of the world and he knew it, but made himself as charming, as benign, as modest, and as disarming as he could. His hair was thinning. It lay flat and glistening. Seeing him from behind, his projecting ears were more obvious. His face was sweaty, probably because of the stifling atmosphere, and maybe also from the tension, the cold exultation, of finding himself the focus of such a prestigious social gathering.

A few days later, my relations with Gerthoffer took a turn for the worse. He had disliked my letter on Schacht's examination. Now came the speech by Schacht's Counsel. Lalouette, to give himself a boost, went and read him the draft telegram I had written on that occasion.

Dr. Dix's speech stood out clearly against the others. He was a Berlin barrister with a flourishing practice. He came to Nuremberg only from time to time to look after the interests of his client, Schacht. In his speech, he distanced himself from the Nazis, and from Hitler himself – clever tactics that the other Counsel for the Defence did not try to adopt, and perhaps could not have applied. Schacht, for his part, was only too anxious to dissociate himself from the other defendants, from Goering in particular, his *bête noire*, since fat Hermann had ousted him from his positions of responsibility.

Dix had given his speech a literary and historical flavour. From the start he piled up quotations, including Latin ones such as "*lucus a non lucendo*" in connection with the Constitution under

Hitler, and the better-known one of Oxenstirn, "*Nescis, ni fili, quanta stultitia mundus regitur.*" He quoted also a "great French thinker" who had said: "*En fait d'histoire, il vaut mieux continuer que recommender.*" Dix drew a parallel between the relationship of Schacht with Hitler and that of Seneca with Nero.

He referred to Wallenstein, probably according to Schiller, for whom "The earth belongs to the Evil spirit". The crowning element of this display of erudite pyrotechnics was a long and famous quotation from Goethe's *Dichtung und Wahrheit*, a quotation that according to Dr. Dix at one stroke explained the Hitler phenomenon and exculpated Schacht. It was the theory of the "demonic", this mysterious force to be found among all corporeal or incorporeal beings, including animals. Men in whom this force appears are not necessarily the most remarkable for their minds or their talents, and they distinguish themselves rarely by the goodness of their hearts. A monstrous force inhabits these men. They exert an incredible power over all creatures, even over the elements. The combination of all moral forces can do nothing against them.

At the mention of Hitler, the "demonic" Goering and von Ribbentrop, who had merely smiled ironically at Latin quotes or Schiller, burst out laughing. Goering slapped his thighs. Lalouette, always concerned with decorum, revised into diplomatic style the text of the telegram I had prepared, substituting: "This quotation from Goethe provoked reactions of irony from Goering and von Ribbentrop." Actually, Goering and von Ribbentrop were probably justified in their reaction: it was difficult to recognise in this literary context the Hitler they had known.

I believe that Dix was carried away by his conception of judicial eloquence and that his literary feats misrepresented an explanation of Hitler, which he developed later with good common sense. Basically, he was pleading that Schacht had committed a gross error and that he had been sincere; Hitler had deceived everyone, he had promised everything to everyone, but failed to keep his word. Everyone in Germany, as well as abroad, had been deceived. Dix went rather too far in comparing Schacht to Faust as deceived by Mephisto.

Dix did, however, know how to play his trump cards. The end of the war found Schacht in a concentration camp. He was arrested after the assassination attempt of 20 July 1944, and was one of the few from the Flossenbuerg concentration camp to escape execution. The mere fact that Schacht was sitting at Nuremberg on the same bench as Kaltenbrunner, head of the police and repression services, illustrated clearly the absurdity of Schacht's trial. Gisevius' testimony proved that Schacht had been an authentic Resistant.

More simply, Dix could have argued that Schacht had lost all of his posts of responsibility a year before the war. Consequently, it was hard to see how he could be treated as a "war criminal". Dix disposed rather offhandedly with the argument that "Hitler could not have re-armed if Schacht had not helped him" by saying, "Well then, one would have to condemn a car manufacturer because a drunken taxi-driver ran over a pedestrian." This would have been enough to make Gerthoffer cringe.

Having provoked Gerthoffer by showing him my two papers on Schacht, Lalouette thought it politic to attempt a reconciliation. "Go and see Gerthoffer," he told me, "And ask him to explain to you how he gathers his documentation for the trial of the German industrialists, where he will play a leading role."

Gerthoffer welcomed me as correctly as he could. He did not talk about documentation. Instead, he gave me a long lecture explaining that the Americans had built up a team of fifty researchers to prepare the trial against German industrialists, that the trial would take place, and that it had to be taken very seriously.

A few days later I met him in a corridor, when I took the liberty of belatedly offering him my respectful congratulations on his Legion of Honour. He did not answer. He was sweating; he turned his back without a word. I began to regret having expressed at Nuremberg so frankly my views on Schacht. In Paris, Fouques-Duparc, when he recruited me, had said, "-And also at Nuremberg, it will be good for you. You will be in a position to form relationships that will be useful to you later on." By way of forming relationships, I had succeeded in turning against me the most eminent magistrate of the French delegation. I decided then that in the future I would use the greatest circumspection and try to please everybody, including Lalouette and the French magistrates. To whom, though, should I give priority?

Leaving the Gerthoffer reception, Lalouette ran his eye around the room. He could not see La Gorce so said to me, "Come and have dinner with us. As it happens I have invited a French journalist." It was a journalist accredited to the trial since its beginning. No one saw much of him. He lived with the many journalists from all over the world in the 'Press

Camp', organised by the Americans in a building I never saw. I imagined it, from what I had heard, to be a *Schloss* in the mediæval style, with crenellations and watchtowers. It was built of dark red stone towards the end of the nineteenth century, by a pencil manufacturer of world renown, at a time when cheap German products were flooding the market. There is little doubt that the Americans had arranged the situation to their advantage. The journalists received the latest news from the trial without having to hound them for information.

We sat in the large dining room of the Grand Hotel. The hotel itself had known better times and seen the upper crust of Nazi society coming for the great rallies. It had become, now, for the Allied personnel involved in the trial, the centre of social life and also of international intrigues. This was most obvious in the ballroom, also the venue for a daily cabaret, with small tables around the dance floor. The music-hall numbers alternated with the tango and other not-so-modern dances, all danced cheek-to-cheek *à l'américaine*. There was a feeling of *déjà vu* – but of where? Of the cinema, of course, on the big screen. The dancers emulated the great Hollywood stars, who played the parts of secret agents in all sorts of cabarets from Tangiers through Alexandria to Berlin.

Those admitted into the large dining room belonged to a select milieu, including diplomats, heads of foreign delegations, and their assistants. Soviet and American representatives could invite each other to dinner and talk. The French journalist appreciated the favour bestowed on him. He sat without saying anything, modest but tense. The menu, written in American though of German inspiration, was refined and ambitious: asparagus soup, steak or *ragout fin* with asparagus tips, and peach melba. It added up to a lot of asparagus. Lalouette deliberately introduced a subject for conversation: "Do you know my friend Gasquel? He writes in the weeklies." Taking some time to find the thread of his thoughts, he added, "Yes, the weekly papers ... which are published once a week." The conversation – or, rather, the soliloquy – fell away. What was Lalouette getting at? His guest also wrote in the weeklies, even in those with a high circulation. We remained deep in our own thoughts. The journalist found the waiting unbearable.

Turning towards me, he said in a friendly way: "You came to Nuremberg recently. What are your first impressions?" I tried to be very careful in my answer. "I was struck by the serenity of the debates, the muffled atmosphere of the courtroom, and the absence of judicial rhetoric." He interrupted: "It is obvious that you have not been here very long." Embarrassed, Lalouette changed the subject – more precisely, threw himself into the real subject:

How will the Trial be seen in an historical perspective and in the perspective of the judgement? ... There are several groups among the Accused. First of all there are the Party men: Goering, Hess, and Ribbentrop, whom we can eliminate. Then there are the military people, Generals and Admirals, just technicians, after all. There are also the diplomats, such as Neurath and von Papen, professionals, who under any regime....

The scale of responsibilities descended from Goering to von Papen. The further down they were, the more inhumane it seemed to "eliminate" them. The journalist held his breath. He hung on Lalouette's every word. I felt he would have thrown his arm around Lalouette's neck, had he allowed himself to do so.

He dared not pull his notebook from his pocket, so remembered every word. A few weeks later, after the end of the public debates and while the judges were discussing among themselves the text of the verdict, I read in the *Journal du Dimanche* a long article under the headline "What will be the judgement at Nuremberg?" The article began: "If one looks at matters from an historical perspective, how does the Nuremberg Trial appear? A man who has been initiated into all of the secrets of Nuremberg and who is also one of the leading experts on Germany and the Germans told me that one must distinguish several groups. First of all, there are the Party men and the main Nazi leaders, whom one can eliminate..." Then followed almost word for word Lalouette's declaration made on that evening during dinner at the Grand Hotel.

Were those views original? Everybody knew how the Accused had been chosen to face trial. Each was held to represent one of the main branches of the government of the Third Reich. The Party: Goering and Rudolf Hess. Diplomacy: von Ribbentrop, von Papen, and von Neurath. The Army: Keitel and Jodl. The Navy: Raeder and Doenitz. Home Affairs: Frick. Finance: Schacht and Funk. The Police: Kaltenbrunner. The Occupied Territories: Frank, Rosenberg, Seyss-Inquart, von Neurath, and Baldur von Schirach. Education and Youth: Baldur von Schirach, again. Propaganda and Idæology: Streicher, Rosenberg (already mentioned), and Fritzsche. Armament and Labour: Speer and Sauckel. Industry: Krupp von Bohlen und Halbach, who, unwell, was allowed to leave the dock.

Lalouette drew a distinction that was as good as a judgement. On the one side were the Nazis too compromised to be saved, and on the other the civil servants who had done nothing but their duties as civil servants. The Generals had drawn up war plans, as was the function of Generals. The Admirals had built submarines – and why not? The diplomats represented their country abroad. This was a sociological distinction and a question of milieu: into one and the same bracket would not fit von Papen and Rudolf Hess, von Neurath and Sauckel, the Grand Admiral Raeder and the vile Streicher. There were men one could meet in society, and there were those of street demonstrations or of local Party meetings. It was as if Lalouette was pleading against any meddling in the noble careers of the army, navy and diplomacy, as who knew where that would lead?

Observing the Accused in the dock, it was not easy to make such distinctions. They looked pretty ordinary, and a paltry lot at that.

However, the date when each joined the Nazi Party or were won over to Hitler could be established. There was firstly the case of Hitler's companions at his beginning in Munich, the *Alte Kaempfer* of the Party, who had been implicated in the failed *Putsch* in 1923: Goering, Hess, Frick, Streicher, and Rosenberg. Then there were those who became Nazis later on yet before Hitler's seizing of power: Frank, Funk, von Ribbentrop, and Schirach. There came those who might have become members of the Party as a matter of social convention because they were members of the government or top civil servants. This was the case of the Weimar politicians: Schacht, von Papen and von Neurath, as well as of the military leaders, apolitical by tradition: Keitel, Jodl, Raeder and Doenitz. Finally, the last group included the rest, such as people who joined for a mixture of motives. Some were opportunists, some of them simply ambitious. Responsibilities happened to come to them, and they like carrying out orders. They are found under any regime, and their political attitudes are of no importance as they merely do a job, as did Kaltenbrunner, Seyss-Inquart, Speer, Fritzsche, and Sauckel.

CHAPTER 8

Hitler's Secret Conferences

After the journalist had taken his leave Lalouette saw Lépinois sitting near the bar cheerfully biting into a hamburger, tomato sauce dripping down his fingers. Lépinois had a round head, flat hair, and thick horn-rimmed spectacles. He was a hard worker. Already a lecturer at the Sorbonne, specialising in "German prose", he had one major preoccupation, which was to finish his doctoral thesis on Austrian history.

Lalouette had tried to allocate to Lépinois the study of the documents submitted to the Tribunal. The documents were piling up on the desk. When the trial came to an end, Lépinois took the train carrying a dozen large parcels, carefully wrapped and tied up. They contained seven thousand pages concerning Seyss-Inquart, the *Anschluss*, von Papen, etc. He confided to me: "I was forewarned before I left Paris to be careful with the Quai d'Orsay. I was told they will make you work for them and you will not have time to work for yourself." Lépinois had, however, made a concession. He had agreed to write a "letter" on the subject closest to Lalouette's heart: Hitler's secret conferences.

Lalouette used to say in his dinner-table conversation, "The most beautiful emotions I had at

Nuremberg ... came from reading documents." He was thinking about the famous Secret Conferences identified by the names of the author of the notes taken at each conference, for example, the Hossbach or the Schmundt document. Before I arrived in Nuremberg, the revelations of the existence of these documents caused a great fuss. To the French, they proved without ambiguity the "crime against peace", Hitler's willingness to go to war. To show you were a true member of the French delegation, one had to be able to quote the Hossbach document on 10 November 1937, reporting the explosive remarks made by Hitler on 5 November during a solemn and exceptional meeting of the highest dignitaries of the Third Reich: Goering; Raeder, Chief of the Navy; von Neurath, Chief of Diplomacy; Blomberg, War Minister, and Fritsch, Commander-in-Chief of the Army.[28]

Hitler said that Germany needed "vital space". The first objective must be to conquer Austria and Czechoslovakia. If not, those countries could become a threat in the course of an attack in the West.

Hence, Austria and Czechoslovakia were subjugated and occupied.

A new secret conference was held at the highest level on 23 May 1939, to which reference is made in the Schmundt document: Hitler declared his intention to attack Poland. And Poland was indeed attacked.

---

[28] *In retrospect, it is difficult to understand Lalouette's enthusiasm, as in actual fact the text of the 1937 Hossbach document had been leaked to the French at the time. Perhaps Lalouette had not been told of this? A further twist in the story is that the Germans knew of the leak within hours, as they were intercepting the diplomatic cipher, and they did nothing about it.*

Once Poland was under his thumb, Hitler called his valiant knights together again. This was on 23 November 1939. The meeting was marked by a triumphant speech. Hitler recounted his international activity since the day Germany had left the League of Nations. Germany had occupied the Rhineland, Austria, Czechoslovakia, and Poland. And now? Hitler gave his chiefs to understand that he wanted to attack in the West.

I could understand Lalouette's emotions as he had lived through those years posted to Vienna, Prague, and Berlin. The essence of his activity, then, had been to dissect the utterances of Hitler and of his entourage, trying to penetrate the mystery of his intentions. Now, these plans of Hitler, which had seemed so complex, so ambiguous, and so full of surprises, appeared after the events to be of a blinding clarity and simplicity. In a few pages, Hitler's grand strategy was outlined in black and white, with no grey areas. He would take first the Rhineland, then Austria, and planned to go even further. From a mysterious and unfathomable genius, Hitler was transformed into a conjurer who, with a few passes of his magic wand, pulled out of the hat one rabbit after another while Europe, dumbfounded and paralysed, witnessed this, saying, "It is not possible! We can't believe it! There must be a trick!"

For the lawyers, the secret conferences were a godsend. What better proof could be imagined of Hitler's and his accomplices' plan of aggression? It was the admission, the confession and – better still – the obvious premeditation... the malice aforethought. The Prosecution seized upon the notes. Donnedieu de Vabres did not, after the Trial, hide his feelings: "Hitler's premeditation in this series of aggression was established in a superabundant way." In actual fact, premeditation was established with the publication of *Mein Kampf*.

For my part I always had my doubts about the significance of *Mein Kampf*. Had Hitler really drawn up a plan for future action? *Mein Kampf* was a confused and complex book. Few had enough courage or patience to read it. Even today I can perceive in it an echo of Hitler's speeches in the Munich *Bierkellers* and a propaganda pamphlet, but was it truly a book revealing his secret thoughts, present and future? In the end, none of his essential prophecies was fulfilled. Had Hitler wanted no war with Britain? He had war with Britain. Did he want no war on two fronts? He had war on two fronts. *Mein Kampf* drew on the lessons from the First World War; it formulated desirable objectives. Were these enough to constitute a serious plan? Was it even proved that Hitler, once in power, wanted war for the sake of it?

Lépinois was as silent on the subject of the Secret Conferences as on the subject of his thesis. He followed the tradition of these academics anxious to keep their distance, those who adopt a cool and haughty air, often a defensive reflex hiding a feeling of insecurity. The only thing he condescended to say about the paper he was writing was, "I have taken my precautions!" Perhaps he was more cunning than Lalouette thought.

Until Nuremberg, in order to decipher the enigma of Hitler's intentions the *Yellow Book* and its fine analysis by the French diplomats posted in Berlin before the war had to be consulted. What they wrote seemed *passé*, but they all wrote well, each in his own style. A piece by Tarbé de Saint-Hardouin came to mind: "Hitler is accustomed to keeping several irons in the fire." This image reflected de Saint-Hardouin's uncertainties. He had a very agile mind in a heavy body that rocked from side to side when he walked, a "trapper's gait", as François-Poncet used to say. For his part the latter contributed the pièce de résistance of the *Yellow Book*. His great letter on his visit to Hitler's Eagle's Nest was destined to take its place in an anthology even before the ink was dry. The professionals will more likely remember the most curious document in the publication, the personal letter sent by Coulondre to Daladier on the eve of the war, telling him to "Stand fast!"

The *Yellow Book* gave a conventional image of the origins of the war. It fixed a certain version of the French position, the official version, accepted as such once war was declared. The reality was probably richer and more complex. I would guess that during the last days of peace, French diplomats were not very keen to align themselves with the British position of unconditional aid to Poland. But this may well never be established.

Today, how to read Hitler's Secret Conferences is clearer. De Saint-Hardouin was right. Hitler did indeed keep several irons in the fire, and he counted on the diplomatic game to reach his goals without having to start the Second World War. He doubtless accepted the risk of limited operations or even of local wars against Czechoslovakia, Poland, or Austria, but a world conflict was not in his plans at the time of the Secret Conferences.

I remember having astonished quite a few historians when I sent a letter to the *Times Literary*

Supplement[29] saying that the Nuremberg Judgement had not declared the Nazi leaders responsible for having started World War II, but guilty of having attacked Poland. The nuance had not been noticed.

After his conversation with the journalist Lalouette was in good spirits. It is always a delicate manœuvre for a diplomat to approach the press and try to influence it, although there must be no lack of journalists who are only too willing to accept the offer of a ready-made article. I remembered the advice of Fouques-Duparc before I left for Nuremberg: "Above all, do not talk to journalists!"

Lalouette approached Lépinois: "Well, *cher ami*, would you like a drink?" Feeling on top form after his success with the journalist, Lalouette was ready to tackle the Sorbonne and the University in general in the person of Lépinois, who was admittedly only a lecturer yet who might be in a position to influence some of the most eminent professors. After all, there were not that many Germanists at the Sorbonne. Also, Lépinois had relations and some support: "I have just seen Monsieur Champetier de Ribes," Lalouette told him, "And he asked me to convey to you the best regards of the Chanoine Desgranges, who talked a lot about you."

Lalouette continued: "A few weeks ago, on this very spot, I had a long conversation with your colleague at the Sorbonne, Professor Vermeil. He said to me, 'No, it is not possible to accept Germany in Europe as before!' And I spent three hours in discussion with him, walking to and fro in this same hotel hall where we now are, and trying to

---

[29] *This took place on the occasion of the controversy about the book on the origins of the war by A.J.P. Taylor.*

demonstrate that in spite of everything we must re-establish our links with Germany."

Was Lalouette going to repeat to Lépinois his three-hour performance? It was getting a bit late, and not very easy to find a taxi to take him back to Zirndoft. It had been a long day. However, Lalouette extended his thinking beyond his previous argument, saying: "The future is to be found in the creation of Europe." A bold affirmation for the time; a thrust to demolish all obstacles on the way to a radiant and grandiose future. Europe? But what sort of Europe? The word had, not so long ago, disturbing connotations, with "Europe" signifying a crusade against Bolshevism. This was no longer the case, or perhaps not yet. Lalouette had more precise ideas. "What kind of peace settlement are we to conclude? When we try to attach Brigue and Tende, we give the measure of our present ambitions. The future of France is elsewhere, but it does not lie in an inordinate ambition, such as wanting to become one of the Four Great Powers. Our place is among the nations of the second rank, wishing one thing: to place France at their head. Take the case of Austria, for instance. What can its future be without France and without Europe?" he wanted to know.

Lépinois nodded. Yes, of course, Austria, what could be its future? With or without France? Lalouette became afraid of having gone too far in his confidences and of finding himself out on a limb. He tried to put Lépinois back in the saddle by asking, "Before coming to Nuremberg, were you present at historical events?" Lépinois answered, "Yes; I was at the sitting of the Chamber of Deputies when the Communists voted against the war." He was visibly still outraged by this lack of patriotism.

Lalouette hesitated for a short time, wondering whether his next words would bruise the delicate feelings of Lépinois, then proceeded: "You know, sometimes, when I think about that period of history, through which I have lived day by day, I cannot but have some doubts. Obviously, I have the soul of a diplomat and it tells me, 'Well, the Prussians, by concluding a pact with the Germans, have acted in a perfectly rational fashion. They followed their analysis of the situation through to the end. From the moment they believed that Chamberlain's and Bonnet's policy had given the Germans a free hand in Eastern Europe, what else could they do? To protect themselves from the Germans, they had to come to a direct understanding with them. They had no choice.' All of the states from Central Europe and the Balkans, one after the other, did just that when Hitler came to power. The Soviets played the diplomatic game: they practised the traditional *Grosse Politik* of the European Cabinets." Lépinois looked worried. How far would Lalouette go in his heresy?

"*Cher ami*," resumed Lalouette, "the *Grosse Politik* of the diplomats is, in the end, something very simple, as is the Grand Strategy of the Generals. It is a question of the to-and-fro. The Soviets understood this. The answer to Munich was the Soviet-German pact. But then, what should have been the answer to the Soviet-German pact?" Here, Lalouette's faced clouded over. Would he dare? Not really. He concluded in a softer tone, "Do not forget in any case, *cher ami*, that French diplomats have never been found wanting in lucidity." To support the clarity of the French diplomats, Lalouette felt he had to dispose of an embarrassing memory, which was the famous letter from Coulondre to Daladier in the last days before the war: "You like fishing, I believe, *M. le*

Président. The fish is biting ... stand firm! Hitler is bluffing."

"Yes," said Lalouette, "We were right to tell the French government to 'be firm'." What, then, were the intentions of the French embassy in Berlin? Did France wish to back to the hilt the Poles in their intransigence? Did France actually encourage them to be uncompromising? Coulondre's letter to Daladier suggests that the "bull from the Vaucluse" was not too anxious to charge into the German trap. There was deep disagreement between the Berlin embassy and the French government, and the Germans knew it.[30]

Coulondre quarrelled with Henderson, the British ambassador, when the latter wanted – at any price – to bring the Poles to the negotiating table, and to make them reach terms with Hitler. At the last minute Coulondre wanted to oppose the handing over of the British ultimatum. Moreover, it was noticeable that the French war declaration was delivered only some time after the British declaration.

Possibly, the French embassy may have employed ultra-secret moves in the hope of combining a general negotiation. It could have been banking on Goering, who had realised the danger of the situation and believed that Britain would indeed go as far as declaring war. Alas, Hitler listened to von Ribbentrop, who maintained that Britain would not fight.

"-But the *Yellow Book*?" asked Lépinois plaintively. "The *Yellow Book*?" responded Lalouette,

---

[30] *The Germans knew it thanks to the phone tapping and telegram decoding done by the Forschungsamt. See the work of David Irving, Breach of Security, London, 1968, with an Introduction by Donald Watt.*

who was reluctant to go too far along the path to revelations. "We could do nothing else." He shrugged his shoulders.

With this remark, he ended the conversation. Lalouette gulped the rest of his whisky; Lépinois swallowed the last drop of his Coca Cola. Each went on his way, Lépinois wishing Lalouette, "A good night! A very good night!"

As it happened, La Gorce was waiting for a taxi so we went together to Zirndorf. The journey cost officially only three marks, a derisory price roughly equivalent to that of a cigarette, hardly more. But La Gorce, again, wished to show himself generous towards the driver. "Why don't you give him two packets of cigarettes," he said. "I will give them back to you." These princely tips gave him a certain air. However, as he did not smoke, he never had any cigarettes handy. I was always the one to give away packets of cigarettes.

CHAPTER 9

Excursion to Wuerzburg

That year, 14 July fell on a Sunday. I wondered if the French planned to celebrate Bastille Day. The circumstances did not really lend themselves to it. There was no monument to the dead of the 1914-1918 war, and there was no fanfare. The two *gendarmes* and the lieutenant of *gendarmerie*, who lived in the villa to ensure Dubost's safety, were content with having a lie-in. The manager of the French canteen in Zirndorf, though, promised to organise in the evening a "*bal populaire et folklorique*", where the folklore would be supplied by three musicians from the village.

The French went to mass in the Zirndorf parish church. The nave had been whitewashed, and the sun's rays shone into the back of the church. It would have been very difficult to analyse the feelings of the congregation. The Germans formed a sort of black stream running along the walls on both sides; they were mainly women, older women, mothers and also widows, whose sons and husbands had fallen on the Eastern front or were still in captivity. The German women showed their sorrow. The Zirndorf priest, with whom I had a brief occasion to talk, remarked, "Ah! Here is another war crime! ... A year after the end of the war, and our prisoners have not yet been freed!" I admired the ease with which he could mention war crimes, when the victims were Germans. It is true that with the Nuremberg trial only a few miles away the press must have used the word so often that it gradually lost its value.

"Moreover, you know," he continued, "I, too, was in the Resistance. It was forbidden to have Catholic boy scouts, but I managed to gather the children discreetly during the holidays and take them for walks in the countryside." He brought our conversation to an end by telling a little Jewish story: "As you are planning to go to Berlin, I must warn you that there they talk a language rather different from ours. In the time of William II, at a reception, two flunkeys who were standing at the top of a large staircase saw the last guest arriving: a Jew. One of them said, '*Ende gut, alles gut!*' (All's well that ends well) – but as he was a Berliner, he said it instead as '*End jut, alles jut!*' As the pronunciation 'jut' could be understood as 'Jude', this suggested 'All is Jewish that ends Jewish!'" The joke was fairly innocent and I heard it many dozens of times later in Berlin. Given the atmosphere of the trial, one came to wonder whether every Jewish story was not necessarily anti-Semitic.

After mass, La Gorce proposed an excursion to Wuerzburg. In all aspects of his life he tried to be at one and the same time conventional and adventurous. He was guided by his perception of 'the diplomat' as well as by a certain notion he had formed of what was likely most effectively to further his career. When he entered the Quai d'Orsay, he wondered whether he should envisage a distant posting, for example, to the Far East, or perhaps to Japan. However, La Gorce decided to stay as long as he could at the *Département* in Vichy and later in Paris. He considered it better to stay close to the centre of power. He flitted about from one office to the other, making himself known and liked, looking for a serious "patron" while avoiding getting bogged down in some over-specialised task. He kept his options open. He realised, though, that a diplomat should not remain too sedentary. Having missed the great adventure of travelling to far-away places, he liked to stay available for any small adventure within a short distance. On this modest scale he had made his own the words of Disraeli, "Adventure to the adventurous." He added, "One must always leave, whatever the circumstances, because things always take a turn for the better and it is always worth seeing new things." Another factor was that during the Nuremberg trial, Allied personnel could travel free on the railway.

Walking through Wuerzburg was more disturbing even than going through Nuremberg, where the old city had become a kind of lunar landscape and it was impossible to recognise the shapes of houses. Nuremberg's various quarters had been transformed into undulating plains covered with debris, carved up into geometrical forms as the streets were cleared, the rubble aligned in dry-stone walls so meticulously built that they presented perfectly smooth surfaces.

After only a year, ruins can already look ancient, their age hard to determine. I could not picture the life of old, as I had not known Germany before the war. At Nuremberg or Frankfurt, and later in Berlin, I saw only dead landscapes, the result of apparently natural decay. In spite of myself I remained unmoved. I could not imagine the moments when the bombs fell.

In Wuerzburg, the front walls still stood, while the roofs and floors had collapsed and lay piled upon the ground. We left the station and took the Kaiserstrasse, which was completely deserted. We had neither map nor guidebook. The façades were still there. At best, we could be archaeologists searching for a long-vanished civilisation. We did not know that Walter von der Vogelweide was buried in the Neumuenster Kirche, next to the cathedral. We did not even know that Wuerzburg was home to Tilman Riemenschneider, the sculptor, who had been mayor of the city. He was arrested and tortured because he had taken the side of the peasants at the time of the 1525 Jacquerie. Still, we saw the immense rococo façade of the House of the Falcon, which La Gorce liked as it was fashionable, elegant and aristocratic. Not far from there the sixteenth-century Chapel of the Virgin had been destroyed in the bombings. On one of the whitewashed walls a clumsy hand had written in enormous black letters the word "*Rache*!" (vengeance).

That which remained intact in Wuerzburg showed that the prince-bishops had left their mark on the city. As early as in the thirteenth century the Marienberg fortress dominated over the town from its high setting. We discovered that there was a *Residenz* to which the prince-bishops had moved in the eighteenth century, preferring the charms of a vast baroque palace to those of the austere fortress.

We crossed the River Main, indifferent to the statues mounting guard on both sides of the bridge. I thought that La Gorce was most at his ease when conversing with elderly ladies over a cup of tea, but he suddenly became as frisky as a horse let loose in a field. I had difficulty in keeping up with him when he started to climb the steep rise leading to the fortress.

Despite the heat, he did not slow down. Some Nuremberg old hands told me that they had seen him in Paris, cycling determinedly up the Boulevard Saint-Michel, very composed, wearing his usual celluloid collar and brown striped suit.

We were not allowed to enter the fortress, which had become a hospital during the war. To the families who came from visiting the sick and wounded, going back to town must have been just like Sunday excursions into the countryside during the war. The small boys in lederhosen jumped about, shrieking for joy. A few years before, their future would have been predictable: Hitler youth, Labour Service, the green-grey uniform of the *Wehrmacht*, and then to the front.

Back at the *Residenz* we saw first the wrought-iron gate, its tormented design evocative of a nightmare. In the staircase, chubby cherubs supported on their fingertips a candle encased in a glass bubble. Finally, we entered the grandiose ballroom, decorated in the Italian style. On the garden side, the *Residenz* was reminiscent of the Palace of Versailles and of the Galerie des Glaces, although the façade appeared heavy with its baroque ornamentation.

The park, with its many terraces, was more theatrical than the one at Versailles. A concert was about to begin. The orchestra of twenty musicians faced fifty chairs on the lawn, of which hardly a dozen were occupied. Were the Germans with their music trying to give the illusion that nothing had changed? Were they trying to recover an identity they had for a time lost? I was reminded of the Sunday mornings in Toulouse during the last year of the Occupation. A military band set itself up at the centre of the façade of the Place du Capitole. For an hour the semi-circle of musicians went through its repertoire, moving from the martial to the sentimental. Did they hope to soften up the French in this way? During the whole hour, the Place du Capitole remained almost completely empty. The French, keeping themselves to the walls on the opposite side of the square, saw nothing, heard nothing, and said nothing.

At the *Residenz*, the sound of music rose from the lawn towards the top terrace, where the audience could sit in a nook of greenery as if in a box at the opera. The whole garden and the building began to tremble in the wind. The façade of the *Residenz* was unstable. It bowed in the breeze as if it were the canvas of a theatre set. Everything seemed filled with light; the stone urns and the truncated pyramids standing on the balustrades became elegant pretexts to accentuate the perspective and give depth to the image. It was a unique moment when all around became animated and in communion with the rest, and when nature, trees and flowers were all finding their places again. I would have liked to approach those blonde young ladies, well built, and with naïve, astonished expressions. They passed by in front of us slowly in groups of two or three for their quiet Sunday stroll. With La Gorce present, there was no question of speaking to them – no women, and above all no familiarities with anyone not belonging to his *milieu*.

From the prince-bishops we had to return to Hitler. I remembered the hope expressed by Fouques-Duparc that "you will then be in a better position to understand Nazism, which remains something mysterious." He underlined those last words by raising his eyes from his dossier dealing with the

Status of Trieste, and stared into a corner of the window at the Quai d'Orsay. His eyes of washed-out blue seemed to lose themselves in an imaginary fog rising from the Seine.

CHAPTER 10

The evening of 14 July

I was disappointed that no patriotic demonstration was held to celebrate Bastille Day. The lieutenant and his two *gendarmes* could at least have saluted the colours. However, as promised, there was a 14 July ball at the Kasino. It was as if to pretend that we were all still in France, and that we could actually go down into the village and mix with the young peasant couples. It fostered a sort of nostalgia and a wish to enter into a deliberate dream. As on the first day in the courtroom of Nuremberg, I felt I was entering a surrealist universe, when the former NCO from the Foreign Legion guarding the door to the ballroom asked, "Why don't you go and waltz around the floor? The room has been decorated with paper chains."

A few people had already arrived. I recognised Evelyne, an interpreter of Polish origin, who had become Parisian again after the Liberation. She was sitting with Katz, who until 1938 had been a German from Nuremberg. He was kind enough to invite me to his table and to buy me a whisky. A few minutes later Lalouette came and asked me to join him. Katz shouted to me, "That's a good one … someone buys you a whisky then you bugger off…"

Lalouette, who heard, said, "You don't really want to spend the evening with that Jew!" The room was beginning to fill up. The band of three musicians from Zirndorf launched into a foxtrot. A few couples skimmed past us. I was surprised to see Frau Pick in her sober olive brown American uniform, her black hair tightly drawn back, as in Caffarelli. Her cheeks were round and rosy. Her dancing partner played no particular part in Nuremberg; he was obviously one of our secret agents. I said to Lalouette, "Here is Frau Pick, whom I mentioned to you the other day." Lalouette stared at her intently; she was not embarrassed. He turned towards me and remarked, "I do not like her. She looks like an intriguer."

Lalouette's comment about "spending the evening with a Jew" was addressed indirectly to Katz. It reminded me again that, despite the circumstances, anti-Semitism in France survived not very far below the surface of good sentiments and of good manners. I remembered the atmosphere I found in Montpellier in 1941, after I had done my time in the *Chantiers de Jeunesse*. My grandfather, anti-Semitic, belonging to another generation, constantly addressed the same themes in his dinner-table conversation. These centred around political denunciations of the Socialists, the State, the Bureaucrats, the English and, curiously, Czechoslovakia, though Occupied. My grandfather expressed himself slowly and ponderously, listening to himself. He had always been unable to pronounce the name "Czechoslovakia" in one go, and always stumbled after "Czecho" as if to prove that even the name of that State was an impossibility.

The unique source of his daily commentaries was the local newspaper *L'Éclair*, printed not fifty yards away from his flat; until we got used to the noise, its rotary press kept us awake every night from ten o'clock onwards. This flat, which seemed to me ancient but which in fact dated only from the turn of the century, had balconies on three sides. The location was not very distinguished; it faced the entrance to the railway goods station. In November 1942 I watched from the balcony as some troops of General de Lattre de Tassigny embarked in cattle trucks to "move off" before the arrival of the Germans, who were then invading the non-Occupied zone.

In 1941, after months spent in the snows of the Jura, pretending to be a soldier yet without weapons, I discovered with delight in Montpellier the relaxed atmosphere of the Mediterranean countries. Here, even in mid-winter, people could lounge about in the sun, pass their time on the terrace of a café or watch a game of pétanque under the plane trees. Not everything was innocent, for all that. One morning I experienced a shudder when I realised that I was in a country friendly to the dictators – and that everybody found the situation quite natural.

Suddenly I saw, sweeping by like a whirlwind, a column of Spanish cars preceded and followed by the black Citroëns of the French *gendarmerie*. I noticed that the uniforms were in unusual colours, red and yellow, as if the officials were arriving for a bullfight. The rumour went around soon after that Franco and his entourage had just driven through the city. This was confirmed by *L'Éclair* a few days later, in an article saying that Franco had gone to Italy to meet Mussolini at Bordighera.

On his way back, Franco stopped at Montpellier and lunched at the *Préfecture*. He had been invited by Pétain, who had come especially for the occasion with several members of his government. A dense crowd gathered on the Place de la Préfecture. Pétain appeared on the balcony. After some hesitation, the crowd applauded and began to shout, "*Vive Pétain!*" Franco joined Pétain on the balcony, so the crowd added, "*Vive Franco!*", laughing, shouting for fun, and possibly with a twinge of bad conscience. It was only a farce. The sun, the harsh light on the façade, and the theatrical and dramatic appearance of these "strong men", the dictators, combined to invite the crowd to let themselves go wild and join in.

L'Éclair, the following morning, told us that while waiting for Franco before lunch, Marshal Pétain had gone for a walk to the Pérou. Taking in the gardens at a glance, he commented, "*La France est belle!*" Another piece of information was how the Vichy government had mounted a gigantic operation to ensure the security of Franco, with a *gendarme* every fifteen metres from the Spanish border to the Italian border. Was this actually possible, even by stationing all available *gendarmes*? However, the Montpellier people derived some pride from such a demonstration of strength. It must have duly impressed Franco, who was quite a connoisseur in this field.

I tended now to react to Lalouette's utterances as I used to with my grandfather's: by identifying myself with all of the enemies they both denounced, and by rejecting all of the so-called values they commended.

Lalouette told me that he was expecting some French performers who were passing through Nuremberg: "I invited them to come here to celebrate 14 July in a truly French atmosphere." Then, to make conversation, he undertook a general survey of the trial, concluding, "In the end Nuremberg is the trial of an absentee – Hitler. The character of Hitler remains mysterious, but ...", pausing for effect. Lalouette used the same trick as had Fouques-Duparc at the Quai d'Orsay before my departure, taking time to glance towards the end of the room where two tricolours were crossed. I felt he was about to say something important. He continued, "But ... it would be possible to make a fascinating portrait of Hitler by gathering the declarations, scattered haphazardly in a number of sittings, of the Accused, his former companions, who had seen him at close quarters." It was a task I dutifully promised to undertake; on thinking it over, though, I became sure that Lalouette's advice would not have got me very far. For one thing, what were the Accused actually saying? It was that Hitler had lied to them, that he had deceived everybody, and that they, too, had been his victims.

Maybe there was a secret to discovering whatever it was that would explain the Hitler phenomenon. In the end, Hitler might reveal himself as an ordinary man, ordinary in his ideas, his projects, his view of the world; a man without originality and, finally, as not very interesting. It could be said that he was a man of limited education, one who took things literally, who could not see the difference between speaking and acting. Whereas many a "right-thinking" bourgeois may have said, "If only one could get rid of the Jews ...", Hitler, for his part, annihilated them.

Without taking matters too far, maybe he was inspired by a "philosophy of action", which would explain his policy. More simply, there could be talk of the gangster-type methods that differentiated him from other politicians. Under Weimar, Stresemann and his successors argued, claimed, and negotiated.

When Hitler was in power he put an end to the chitchat and proceeded to act. He did not ask for equality of right; he took it. He gave himself the right to re-arm; he re-occupied the Rhineland, and he carried out the *Anschluss* into Austria. Hitler would have taken the *Sudetenland* had France and Britain not done everything in their power to give it to him, with the consent of the Czechs. The world marvelled at Hitler's audacity, his cleverness, and at his Machiavellian methods, even when the simplicity and rusticity of his tricks were more relevant. Similarly, in internal politics he wasted no time in confabulations with politicians, because he simply made people toe the line.

Today, I still remain sceptical of the value of the research into the origins of Hitler's ideas. Did he truly espouse the ideas of an obscure sect founded by a former monk? There are fewer hidden sources that might have shaped his thinking and inflamed his imagination: the story of Max and Moritz, for example, a work for children by the anti-Semite Wilhelm Busch, which nowadays sells very well in West German shops. It is an apparently innocuous work, the equivalent of the *Sapeur Camembert* or the *Famille Fenouillard* in France. Below the surface, though, the story of Max and Moritz can take a rather frightening anti-Semitic turn when the reader considers that, one day, a man would have the power to transform it into reality.

Max and Moritz are two little boys. They are very cunning, too cunning (as the Jews are said to be). They are so cunning that they play dirty tricks on the widow Bolte and on schoolmaster Laempel, who are quiet, steady and decent Germans. Max and Moritz believe that they can carry on behaving like this until the master baker seizes them by the collar, rolls them in flour, and puts them into the oven. It is already the "final solution", including the furnace of the crematorium. In the work by Busch, the story ends up with the whole village rejoicing and saying, "Thank God! An end has been put to those who were harming us!"

The French performers had not turned up. Lalouette scanned the crowd in the room searching for people who would come and join him at his table to make up a "party". His choice fell on a General of the French zone administration, a quiet, fat giant of a man, with eyes as black as olives, who was a visitor to the Trial. For the previous three days he had missed not one minute of the sittings, looking longingly at the Defendants' bench as an owl watching for mice. Fuster nicknamed him "the satrap", as he had been told that the General was the big chief of the Occupation in Wurttemburg. Lalouette asked me to invite "the satrap" to his table.

The satrap proved actually to be the Director of Prisons for the French zone in Austria. To liven up the conversation, he talked about some of his top prisoners. One of them had, before the war, been a hotelkeeper in a ski resort. In the war he became a policeman. The satrap told us in detail of the tortures inflicted by the former hotelkeeper on his "clients". The torture consisted of progressively tightening a screw until the testicles burst. The art of the torture resided, of course, in making it last as long as possible. Several attempts could even be made.

I noticed Lalouette's repugnance at listening to the satrap as soon as the conversation turned to prisons. I saw his face, usually blotchy, becoming paler at the turn of each screw and wondered how much more he could bear to hear. The satrap reached the moral of his story: "How could it be that a hotelkeeper practised such tortures, while in his profession all of his efforts were directed at rendering the stay of his clients as comfortable and as pleasant as possible?" Who knows? Perhaps the war gave this man the opportunity of taking his revenge or playing out his dreams and his nightmares.

Fortunately, Dubost came to relieve us of the satrap, who seemed well on the way to treating us to his horrific stories for the whole evening. The satrap must have been a high civil servant within the prison administration of France then sent to Germany – or, rather, Austria – to perform there his delicate functions. Dubost, always anxious to make himself popular with the civil servants of the Justice ministry, believed it was imperative for him to take possession of the visitor for the rest of the evening. With no regret, we watched them leave.

The performers finally arrived. Clearly, Lalouette had met them several times before in Nuremberg, when they were at the Grand Hotel at "cabaret" time. They belonged to three generations. "Granny", barely fifty, sat opposite Lalouette. I was lucky enough to sit by the granddaughter, an eighteen-year-old blonde with a calm, limpid face. She had been brought up by very strict parents who were still young and whose faces expressed seriousness, the habit of discipline, and the taste for a well-ordered life. Granny was the one with flashing eyes. Lalouette led her onto the dance floor.

We might well have pretended we were at a village dance in France, though the illusion slowly faded. Lalouette had to force himself harder to remain jovial with the French artistes. The parents were fearful that their blonde daughter might find it too warm if she danced too much. Only Granny kept on smiling. Everyone felt that the fun of patriotic fraternisation wore off by lasting too long. Lalouette proposed to go back to the Grand Hotel in Nuremberg to finish up the evening. The group took two taxis. At the Grand Hotel I regained my freedom, and bumped into La Gorce. He had been with a friend for a walk in the ruins of the city. They counted three inhabited houses; the third was a brothel. The evening was so warm that the girls were sitting on a bench outside, facing the city walls from where the passers-by could observe them. "They are living testimonies to a routed army," La Gorce's friend said. "These poor girls are like scarecrows, with their distraught faces, their feverish eyes ringed with deep, dark shadows, and their empty stares. They seem to make a tableau vivant depicting the horrors of war. Who would dare go anywhere near them and take the risk of touching them – even without having to pay! ... Are you going back to Zirndorf? We'll give you a lift."

The taxi dropped us off at the Kasino in Zirndorf. In the clear warm night the sound of crickets was everywhere. It was a reminder of the summer evenings in the south of France near Villeveyrac at my grandfather's when I was a child. In the distance, Sète Mountain seemed an enormous monster crouching in the dark, speckled by dozens of lights from isolated cottages.

We went up to the Dubost villa. Curiously, at the gate American military policemen asked for our identity cards. Dubost told us that on this Bastille Day the Americans were worried about finding the French *gendarmes* at their posts to ensure the French prosecutor's safety. They had left behind two of their own policemen to teach a lesson to our *gendarmes*.

Dubost was, as every night, ready to launch into a long conversation. It was a way for him to conceal his idleness. La Gorce, however, delighted to find himself in the presence of an 'important' person, lent himself gracefully to listening to a general survey of the Trial. Moreover, in return, he expressed himself very frankly. La Gorce thought the Trial "premature", and that holding it several years later would have allowed an "historical perspective". It was a way of saying that he was absolutely against the Trial. Dubost, for his part, acknowledged that there were arguments for and against. "Yes," he said, "but if one entered into detail, if one wanted to understand everything, one could never condemn."

I was looking for a pretext to pass the time. I accompanied La Gorce to his villa. The night was to be very long. Dubost was to settle in the bedroom I shared with the younger members of the delegation to be sure of a captive audience. Through his conversation, he was to offer us an *ersatz* and verbal version of the traditional 14 July fireworks that had not taken place.

La Gorce's villa was the first on a modern housing estate. The last was occupied by a lady from Berlin, elegant, very blonde and slim, living alone with mother; she was someone who liked an active social life. That evening her American friend, an NCO, was due, loaded with parcels from the PX. I could see that I was not wanted.

Walking back to my villa, I was thinking of Goering and his companions, alone in their cells. Each was watched around the clock by an American soldier. Did they think about their imminent death? Did they reconcile themselves to their fate? One day at Caffarelli, one of the internees escaped; he was a former Gestapo agent fallen into disgrace, probably because he had shown himself to be too greedy. In the prison he adapted easily to the existing conditions, had become the favourite internee of the *Unteroffizier*, and would have acted as boss were it not for Petit-Louis and his men. However, along with the little Czech doctor he was the organiser of the black market. "Here, you can have anything you want," he told me when I arrived, "wine, cigarettes ... at the same price as outside." As the Gestapo had emptied my pockets, the prices "as outside" were of no great advantage to me.

His escape took place a few weeks after my arrival at Caffarelli. He had quite simply jumped over the wall. I never knew why. Had he been warned of an impending danger? He put on his best clothes and for the whole afternoon stood near a window, motionless, staring at a point on the other side of the street, nervous and trembling like a cat ready to pounce. The soldiers noticed his escape before we did. At evening rollcall, the *Unteroffizier* appeared in full rig-out, wearing his helmet as if about to go onto the attack. I hardly had time to shout my "*Stilgestanden!*" when he yelled, "*Man hat mir eine grosse Schweinerei gemacht!*" ("Someone has pulled a dirty trick on me!").

The scene moved on as the *Unteroffizier* went into another room to renew his squawking. I did not understand what was going on. When calm was restored, the rumour went around that the ex-*Gestapist*, the 'don' of the black market, had disappeared; in reprisal, the following morning the *Gestapo* was to shoot the youngest among us. This seemed to me absurd, but my comrades seemed to take it lightly. Yet rumours that had previously circulated in our little milieu had always proved correct.

Thinking it over, I suddenly realised that I was by far the youngest internee on the Aryan side. The Parisian explained to us that the Gestapo, before executions, used to pin a red target in the shape of a heart onto the chest of the victim.

Was it really the end for me? I managed to convince myself so, for I considered that it was better to prepare myself mentally for the worst now so as not to be surprised by the event. I lay down on the straw, as I did every evening, but in the knowledge that this time would be my last. No, I would not be able to sleep. I felt myself tense, even if I showed no emotion to the others. I took care not to let them know that I already felt condemned. The noises from the city, which also did not want to go to sleep, rose through the open windows. Petit-Louis conferred in a corner with his trusted lieutenants.

Then I was overcome by a feeling of peace, an utter calm. There was no longer anything in front of me. The whole future counted for nothing. It stopped and remained fixed, immutable. In the end I simply dropped off to sleep, perfectly sure that I would die the following day. I woke up rather late. I forgot that this was to be my last morning. I had to force myself to acknowledge it and even then could not believe it. Actually, nothing happened: it was a day like any other. The Gestapo let it be known that it had lost interest in the ex-*Gestapist*; his escape was the business of the *Wehrmacht*. Anyway, he had escaped precisely the day before he would have been freed.

Back at the villa I saw that I had guessed right, and Dubost was indeed holding court in our bedroom. Another short night! Did he have nothing to do during the day? Once more, he was treating his small circle to a tale of his feat at assizes. Through evoking his past successes, he was freeing himself from nerves on the eve of his final assault against Goering.

You had to know your juries, he was saying. Juries composed of peasants, for example, were merciless in condemning arsonists who had destroyed crops. You had also to outsmart the barristers, who played the sentiment card to juries. Some prosecutors – and he was not one of them – used feints, perfectly legitimate ones. During the course of the debates, they would direct their attacks towards a certain objective then during their closing speech would abruptly change their argumentation. This way, they would upset the barristers, who had no time to alter their carefully prepared speeches. It was even possible, he maintained, to change the count of the indictment and accuse the defendant of a different crime – during the sitting and at the very last moment. The barristers would, no doubt, protest furiously, but the *Court de Cassation* would take no notice of them.

Changing the subject, Dubost talked about his family, whom he had left in Paris. Was it another cause for worry for him? Under his tough-guy exterior Dubost was, I thought, a soft-hearted man. He certainly needed the human warmth he found in a group of listeners. During the day he lectured to the French magistrates, who had come for a short visit to Nuremberg. In the evenings, he fell back on those who were, as was he, playing a small part in the Trial. There was in our room a young translator, rather astute looking, Yugoslav on his mother's side, who spoke fluent German. He was Dubost's most respectful, patient listener. Some time later he was expelled with scant ceremony from the delegation and sent back to France – as soon as the intelligence services discovered that he had volunteered to work in Germany during the war.

Towards midnight, Dubost suddenly decided to do something to celebrate 14 July. "Let's go and fetch Ginette!" he said. The suggestion was ignored.

CHAPTER 11

Von Rundstedt: No Brutalities in the West

Lalouette danced very formally with Granny at the 14 July ball, back arched and chin held high. He looked at the two crossed tricolours on the opposite wall. I reflected that he was a reserve cavalry captain, a fact of which he often reminded me. I wondered whether, in the patriotic atmosphere of 14 July, there lay under the trappings of a diplomat with his inscrutable face the slumbering soul of a hussar, which might awaken, if only for a moment. As the couple danced closer I could hear Lalouette murmur to Granny, "I love France."

I relived in my memory the various Bastille Days of recent years. That of 1940 felt closest to here. On 14 July 1940, I was in Châlus in the Limousin. I had arrived there a few days earlier with a few thousand others from the artillery depots of La Rochelle and Rochefort freed by the Germans; they had so many prisoners that a few thousand more or fewer made no difference. In the non-Occupied zone, a French cavalry unit took charge of us. I admired the young officers, who, despite everything, managed to keep their cool, as well as their horses and their haughtiness. Their uniforms were admirably cut by a civilian tailor, the silk shirts were of the shade of weak tea, and their riding boots made to measure, gleaming. They observed very strictly the principles of the French school of equestrianism. It required them to keep the heels low and to make their close trot really close, the buttocks following every impulse from the saddle. Elbows were held tight to the body, while the little finger exerted precise and discreet control on the rein. The cavalrymen paid us a visit every day in the farms where we were located. Their arrival was signalled by the rhythmic jingling of the curb chains.

On the morning of 14 July 1940, soldiers and officers from the most diverse units, wrecks and remnants of the routed army, were mooching around in the Châlus streets when a bugle call came up from the fairground. A ceremony was taking place. The colonel, a captain and a few men were laying a wreath at the 1914-1918 war memorial. The whole happened in discreet fashion, almost on the sly.

Hearing the bugle call, hundreds of soldiers ran towards the fairground, used during the week for the cattle market. The bugle played the Last Post, arousing deep-seated instincts. The soldiers were in an ugly mood. Anger drove them. There were resentment at those last weeks, frustration as a consequence of the defeat, and hatred of the army and its chiefs who had led them into a humiliating and pointless war. The soldier had only one thought in mind: to go home. The ceremony, however modest, was to them a form of provocation. I felt an elementary emotion surging through the groups, probably very similar to that which provoked the 1917 Russian Revolution.

The captain walked across the fairground towards his mess. He was suddenly surrounded by the swarming mass of soldiers, threatening and almost insulting in their demand to know "When are we going to be demobilised?" Talking to three soldiers in an informal tone, being friendly, and addressing all three, the captain responded, "But I too would very much like to go back home and see my wife." He managed to calm them down. Did he really share their preoccupations, as he made them believe he did?

The cavalry had a long aristocratic tradition. They looked dapper even in defeat. When they thought of Germany, they looked with some nostalgia at the Prussian *Junkers*, a caste they assumed to be identical to themselves and which, faithful to its ideals through the last centuries, had caused the rise of both Prussia and Germany. Was not Prussia "an army possessing a country?" France's destiny would have been different if it had remained faithful to a certain ideal.

Prussia's ideal was evoked at Nuremberg by Marshal von Rundstedt during his cross-examination by a member of the British delegation, Peter Calvocoressi.[31] The Prussian Marshal was not an easy character. He attended not as a Defendant, but as a witness in the case against the General Staff. He did not come even as a defeated man. He had achieved notable successes, in particular in the Ardennes breakthrough during the last winter of the war. He posed as the most senior of the German Generals, as the man of an earlier generation who believed in chivalry in warfare, one who had known the cavalry charges and also the bayonet charges of 1914. Von Rundstedt was an old soldier who had always tried to train the young officers according to the old military traditions. In brief, von Rundstedt

---

[31] *The German edition of the Trial describes him as "Fregattenkapitaen", an obvious mistake as he was a barrister in civilian life and had worn RAF uniform during the war.*

was a figure awe-inspiring enough to terrify subordinates. The haughtiness, the jerky delivery, and the rough-hewn features of an impassive face combined to make one feel that he was a real Prussian.

Calvocoressi began to question von Rundstedt, although it was not immediately clear where he was leading. He was trying to define the relationship that existed between the Generals and Hitler. He mentioned the word "politics" and alluded to General von Seeckt, which gave von Rundstedt the opportunity to invoke the Prussian tradition of adopting a non-political stance (the *"Nur Soldat"* [just a soldier, following orders] of von Seeckt):

It is a very old Prussian tradition that the officer has not to be concerned with politics and General von Seeckt has supported in the most loyal fashion the Weimar government according to the Constitution; he supported it as much against the Right in Kapp Putsch as against the Left during the uprising of the Communists in the Ruhr.

Calvocoressi was trying to encourage von Rundstedt to say that he supported Hitler because Hitler had succeeded where Kapp had failed. This gave von Rundstedt another opportunity to justify his position:

I must take note of the fact that Hitler was called to the government under Hindenburg legally, by the majority of the people and as head of the most important party, in a perfectly democratic and constitutional fashion and not as a result of a Putsch ... We have done our duty because Hitler was legally appointed by Hindenburg. After Hindenburg's death and by virtue of his will, Hitler could appear as the Fuehrer.

Von Rundstedt tried to adopt a rigid and unassailable stand, the legal character of which was perhaps not very firm; did the Nazis actually obtain a majority before coming to power, and was Hindenburg's will enough to make Hitler the Fuehrer? Von Rundstedt's legalism and democratism were in answer to Calvocoressi's remark reminding von Rundstedt that Marshal von Blomberg, the War Minister, had said that the Generals had no reason to oppose Hitler, who was giving them exactly what they had always asked for.

As a result of the exchange on the attitude of the Generals in political matters, von Rundstedt established an absolutely watertight system of defence. It held that the soldier is not a political activist; he may, admittedly, have political views (condemning the excesses committed by the Nazis, for example), but he must keep them in his heart of hearts. He may neither express them nor translate them into actions. Such was the Prussian tradition; such had been General von Seeckt's attitude under Weimar, as von Rundstedt understood it. Previously, when a Counsel for the Defence asked him, "Did you not think to remove Hitler by force?" von Rundstedt answered, "That would have been purely and simply treason."

This is why, at a certain point in the cross-examination when Calvocoressi asked, "You consider yourself a patriot, don't you?", it could have been predicted that von Rundstedt would give a ready-made and scathing answer. Raeder, whom I had observed as he followed the exchange with an ironic smile on his face, buried his head in his hands. In politics Calvocoressi was a Liberal. He saw no reason to act deferentially in the presence of the military and, above all, he believed that each should act according to his conscience. There was then little likelihood that he would have anything at all in common with von Rundstedt.

What neither Grand Admiral Raeder nor Marshal von Rundstedt suspected was that they were facing in Calvocoressi somebody unusually well informed. During almost the whole war, he had read and exploited the *Wehrmacht* wireless traffic, enciphered by the Enigma machine. The British had actually succeeded in intercepting and deciphering German military communications, one of the most remarkable feats of the war. In the eyes of the Prussians, Calvocoressi must have passed for a civilian, even if he were wearing a military uniform. Moreover, a music enthusiast, Calvocoressi was personally inclined to take a greater interest in German music than in the German army. He spent his evenings during the war listening to musicians of the Viennese school, a way of evoking another Germany. Calvocoressi had acquired in Buckinghamshire a fairly large house a few miles from Bletchley, where the Enigma signals were decoded, and provided billets in his home for those of his colleagues who shared his interest in music or could play an instrument. Calvocoressi's task had been to analyse the deciphered materials, which, unknown to the general public, provided guidance for an attack on the weaker sections of the German forces.

Given that my life underground had been useless, I could see a parallel: I assumed the imaginary character of 'Roger Bousquet' and spent my evenings reading the German Romantics. Of the dozens of authors whose company I kept, I identified myself more closely with one of Jean-Paul Richter's characters. This was Wutz, the little schoolmaster who, solitary the whole winter long, studied publishers' catalogues. Because he had too little money to afford the books they advertised, he re-created in his imagination the works of which he knew only the titles...

Towards the end of the cross-examination, Calvocoressi tried to discover why the German soldier, so disciplined, had committed brutalities. Von Runstedt answered, "Within the territory under my command, there have been no brutalities."

No brutalities in the West? The memory of the Oradour-sur-Glane massacre and of the killing of *maquisards* sprang immediately to my mind. In the villages of the Lot-et-Garonne or the Dordogne, there are all too many monuments or simple plaques commemorating shootings by the Germans, such as the memorial to four young men killed during the fighting or after, and women and children who were "victims of German barbarity". Many of the crimes cited at Nuremberg seemed distant; nevertheless, the brutal repression of the Resistance was too close to be forgotten. The victims left behind families who were still traumatised. These families could hardly have been persuaded that it was justified, legitimate or 'normal' to execute *maquisards* once they had been taken prisoner and therefore rendered harmless. Would the judgement determine that *maquisards* were *francs-tireurs* (in it only for the money) and as such traditionally not protected by the laws governing warfare?

I would have been very wary of mentioning this aspect to Lalouette. Although I knew little of his career during the war, I sensed that his sympathies had never been on the side of the Resistance. The Quai d'Orsay people, even the Resistants among them, displayed a certain snobbism towards the Resistance, which they considered as slightly vulgar.

CHAPTER 12

Sauckel, the Recruiting Sergeant

From where I was sitting, it was easy to observe Sauckel in the second rank of the Accused. He was always out of line: constantly attentive, he leaned forward in order to follow better what was going on. He tried his utmost yet right until the end he failed to understand what was happening to him. He believed that he had done his best during the war. He had done his duty as a recruiting sergeant to supply labour to the German economy and he had done what he could to ensure good living conditions for the foreign workers in Germany.

Of all of the Defendants, Sauckel was the only one who could pass for a manual worker. In fact, he had started out as a sailor. He was obviously out of place among the aristocrats, the ambassadors, the admirals, the generals, and the highly placed civil servants surrounding him. Even the defence lawyers looked down on him. What could they have in common with this man? Furthermore, historians for the last forty years seem to have had nothing but scorn for this little man. They ignored him; he was not interesting.[32]

---

[32] *One example is the fact that the book by Joachim C. Fest, The Face of the Third Reich, does not mention Sauckel's name once.*

To several million men during the war, Sauckel actually was important. At Nuremberg, my gaze kept falling on him, an obtuse Nazi with a polished skull, a toothbrush moustache that schoolchildren in my time called "snotty-nosed". He was, though, a sincere Nazi. To a greater extent than the other Defendants, he was probably typical of the millions of Germans who had followed Hitler without knowing or understanding where they were being led.

I sometimes reflected that, of all those present in the Courtroom, I was most probably the only one who had suffered from Sauckel's activities. It was a question of age, of belonging to the class of 1940.

During the early years of the Occupation, Hitler granted France a privileged status; then, in 1943, he decided that France should be treated as the other Occupied countries. Sauckel received a directive from Speer to that effect. Consequently, Sauckel was sent to Vichy to "negotiate" the sending of French workers to Germany. That was his crime. Small wonder he did not consider himself a criminal. Strictly speaking, at least in France, he did not have to force young people to leave for Germany. The recruiting was done by the French authorities, and the recruits were simply invited to catch a train for Germany on such and such a day at such and such a time. It could have been claimed that they left of their own free will.

In July 1943, I was called up to work in Germany. The Government of the *Maréchal* presented the *Service du Travail Obligatoire* (STO, or National Service) as a patriotic duty. Was it mobilisation in wartime? The procedure of registration and the medical examination of batches of naked young men, orchestrated by the *gendarmes*, made it seem that a real recruiting board was officiating. As early as in 1940, when the French army was truly routed, the Reynaud government had called me up to join the contingent of the "Marie-Louise".

I was called up again in 1943, less passive then. I finally understood that the youngsters of my age were just pawns being pushed around shamelessly by Generals and Ministers in some of their less admirable moves. In 1940, Paul Reynaud subsequently thought of sending us to North Africa to continue the war from there, supported by the rest of the French overseas empire. Reynaud himself stayed in France. Once the Armistice was concluded with the Germans, the Vichy Government, in their turn, in order to keep our year group busy, had a brilliant idea: to create *Chantiers de Jeunesse* (Youth Camps) instead of military service and, supremely cleverly, prepared under the very noses of the German secret service a secret army for the day when...

The day when – what? Actually, nobody seriously believed that such a day would ever come. Meanwhile, a task must be found to occupy those twenty-year-olds. In a moment of inspiration, Paul Baudouin, a Minister of the *Maréchal* suggested using them to build the Trans-Saharan railway. A grandiose task, indeed. Fortunately for me, the idea was quickly forgotten. Besides, the Germans would not have allowed the transfer of soldiers to North Africa on such a scale. I congratulated myself for the second time within a few weeks at again having eluded the risk of ending my days on African soil.

Was I in 1943 really likely to take seriously the patriotic call of the Vichy Government asking me – ordering me – to go to work in Germany? This would, we were told, have hastened the return of "our dear prisoners", for whom the *Maréchal* showed the greatest solicitude whenever he could. I had already been a prisoner of war for a few weeks in 1940, and had no desire to find myself in a similar predicament by a sort of "exchange" with my unfortunate former comrades. The whole notion held a hint of blackmail, with the Germans using prisoners of war as human currency to buy in more labour for their economy. Frankly, I could not see myself turning out shells in the Ruhr or tightening bolts in Stuttgart in order to aid Germany's victory.

I experienced not one second's hesitation in becoming a *réfractaire* (objector) at the very last moment. I had completed the preliminary formalities preceding a departure for Germany, which were presented officially as a *recensement du contingent* (registration of the battalion) under the pretence that we were being called up for military service. I left for Toulouse, where suddenly things appeared in their true colours: the Vichy authorities were putting me into the hands of the German labour services, those of the very same Sauckel whom I saw in front of me at Nuremberg, and the Germans were making me sign a work contract. I understood immediately that to sign that contract meant I was placing myself "voluntarily" under the thumb of German law. Therefore, I would enjoy none of the legal guarantees protecting prisoners of war under international conventions.

As it happened, I was by then a young lawyer who had gained his doctorate a few days earlier. I had no difficulty in searching my memory for recollections of international law, from which it appeared that the occupying power had no right to transfer the civilian population to Germany to make them work for the German war effort.

So, I would become a *réfractaire* – but *how*? On the eve of my presumed departure the Resistance sent a sign in my direction: if I did not want to go to Germany, they could help me to hide. I was accommodated for a few days near Port-Sainte-Marie by a small landowner who obviously belonged to a rather mysterious organisation. I worked on the farm to justify my presence *vis-à-vis* the neighbours. The season came for the communal threshing. Two girls from Agen, whom I had seen at a newspaper stall near the railway station, came to brighten up the meal, always a real banquet on those occasions, a joyous affair with about twenty farm labourers who helped out. The girls from Agen sang light-hearted songs. We waltzed on the grass. Guests helped themselves freely from the packets of *gris* tobacco spread out on the table, a windfall in those days of rationing. The daughter of a neighbouring landowner tried to attract my attention, but I took no notice as I was far more preoccupied with what was going to happen to me.

I shared the family life. The wife was slightly worried about the comings and goings in her house. She could not see why the girls from Agen were there. I remained preoccupied. My host asked at the evening meal, "So, the wine; do you take it in the glass or in the plate?" I answered without thinking, "In the glass!", not realising that I was missing the opportunity to make *chabrot*, also known as *chabròl*. This is when a glass of red wine is tipped into the dinner plate to mix with the last good drops of gravy, and is then drunk from the plate. Two days went by. I was confined to a room. Twice a day, I was submitted to questioning, which seemed to me very elementary, and of which the meaning was unclear.

They asked a few trick questions. I was told that Toulouse railway station had just been bombed by the British. "Well, that is strange," I said, "as less than a week ago I spent the night at the Terminus Hotel, which is located in the station itself. I must have had a lucky escape!" It was to judge my reactions, for Toulouse had indeed not been bombed. The questions continued. The examiner was a strong lad who was, I thought, of German origin. The small landowner who was my host protested his loyalty and told the German, "For myself, you know, I am Republican!" And when we were alone together, my host said – as if he wished to increase his own admiration for an examiner, "You know, he has fought in Spain, and when he goes to work in the fields he is always armed!"

The third day of questioning brought what seemed to be the essential issue: "What is your attitude to the working class?" I was truly taken aback and began to splutter. My answers were, however, found satisfactory by my examiner, who was now accompanied by another character with a more discreet profile, probably higher up in the hierarchy. I was considered as obviously sincere in my answers and they were ready to accept me – but for what? I mentioned that I wished to cross into Spain and join General de Gaulle's camp. "It is finished," they told me. "This is no longer the thing to do. There is now an agreement among all of the groups: we resist in France, on the spot."

I learned gradually what was expected of me: to join the others in the Landes forest, to dig a hole in the ground, and to wait for the landings. That did not seem to me a serious proposition. In the end, my questioners dotted the 'i's for me. The objective was to "punish the traitors".³³

When I think it over again nowadays, I can see that my questioners, in spite of the apparently slow and careful initiation, had gone too fast over uncharted ground. The idea of "punishing the traitors" worried me.

I was too much of a *petit-bourgeois*, too prudent, to throw myself into that adventure. For them it was different. They were professionals. The years of struggle, the long-practised discipline of being an "illegal", had hardened them. I admired their focus on security as well as the care with which they followed procedures. For example, before making a telephone call, they put down in writing exactly what they wanted to say, so as to be sure not to say more; also, they used a network of mailboxes to transmit written messages. I was impressed with the way they kept cool heads. Thanks to them, I understood that the important feature of being in the Resistance was not to fight the Germans, but to be

---

³³ *Was I wrong to take this as a strict directive? Years after the Liberation, "Punish the traitors!" was displayed as a slogan on giant banners at Communist mass-meetings, but it seemed by then to have lost its urgency and relevance.*
On Sunday 27 June 1943 after mass, General de Gaulle used the same language in a speech in Tunis: "We have ... to punish the traitors" (Mémoires de Guerre, paperback edition, Vol. 2, p. 150). What de Gaulle actually meant by "traitors" was spelled out in a decision of the Algiers Committee of 3 September 1943 proposing: "To make sure as soon as circumstances allow, that Justice is visited on Marshal Pétain and those who are or were members of the pseudo-governments formed by him, who have capitulated or made an attempt against the Constitution, collaborated with the enemy, delivered French workers to the Germans and made French forces fight against the Allies or against those Frenchmen who had kept on fighting." (Ibid., p. 161.) The clarification was quite precise and restrictive.

there, and to be ready to intervene on the day of Liberation after the Germans had left. I was wrong to see in this the revelation of a political calculation, realistic and almost cynical. To these people, fighting the Germans – as they understood it – was merely a phase in an historical evolution, one that would bring other changes and about-turns.

I decided to leave them and to go underground on my own. I thought I could hide more effectively in Toulouse by merging into the mass of the inhabitants. I explained this frankly; they took it very well. The smallholder led me back to my family, cycling in the middle of the night, taking roundabout roads through the hills of the Gers. These excessive precautions made me think that we were doing something dangerous. I was anxious to regain my independence as soon as possible, and feared that by staying too long in their group I would reach a point of no return. I wondered many times then and later whether they would hold it against me after the war. I was somewhat ashamed of myself. I would have liked to be another kind of person, someone who would have thrown himself into communal action.

- But where would that have led me?[34]

Against Sauckel, the Prosecution was very effective. I was not at Nuremberg when Sauckel was

---

[34] *I saw my host again after the Liberation. Everything had gone all right, and their group suffered no losses. However, he was denounced by the road-mender, who had noticed unusual comings and goings around the house, but got off without too much harm. Incidentally, the road-mender would no longer have the opportunity of talking too much. My host, what was he doing nowadays? As before, nothing had changed. Oh yes, he had bought the estate of his neighbour, the old lady I saw on the day they were threshing the harvest.* [34] *After a few months, the STO had become a farce thanks to the natural lack of discipline of the French. Not even ten per cent of those called up agreed to go to Germany. Instead, by and large, they joined the Resistance.*

cross-examined; from the transcript, it appeared that Herzog, on the French side, had proved that workers had been forced to go to Germany, and that the *Wehrmacht* and the SD had been used to that effect.

This was not, however, my experience. Only the French *gendarmerie* was after me. They traced my last residences in the Occupied and non-Occupied zones; they also enquired about me and no doubt wrote substantial reports, although did not try too seriously to arrest me.[34]

Herzog also proved that the Gestapo searched for escaped workers. This was probably true in Germany. Sauckel said that there was no other way of proceeding. I am sure that some of the foreign workers eventually found themselves in concentration camps. In my case, the Gestapo arrested me in France more by luck than by design.

– Servatius, Defence Counsel for Sauckel, tried unsuccessfully to erase the impression left by the written testimony of a doctor at the Krupp works. In it was described the poor treatment received by foreignlabourers, who suffered from tuberculosis, typhus, infected food, and bad lodgings: in extreme cases, these were old latrines after the bombings.

That French workers were badly treated was no surprise to me, as by signing a contract with the Germans they forfeited any special rights to which they may have been entitled. They fell entirely under German law. They lacked the protected status of prisoners of war. This consideration was uppermost in my mind when I decided not to go to Germany when called up, allegedly to take the place of a prisoner of war.

Not all slave labourers (*déportés du travail*) were badly treated. I had a colleague after the war who had been very happy working in a factory near Minden; he told me rather pointedly that there was no reason to refuse to go to Germany. He believed in Germany's ultimate victory and had been planning for after the war, for his future career to continue within the complex of industries where he worked.

Sauckel was tackled by the Russian, Alexandrov, too. This turned into a four-hour slanging match, in particular about statistics. The President, Lawrence, intervened to say that it was irrelevant whether there had been five or seven million slave labourers in Germany.

The aristocratic US Judge Biddle was irritated by Sauckel's vulgarity in shouting at Alexandrov. He undertook to re-examine Sauckel the following day, after which he wrote to his wife: "The French and the Russian had been quite inadequate and I decided to go to town on him and spent a couple of the hours studying the case last night. I really got him. He was frightened, brief and totally unresponsive. If I raised my hand he would stop in the middle of a sentence ... it took three-quarters of an hour, and I thoroughly enjoyed it and felt pleasantly relaxed as a result."[35]

Sauckel was eventually hanged. He was not solely responsible for the deportation of workers to Germany. He had under his control a number of commissions, Germans participating in the recruiting, who were fanatics, most of them. They put a black mark against my name on their lists because I wanted to delay my departure in order to undergo

---

[35] *Quoted by Ann and John Tusa, The Nuremberg Trial, p.380 from the Biddle Papers, letter of 31 May 1946, Box 19.*

an operation. Among those commissions there was in Toulouse a Vichy element composed of pleasant young men, who told the candidates quite openly, "You do not need to go. Trains are leaving practically empty. Ten people are going when there should be several hundred." The advice was enough. It did not need much repetition.

Sauckel's boss, Speer, sitting a few places away along the same bench, had managed his defence much more effectively.

Speer was helped in this by the US Prosecutor, Jackson. Was there, as has been suggested,[36] a "secret agreement" between Speer and Jackson, or perhaps a tacit agreement that Speer would "talk" and that in exchange Jackson would be "understanding"?

On the face of it, Jackson in his cross-examination showed himself remarkably incompetent – if his aim was indeed to obtain a condemnation:

As I understand it, you were struggling to get manpower enough to produce the armaments to win a war for Germany ... I am not suggesting – I repeat, I am not suggesting – that this was your responsibility. I am suggesting that this was the responsibility of the regime ... Your problem of creating armaments to win the war for Germany was made very much more difficult by this anti-Jewish campaign which was being waged by another of your co-Defendants.

Entering into the spirit of the game, Speer replied, "If the Jews who were evacuated had been allowed to

---

[36] See Adelbert Reif (ed.), *Albert Speer: Kontroversen um ein deutsches Phaenomen*, Munich, 1978, pp. 223-230.

work for me, it would have been a considerable advantage to me."

This was a clever answer. It suggested that Speer would have given the Jews a regular job without their leaving their homes.

When the issue of the bad treatment of foreign workers was raised, Jackson went out of his way to excuse Speer: "I am not attempting to say that you were personally responsible for these conditions." In the course of the cross-examination by Jackson, Speer made the key statement:

Even in an authoritarian system the leaders must accept a common responsibility, and it is impossible for them to dodge that common responsibility after the catastrophe, for if the war had been won the leaders would also presumably have laid claim to common responsibility.

Jackson, as well as the judges, was obviously delighted with this statement. The Defendants were correspondingly dismayed. Goering expressed their anger.[37] By proclaiming a "common responsibility", had Speer indeed implicated himself and acknowledged his own personal responsibility? As the other Defendants, he certainly intended to accept responsibility only "within the framework of his functions." However, the American Prosecutor went so far in excusing him that Speer felt impelled to tone

---

[37] *That evening in his cell, Speer confided to Gilbert, the prison psychologist, that in the dock Goering "announced to the others in a way that I would be sure to hear that even if I came out of this trial alive, the Feme (kangaroo court) would assassinate me for treason." Speer had breached the united front that Goering wanted to maintain against the Prosecution. (G.M. Gilbert, Nuremberg Diary, London, 1948, p. 249.)*

down slightly the impression left by Jackson. This he did rather carefully:

First, I would like to say, as you have so often mentioned my non-responsibility, that in general these conditions were true; on the basis of my statement yesterday, I should consider myself responsible. I refuse to evade responsibility. But the conditions are not what they are here said to be. Only individual cases have been cited.

Speer did not like specifics.

Jackson avoided tackling Speer too rigorously on the two points that would have been most damning for him: the employment of slave labour in the armaments industry, and the deportation of the Jews.[38]

Speer actually saved his neck, yet he was the one really responsible for the deportation of French workers to Germany. He gave the image of being a nice young man, decent and gifted. In spite of his close association with Hitler and of his belonging to the Party, he was not stained with Nazism. He was the artist, the architect, who had attracted Hitler's friendship. This was, rather, a *camaraderie* between artists. In his memoirs, Speer comes close to stating that he had been perverted by this friendship.

Furthermore, Speer enchanted his judges when he told them that, towards the end of the war, how he attempted to assassinate Hitler by introducing poison gas through the air vent of the bunker. The

---

[38] *More recently, the actual part played by Speer in this, and also in the building of concentration camps, has been described by Matthias Schmidt, Albert Speer: The end of a myth, London, 1985. It shows how Speer, in his late writings, doctored the documentation.*

reason? Speer was horrified by the scorched-earth policy of the last month of the war, and the destruction of Germany's economic infrastructure. Hitler wanted to drag Germany down with him into the abyss.

Cynics may have observed that Speer, even at that late stage of the war, showed no objections to the crimes against the Jews, the Poles, the Russian prisoners of war, or to the concentration or extermination camps. He objected to the scorched-earth policy which, by destroying German industry, was destroying his power bases; hence his *volte-face*. Speer was, in the eyes of the judges, a professional middle-class man.

Who would condemn to death an architect who had done nothing but practise his skills? Yet in the war he had become a technocrat responsible for the forced labour programme... For Speer, all of this meant only twenty years in prison, and not the death sentence pronounced on his subordinate Sauckel.

In his memoirs, where he painted a detailed and unfavourable portrait of Hitler (who came from the lower class), Speer admitted that he could not recognise as himself the man he had been. When during the war he was at the height of his power, he was considered in top Nazi circles as the likely successor to the Fuehrer, should something happen to Hitler. For this reason Himmler courted his friendship at one point. And it is remarkable that, despite everything, Speer always managed to present a good image. One proof of this is found in the fact that the plotters of 20 July 1944, without asking his permission, put his name down as a Minister on their Cabinet list.

Jackson's attitude seems difficult to understand, unless he was determined to get a "confession" at any price. An American author offers an explanation: Jackson had just suffered a serious setback in his career. He had hoped to be appointed Chief Justice of the US, but on 6 June 1946 President Truman designated Fred Vinson, Secretary of the Treasury, for the post. As a result, "all the heart and fire had gone out of the American Prosecutor."[39] However, Speer gave Dodd, one of Jackson's assistants, originally assigned to deal with him, to understand that he would prefer to be cross-examined by the chief US Prosecutor. This could have been due to vanity on his part, a desire to be treated on the samefooting as Goering, or possibly that, after the disaster of Goering's cross-examination, Speer perceived that Jackson would pose little danger.

---

[39] *Robert C. Conot, Justice at Nuremberg, London, 1983, p. 442.*

CHAPTER 13

Jodl: Commandos and Terrorists

Jodl's Defence Counsel was someone he knew. Jodl was charged on four counts although he was condemned to death mainly, it would seem, because he signed the Fuehrer's Order on the Commandos. He had, however, the sympathy of many, including his Defence Counsel. This was not so for all of the Defendants. As Counsel he had chosen Dr. Exner, a law professor, who appeared in Nuremberg wearing a purple gown. Exner had known Jodl some twenty years earlier.

I made his acquaintance about 20 years before in the house of his uncle, the philosopher Friedrich Jodl, in Vienna. There I had a conversation with him on training for the career of an officer. The young captain spoke with such moral earnestness, and what he said was so far from anything that could be called militarism, that I have always retained it in my memory. I then lost all contact with him until last autumn, when I received the surprising summons to defend him here. My first thought was, 'This gallant soldier must be helped!' But I doubted whether I should undertake this, as I am not a professional attorney. But when I met him in the courthouse for the first time, he said to me something that swept away all of my doubts: 'Rest assured, Professor,' he said, 'If I felt a spark of guilt in me, I would not choose you as my Defence Counsel.' ... Your Honours, I believe that these are the words of a gentleman, not a criminal.

When it came to it, I was not satisfied with my account of Exner's plea. He placed great emphasis on the fact that when war broke out, Jodl was on the point of leaving for a cruise in the Mediterranean – proof, said Exner, that Jodl did not see the war coming, that he did not want war, hence that he was not responsible for the war.

The argument was certainly authentic. When I put it on paper, though, it seemed somewhat trivial. The Defence Counsel spent too much time justifying the defence for his client regarding every act of aggression committed by Hitler, beginning with the Rhineland, then Austria, Czechoslovakia, Poland, Denmark, Norway, and Russia.

Without doubt, Exner was sincere in his efforts in Jodl's defence. Nevertheless, observers felt that Exner identified himself too closely with his client; by justifying all of the plans for conquest since 1933, he seemed to re-awaken all of Hitler's theses. Tactically, this was not a very clever thing to do. It would not impress the judges favourably. The judgement showed that Jodl was condemned on very precise grounds and, in particular, on the issue of the Commando Order. Admittedly, within the framework of World War II with its millions of dead, that Order may appear to be only a minor episode, but it turned out to be crucial for the Nuremberg Trial.

The Prosecution occasionally described Jodl as Keitel's Chief-of-Staff in the *Wehrmacht*'s-*fuehrungstab*. At the beginning of his cross-examination Jodl made a special point of indicating that Keitel was Chief-of-Staff, as *de facto* War Minister under Hitler, and that Jodl himself was merely in charge of the planning of operations. This was perhaps a way of limiting his responsibilities. He did not feel guilty, he claimed, because he had always tried personally to conform to The Hague and Geneva Conventions, the texts of which he always kept on his desk. On the other hand, he was a soldier, and his first duty was to obey. This was his dilemma. He tried to resolve it.

Jodl was very different from Field Marshal Keitel, who had the reputation of lacking character and of being unable to say "No" to Hitler. Keitel showed at this trial this same weakness in that he acknowledged his "responsibilities". He admitted to being responsible ("responsible within the framework of my function") for having, for example, signed the execution orders of Soviet prisoners. The war in Eastern Europe, incidentally, reached a degree of ferocity unequalled in the West, a fact that throws some light on von Rundstedt's statement that "In the West under my command there have been no brutalities."

At Nuremberg, Keitel was on the edge of falling apart altogether. He let it be known to the Prosecution that he was ready to tell everything and thus clear his conscience. However – further revealing his lack of backbone – he wanted first to warn Marshal Goering, whom he considered still as head of the military hierarchy. Goering answered, in substance, "We are all in the same boat, so if you make it capsize we shall all drown."

Jodl was a firmer character, less subservient to Hitler. Although they had daily contact, Jodl never felt close to him. On many occasions they clashed.

Jodl tried for a long time to leave his post and to fight at the head of a unit at the front.

During cross-examination Jodl defended himself vigorously, adopting the principle of offensive-defensive. He was often scathing. When he was accused of having signed the decree on the execution of the "partisans" who had been taken prisoner, he answered:

It is established by international law that the inhabitants of an occupied territory must follow the orders and instructions of the occupying power, and any uprising, any resistance against the army occupying the country, is forbidden; it is in fact partisan warfare, and international law does not lay down means of combating partisans. The principle of such warfare is an eye for an eye and a tooth for a tooth, and this is not even a German principle.

Similarly, on the topic of the political commissars, he answered rather weakly that Germany had experienced the activities of the commissars at the time of the Soviet Republic of Bavaria (in April-May 1919).

The member of the British Prosecution team who cross-examined him, Roberts, was rather heavy-handed. Jodl was able to parry many thrusts. Roberts said, "I suggest to you that nowhere at all within international law will you find that the shooting of hostages is legalised." Jodl answered, "Then it is not with certainty prohibited anywhere in international law. I believe it is an open question." Roberts was careless enough to ask him, "How many civilians, how many thousands, do you think were killed in the first movement of that 'interlude' in the bombing of Belgrade without warning?" Jodl replied,

"I cannot say, but surely a tenth of the number killed in Dresden, for example, when you had already won the war."

As far as pursuing the war against Britain was concerned, Jodl wrote, "If political means are without results, England's will to resist must be broken by force ... [by] terror attacks against English centres of population." Roberts asked him how he could justify such a plan; Jodl replied, "I admit having voiced a thought that was later put into practice with such perfection by the Anglo-American Air Force." Jodl thus managed to introduce the *tu quoque* argument, which the Tribunal decided not to accept.

If the order of the Fuehrer on the Commandos, countersigned by Jodl, was quoted so often at Nuremberg, the reason was partly because its existence was known to the British and the Americans during the course of the war. The Germans had already announced their intentions on the radio in a *Wehrmacht* communiqué of 7 October 1942. In it, the last sentence was added by Hitler: "In future, all terror and sabotage troops of the British and their accomplices who do not act as soldiers but as bandits will be treated as such by German troops and will be ruthlessly eliminated in battle wherever they appear."[40]

---

[40] *The nuances – or the absence of nuances – of the vocabulary must be appreciated. Armed groups of Resistance are called by the Germans "bands", and their members are consequently "bandits". The Russians talk of "partisans". So, for the war in Eastern Europe, there was the pairing bandits-partisans. For the war in Western Europe, the common usage is slightly different. To the Germans, the British commandos – and their "accomplices", meaning the French Resistants in particular – commit acts of "terrorism" and "sabotage". Armed Resistants are thus called "terrorists". The French talk of the "maquis", whose members are "maquisards". When the Germans talk of "terrorists", the French "maquisards" must be understood.*

Furthermore, during the war the British deciphered the radio communications of the *Wehrmacht* (the Ultra decipherings). This was still a secret at Nuremberg. The British had long known the text of the Commando Order itself of 18 October 1942, in its various versions. They attached all the more importance to it since it concerned their own people.[41]

The Fuehrer's Order of 18 October 1942 obviously violated international law, or what are accepted as the laws and customs of warfare. It ordered the execution of commandos, of the troops committing acts of terror and sabotage, whether they were soldiers outwardly in uniform or not,[42] and whether or not they were armed. If these members of commando units appeared as if wanting to surrender they should, as a matter of principle, be shown no mercy.[43]

Historically, the Commando Order was a consequence of the Dieppe raid of August 1942 by Canadian troops. The reports that reached Hitler afterwards stated that Allied commandos had been given the order to execute their prisoners should the

---

[41] *On 18 October 1942 two orders were issued, one destined for the troops (Nuremberg doc. 498 PS) and the other for the Commanders-in-Chief (doc. 503 PS). The expressions in both texts are quite sharp: "bis auf den letzten Mann niederzumachen" (hunt down to the last man) (498 PS) and "ausnahmlos bis zum letzten Mann niedergemacht" (without exception hunted down to the last man) (503 PS).*

[42] *The phrase "outwardly in uniform" may seem bizarre. Jodl, according to his declarations in Nuremberg, was preoccupied by the fact that members of commando units could wear civilian clothes under their uniform.*

[43] *In the text of 18 October 1942 the "terrorists" (masquiards, for the French) were not mentioned. There were at that time in France almost no maquis – or very few. Hitler's instructions were renewed after the Normandy landings; the July 1944 text mentions several times the "groups of terrorists and saboteurs", a reference to the masquisards. The repression of both the Commandos and the Resistance was thus settled in one document.*

situation require it.⁴⁴ In retaliation, Hitler gave the order to execute Allied commandos. As usual, Keitel submitted himself blindly to Hitler's will. On the other hand, Jodl initially expressed his opposition to such an order, yet in the end he had to comply.

The objections raised by Jodl were pertinent. The Order of the Fuehrer went too far by commanding that all commando troops be massacred and soldiers shot after being taken prisoner. Jodl was perfectly conscious of the legal issues involved in the Order, although said that he had to transmit it: "If I had refused to transmit an order of the Fuehrer, I would have been arrested immediately." He was hoping that the Order would either not be applied or, if so, only rarely: "I intended in the execution of this Order to adopt a very magnanimous attitude and I was certain that the Commanders-in-Chief would do the same."

Jodl discovered a way both to be magnanimous and to avoid the application of the illegal order. He achieved this by mentioning in official reports "groups of reconnaissance" instead of "groups of commandos". The matter would thus not need to be referred to Hitler.

I do not believe that Jodl succeeded in persuading the judges of his innocence, or even of his almost-innocence.

---

⁴⁴ *According to Jodl, there was no order of capture that decreed death for German prisoners of war, although this was mentioned as a reason in the Commando Order. It was, rather, that the commandos had orders to shackle their prisoners. Jodl said that he had hidden from the Fuehrer the fact that the British shackled their prisoners in such a way that they would strangle themselves or one another.*

One of Jodl's stronger arguments was his directive of 6 May 1944 ordering that guerrillas in France and Yugoslavia were to be treated as prisoners of war.[45] He read this passage:

All partisans captured in enemy uniform or civilian clothing or surrendering during combat are to be treated in principle as prisoners of war. The same applies to all persons encountered in the immediate area of fighting, who may be considered as supporting the partisans, even when no combat action can be proved against them. Partisans in German uniform or in the uniform of an allied army [i.e., a German ally] are to be shot after careful interrogation if captured in combat. Deserters, no matter how they are dressed – and may I add, even if dressed in German uniform – are, in principle, to be well treated. The partisans must hear of this.

Jodl explained how he came to issue this directive, which he submitted neither to Keitel nor to Hitler:

I took this unusual step because I became convinced after the shooting of the English Air Force officers at Sagan that the Fuehrer no longer concerned himself with the idea of human rights; also because after 1 May 1944 I myself felt responsible for issues of international law, as the 'Canaris' department had been dissolved on that day and the foreign section, together with the international law department, had come under my command. I was resolved neither to tolerate nor to participate in any such violations of international law on our part, and I acted accordingly from that day up to the end of the war.

[45] By then, the Russian advance was such that partisans found themselves in the zone of operations; the directive failed to cover them.

The existence of the 6 May 1944 directive was confirmed by my reading more recently of the War Diary of the 58th *Panzerkorps*, with its headquarters near Toulouse. The entry of 5 July 1944 indicated that Keitel had reiterated the Commando Order of 18 October 1942 and that, in consequence, "document 503" should be wiped out. This latter document was, it seems, Jodl's directive of 1944 favourable to the partisans.

Keitel had, in reiterating the Commando Order of 1942, made things worse. It said that the groups of terrorists and saboteurs had to be executed in the course of the fighting, and that the troops had immediately to be informed that their duty was to "wipe out" terrorists and saboteurs. The Commander-in-Chief in the West had to report every day to the *Oberkommando der Wehrmacht* (Supreme Commander of the Armed Forces, or OKW) on the number of saboteurs who had been "liquidated" in this way.[46] The diary also says that "local residents, not belonging to the army of a state at war with us, have no right to fight against Germany on French soil; if they do, they are *francs-tireurs* (in it for the money)".[47]

The Commander-in-Chief in Western Europe, von Rundstedt, gave the order to proceed with extreme rigour against *maquisards* in the South. The centres of insurrection must be eliminated forever;

---

[46] *The order was transmitted by Army Group G (Southern France) on 29 June 1944 (War Diary, Army Group G, p. 235).*

[47] *War Diary, Army Group G, Annex 8. This reasoning was in 1944 not totally convincing. To say that Pétain exercised government functions under the overriding authority of the Occupying power suggested that France, the same France that had signed the Armistice, had ceased to be a sovereign power. Moreover, Germany had formerly accepted that the French troops fighting under General de Gaulle had the status of combatants.*

the Resistance must be crushed – and quickly. The most severe measures must be taken to intimidate the inhabitants of the affected areas so as to make them lose any desire to welcome Resistance groups and be governed by them. It was essential in this critical moment to act harshly and brutally in order to remove the danger threatening the rear of the German troops, and to avoid having to shed even more blood later on among the soldiers and the civilian population. This instruction also said that partial successes were not enough.[48]

Von Rundstedt invited the troops under his command to act brutally. His statement at Nuremberg that "Under my command, there have been no brutalities in the West" cannot be taken at face value.

As for Jodl himself, everything he said may well be taken at face value. He was anxious to observe the prescriptions of international law; he managed in May 1944 to introduce a directive that indeed went beyond the requirements of positive law; he had a keen sense of legal niceties, and he knew the German army regulations backwards.

However, there was another aspect of his personality, full of equivocations. In the cross-examination by his lawyer, Dr. Exner, Jodl refused repeatedly to state clearly whether a certain measure taken was legal or illegal. Jodl was trying to create a grey area around the legal demarcations. Even on the issue of the Resistance, on which he had in May 1944 adopted a laudable position, further examination revealed that he justified the sudden

---

[48] *War Diary, Army Group G, 11 June 1944.*

increase in the number of people killed in France after the landing by the fact that they were "insurgents", thus deserved no quarter.

Whenever he disagreed with Hitler, Jodl always tried to avoid confrontation. This was how in January 1945 he had persuaded Hitler not to repudiate the Geneva Convention on the treatment of prisoners: "If I had come to him with moral or purely legal arguments, he would have said, 'Spare me this foolish talk', and he would have proceeded with the renunciation of the Convention ... Someone had to prevent his throwing out our proposals in a fit of rage and immediately decreeing renunciation. That was the approach best followed. If one cannot do good directly, it is better to do it in a roundabout way than not at all."

At the end of his cross-examination, Roberts challenged Jodl to expound upon his ambiguous attitude towards Hitler. He reminded Jodl that, after the failure of the plot against Hitler, he had stated in a speech: "The twentieth of July was the blackest day German history has ever seen, and will probably remain so for all time."

Roberts: "Why was it such a black day for Germany? Because somebody tried to assassinate a man whom you now admit was a murderer?"

Jodl: "It is not the task of a soldier to judge his Commander-in-Chief. May history or the Almighty do that ... [Hitler] came to power borne up by his love of the German people. I saw it. He was almost overwhelmed by his love of the people and of soldiers."

Roberts: "You have forgotten the SS, the Gestapo and the concentration camps for political opponents, have you not?"

Jodl: "I have told you how unfortunately little I knew of all these things – almost nothing. Of course, knowing them, all this takes on a different aspect."

At the end of the testimony, Jodl believed that he had won against Roberts and that nothing could be proved against him. According to Fritzsche, one of the co-Defendants, Jodl was sure he would not be found guilty. But the judges had their doubts. Biddle confronted him with some hostile questions, one of which concerned Russia. He asked:

What I want to get at is this: you were afraid that Russia was going to attack. If that was true, why didn't you advise Germany to attack at once? You were afraid that Russia would attack, and yet you say you advised against moving into Russia. I do not understand.

Jodl might not have understood the point of what the American judge was asking. That attack was better than defence? That preventive war was justified? Sure of himself, a man of inflexible character, Jodl chose neither to repent nor to renounce his past. In his final declaration, he maintained his positions:

In a war ... in which partisans used every single means of violence that seemed expedient, harsh measures, even though they may appear questionable from the perspective of international law, are not a crime in morality or conscience.

Jodl then evoked "necessity" to justify measures that could, from the perspective of international law, appear questionable.

CHAPTER 14

The Realities of the Fight against the Resistance after the Normandy Landings

While Jodl and Exner were arguing whether or not "terrorists" and "partisans" were protected by the laws of war, I remembered those days of 1944 after the Landings, when armed Resistance became a general phenomenon in France. To me, the realities of the fight against the Resistance appeared very simple. I knew what my fate would have been had I joined a *maquis*, as perhaps I should have done.

In 1943, on the point of leaving for Germany, I chose to become a *réfractaire* without making up my mind to join a Communist *maquis*. In 1944, though, reasons for going over to the *maquis* were very different. The problem was not about escaping from the Germans. After the 6 June 1944 Landings, the French rediscovered the state of mind they experienced in 1914 and were leaving home in order to fight. This was particularly true in the countryside, yet was not so in Toulouse: there, apparently nothing had changed. Life continued as before.

I was unaware of the mass exodus to the *maquis* of thousands of Frenchmen and –women of all ages, and missed for the second time the opportunity of joining the Resistance. However, I sensed around me in Toulouse something of a change in attitude. Those who had always believed in an Allied victory felt justified – their hopes were being realised, while those who had bet on a German victory were now beginning to doubt that it would happen.

I heard the news of the Landings that same afternoon, while I was in a bookshop that specialised in religious works and devotional objects. I was the only client. The lady who owned it was talking in a low voice, as if in church. Suddenly, her husband, a small man, bald and frail, erupted into the shop, half dancing, so agitated was he, and shouting uninhibitedly, "That's it! They have landed!" and he kept repeating, "That's it! This time, that's it!"

A few days later, my (still very right-wing) uncle came to visit my Toulouse retreat. It surprised me, and I could not guess at his intentions. He began by giving me news from the Lot-et-Garonne, where the situation had become dramatic. There had been, to start with, the "execution" of the village mayor's clerk, Poulanges. Two young men, towards midday, entered his office, which was located in an annexe of the school. With no explanation, they "sprayed" him with their Sten guns. They then walked away, pushing their bicycles, in full sight of the village and in particular of the dressmaker, Madame Cavaillé. She spent her days working beside her window, taking advantage of the daylight and watching all of the comings and goings at the school. The sheer impudence of the act of shooting made a huge impression in the village.

Also, continued my uncle, his father-in-law, Etienne Bouet, had seen the Landings as the sign to join the *maquis*. Bouet was a hero of the 1914 war. Politically, he belonged to the extreme right wing. He was involved in street battles against the Reds at the time of the Popular Front, and even earlier. He would have liked, in June 1940, to resume the fight and cross over to England. During the whole of the Occupation, Bouet dreamed of "killing Boches" as in 1914. "In the Gers," said my uncle, "things are hotting up. My father-in-law is always armed now when he goes out. The other day, he was with Major Marcellin. On the road they met a Milicien of their acquaintance and asked each other, 'Shall we knock him off?' But they did not do it."[49]

My uncle also talked of his son, Jean, who was still of school age and had spent the year in Toulouse preparing for one of the Grandes Écoles. Jean had just gone home to the Lot-et-Garonne because the Director, fearing Allied bombings in Toulouse, closed the *lycée* early for the long holidays. People in the village who, on the whole, joined the Communist FTP (*Francs-tireurs et Partisans*) asked my uncle about Jean: "What is he doing? Why doesn't he come with us?" This created something of an embarrassing situation for the Château, which was supposed to lead by its example of patriotism.

A few days later, I gathered the object of my uncle's visit. He had been sent to tell me that it was now my duty to join the *maquis*. It introduced a new episode, then, in the history of my year group. I had been called up needlessly in 1940, taken prisoner, sent to the Youth Camps to prepare the revenge

---

[49] *Etienne Bouet was doubtless an unusual man. He was about seventy years old and almost completely deaf. However, he tried as early as in 1943, in association with a neighbour from the nearest village, Major Marcellin, a prisoner of war recently released, to create a maquis. After the Landings he joined a maquis organised by Dr. Reynaud, a local GP who had been in trouble with the Vichy. Bouet shared the life of the young maquisards, insisting that he should also do night duty at the outposts.*

against the Germans, called up anew in the spring of 1943 to go and work in Germany, taken over by the Resistance wanting to found a *maquis*, and now I had to volunteer for the final fight to expel the Germans occupying France. My uncle did not dare in so many words to tell me to join Etienne Bouet's *maquis*.

It is true that I wanted to show my gratitude to Bouet for, in July 1943, he had provided me with a false identity card (of not very high quality) and I told him then, "I will join you when the day comes, if you call on me." I renewed this offer to my uncle "should the call come". My uncle still seemed embarrassed, and now I understand why: he wanted me to throw in my lot with the *maquis*. I should have done so spontaneously, carried along on the wave of enthusiasm, without question, and without waiting for a call. He did not say as much, though. He did not want to take upon himself the responsibility for launching me into an adventure that could go wrong, yet at the same time needed to feel that he had fulfilled his mission.[50]

Actually, Etienne Bouet's Resistance took a tragic turn. I did not know this when I was arrested some time later by the *Gestapo*. During my stay at Caffarelli, my landlady, Madame Person, visited me, and told me she had news of my family. From what she said, I understood that my uncle had joined the *maquis* and been killed in the fighting. I discovered my mistake after the Liberation when, on my way to the Lot-et-Garonne now that the trains were starting to run again, I stopped at Agen to visit a friend of the

---

[50] *Retrospectively, I feel justified. A few days after the Landings, General Koenig, appointed Chief of the FFI (i.e., the maquis) by De Gaulle, concerned by the mass of Frenchmen and –women going over to the maquis, had ordered the new maquisards to go back home immediately and to undergo training before thinking of fighting the Germans.*

family. She told me, "But your uncle is not dead; Etienne Bouet and his grandson Jean were killed. My brother, Jean Bernard, who was in the same *maquis* at Meilhan, came out unscathed, but I lost my fiancé, who was the grandson of General Gras, the one who invented the rifle of the same name, thanks to which we won the 1914 war."

She told me this without emotion. To her, it was already ancient history. The fight in which she lost her fiancé took place on 7 July and it was already the end of August. A chapter of history was ended.

A few days later I went on a pilgrimage to Meilhan, in memory of local *maquisards*. I happened to go at the same time as the families of the victims. The *maquis* had been set up in abandoned farm buildings located on two bare hills that overlooked the surrounding hillocks. The landscape was dotted with a few sparse hedges. Obviously, the location was chosen for its vantage point. It was a fortified keep, the static defence – the very opposite, it occurred to me, of the guerrilla concept, which would have suited a *maquis* better.

On the morning of 7 July 1944 the Germans attacked with artillery. One of the first shells fell on a munitions lorry that had stopped there for the night. It blew up, and with it went the main base of operations. Etienne Bouet and Major Marcellin left their trench and walked towards the Germans. It was as if they wanted to draw the attention of the attackers towards themselves in order to give the others a chance to escape by road.

On the other hill, my cousin Jean Seguin had been given the task of supplying the machine, firing through a slit in a dry-stone wall. The Germans went on the attack. A few maquisards were able to run away, among them Jean Bernard. No others. The Germans spent the rest of the morning counting the dead and the weapons. They took a few young *maquisards* prisoner. They executed them.

I saw the wall behind which Jean hid during the battle and, a few steps further, the small farm building where he spent the preceding night. It was ravaged by the artillery then by a fire. The first floor had collapsed. The inside of the building looked like a hollow tower. I saw, too, hardly two hundred metres below, the ditch where Jean Bernard had hidden. He passed Jean Seguin when the attack began. They smiled at each other.

On this day of pilgrimage, some of the survivors came to meet the families. They were young and discreet, almost completely silent. My uncle talked to an older man with a rough and open face. He asked him to tell him about the fight. The man's face lit up when he relived the action. He added that he had, afterwards, joined another *maquis*, which took several Germans prisoner. "I hope that you were able to entertain them!" said my uncle. "Oh! As far as that is concerned, they had no grounds for complaint!" answered the survivor, with a hearty laugh.

The war diary of the 58th *Panzerkorps* carries a report on the operation against the Meilhan *maquis*, which was carried out by the 116th Reserve Battalion attached to the 28th Reserve Infantry Regiment. The Fifty-eighth had its headquarters near Toulouse, and was responsible for the southwest of France. The Meilhan task took place within the framework of a "cleaning-up operation" of the area between Garonne and the Pyrénées.

The Germans had very limited forces, and only light weapons at their disposal. To get from place to place they used lorries fuelled with charcoal, which were commandeered on the spot, by the day, along with their French drivers, meaning that they were reduced to launching their attacks by bicycle.

The 28th Infantry Regiment had been transformed into a number of mobile groups reacting quickly to the latest information. Their sources were the local French *gendarmerie*, the *Miliciens*, the *Gestapo*, the *Geheime Feldpolizei* (Secret Field Police) and their own intelligence gathering. This flexible organisation allowed them to achieve immediate successes. Colonel Hennenbruch received his order on 3 July, and by 5 July his regiment was engaged in the Saint-Pé area. The 116th Infantry Battalion was routing a forest four kilometres west of Lannemezan; on the morning of 7 July it attacked the Meilhan *maquis*.

The German report is merely an inventory:

7.7 Operation of the 116th Reserve Infantry Battalion against a camp occupied by about 76 terrorists east of Meilhan (54 km east-north-east of Tarbes).

<u>Enemy losses:</u>　　　60 dead (52 counted), 4 prisoners

<u>Our own losses:</u>　　　1 dead, 5 wounded

Captured equipment:

    8 repeating rifles

    24 Sten guns

    3 machine guns

    1500 rounds, rifles

    2000 rounds. Machine guns: ammunition and magazines.

Destroyed equipment:

2 small vans

2 lorries, 1 motor car, 2 motorcycles, ammunition and petrol dump

Damaged equipment:

1 lorry (petrol), 2 cars (petrol) 1 motorcycle.

In the German archives, the operations appear as an important success. There is an impression that it was rather a massacre than a battle.[51] In the stories told by the survivors, collected and published by Françoise Chevigné, mother of one of the victims, the fight assumed gigantic proportions.[52] The *maquisards*

---

[51] *The Germans knew the actual strength of the maquis, which was 75, but how could they know that 60 were killed if they counted only 52?*

[52] *Françoise Chevigné was from Lombez in the Gers, as was Dr. Raynaud, Chief of the Meilhan maquis. Her book is La Tragédie de Meilhan (Histoire du Docteur Raynaud et ses compagnons), Toulouse, 1945. Françoise Chevigné was the pen name of Mme. Becanne.*

certainly fought the best they could, but in their memories they exaggerated the opponent's losses: "The Germans had, it is said, more than 150 killed and many wounded among the 1500 to 2000 combatants" wrote one of the survivors,[53] while the German report mentions one dead and five wounded.

On the day when the families visited Meilhan, fearsome rumours were going around, their sources were allegedly witnesses. One was that the Germans had, after the battle, brought back some of the young *maquisards* to the farm building where Jean Seguin had spent the night. The Laborie couple lived in a farm nearby and must have been the witnesses with whom the rumours originated. Their story, as reported by Françoise Chevigné, was the following:

They saw the Germans bringing back to the Larée Farm most of the young men they were able to find and seize in the neighbourhood, treating them with unspeakable brutality, pushing them inside the house, throwing grenades, shooting bursts with their submachine guns on the throbbing mass of the able-bodied or wounded men gathered in that place.

The Germans then went to fetch armsful of straw and put them against the wall to start a fire in the building. The Labories heard the victims screaming. After the battle, the first rescuers arriving on the spot removed a few bodies from the burning farm before the roof collapsed.[54]

Several months after the war, in France for a short stay, I spent the night in the bedroom Jean Seguin occupied before his departure for the *maquis*.

---

[53] *Chevigné, p. 52.*
[54] *Chevigné, p. 55*

Everything was left as it had been on the morning he left. His mathematics books and lecture notes were still where he had put them. On the shelf above were carefully arranged his scout hat and khaki shirts with the badges he had gained over the years, of which he was very proud. The room itself had not changed since then. The same vases, blue and gold and with broken handles, stood reflected in the immense mirror on the wall, along with a branch of boxwood, blessed on a Palm Sunday and there since 1944.

Several of the Germans who took part in the operation against the Meilhan *maquis* were on 22 November 1947 found guilty by the Toulouse Military Tribunal. It was a year after the Nuremberg verdict, but the French Tribunal seemed to fail to take into account some of the principles implicitly recognised by the International Military Tribunal.

The Toulouse judgement presumed that *maquisards* enjoyed the protection of the "laws and customs of war". This was not considered so at Nuremberg by the French judge; even the Russians acknowledged that in the current understanding of international law "partisans" were not protected.[55]

In fact, what was surprising about the Toulouse Tribunal's judgement was its lack of severity, given the circumstances. The Courtroom was packed with the families of victims, confidently expecting the death sentence for all of the defendants. The French barristers had been appointed officially as defence counsel and did their best, knowing that in this hostile atmosphere all they

---

[55] See Arcadi Soltorak, *Le procès de Nuremberg*, p. 254.

could hope for was perhaps to save the heads of their clients.

The Toulouse judges rendered a verdict that was strict on the principles: the four defendants were "war criminals", guilty of having violated the laws and customs of war, and guilty of complicity in the "murders" of about 60 Frenchmen, members of the Resistance. The judgement did not distinguish between the victims killed in combat and those killed after being captured.

In practice, though, the judges avoided pronouncing the death sentence yet still distributed apparently stiff punishments. They gave the defendants the benefit of the *excuse absolutoire* because they had obeyed the orders of their immediate superior, Captain Boehme. It was an excuse not recognised at Nuremberg, but once accepted it would have been logical to free the defendants. The Toulouse Tribunal also admitted that the defendants had not acted with intent; anyway, they were accused only of complicity.

The sentences passed were:

Lieutenant Johannes Fritsch and Second Lieutenant Ernest Schwinger, both aged 23, both students when drafted into the *Wehrmacht*, were sentenced to life with hard labour;

Lieutenant Georg Lesch, aged 32, career officer, was sentenced to 20 years' hard labour;

Sergeant-Major Hoehnel, 33 years old, a clerk in civilian life, was sentenced to five years' hard labour.[56]

It was a compromise that did not follow popular passions yet where human considerations weighed heavier than legal ones. Also, the passing of time played a part. More than three years had elapsed since the massacre.

The question remains whether the real culprits were found guilty. The defence counsel for Second Lieutenant Schwinger, who remembers the case clearly, told me that his client maintained that he had not taken part in the execution of prisoners, that he was not there when the prisoners were executed, and that he did not even know that executions had taken place.

---

[56] *The variation in the sentences could be explained thus: Lesch and Hoehnel, who received the mildest sentences, benefited from "extenuating circumstances". Hoehnel was an NCO and as such could less easily avoid submitting himself to the obligations of military discipline. As for Lt. Lesch, he had not been at Meilhan – he was accused of complicity in burning houses at Tilhouse in the Hautes-Pyrénées on 29 June 1944.*

CHAPTER 15

Necessity Knows No Law

Legal technicalities concerning the application of the laws and custom of war were one influence on the Trial. There were situations when the German Generals could have invoked the principle of "necessity". On 11 June 1944 von Rundstedt implicitly relied on it when he gave the order to wipe out the terrorists, adding, "Half-successes are not enough."

Not kennt kein Gebot (necessity knows no law) was a dictum favoured at one time by German lawyers. It sounded so authoritative in German that it could be taken as the expression of popular wisdom, simple and irrefutable. Admittedly, necessity may be a defence to any criminal charge – and not merely in time of war; it may be only exceptionally invoked. British law, for example, contains a case of three men drifting in an open boat, two killing the third to eat his body. It was judged to be murder.[57]

The issue addresses the extent to which it was necessary to proceed brutally against the *maquisards*. "Brutality" is not a legal concept; its lack of legal character is no basis for allowing such behaviour. It was Jodl's opinion that everything that

---

[57] *R v. Dudley and Stephens, 1884*

was not forbidden was allowed, or at least was not punishable. Such was the case of reprisals, of taking hostages, and of other wartime circumstances.

"Necessity", on the other hand, could be a dangerous principle, as combatants could apply it as an easy excuse whenever they were confronted with a difficult situation.

What sort of threat was the Resistance to the *Wehrmacht*? On both sides was a tendency to over-estimate the danger presented by the partisans. Jodl mentioned a figure of between 50,000 and 500,000 German soldiers killed by the partisans in Russia, which justified *a posteriori* the severity of German repression on the Eastern front.

Historians favourable to the Resistance have said that the partisans played a decisive role in liberating France and in ensuring the success of the Normandy Landings. They did not, perhaps, realise that by stating this, they were also giving the German Generals the excuse of having repressed the Resistance for reasons of military necessity.

Given the German military archives of the time, whether the *Wehrmacht* was really threatened by the Resistance must be considered.

It is impossible simply to generalise, as the role of the Resistance varied considerably according to regions and to the periods of the war. Eisenhower gave full marks to the Resistance in an often-quoted text, which many consider as indisputable proof: "The organised forces of the Resistance have played a very considerable part in our final complete victory." Greater attention should be paid to the words "organised forces" because, as stated in an American report of 11 July 1945, "Without the organisation, the communications, the equipment, the training and the leadership supplied by the SOE [Special Operations Executive] ... the Resistance would have been of no military value." Actually, it is more than probable that the Americans remembered the support they received from the Resistance troops in Brittany, close to the US' own zone of operations in Normandy.

The American report also mentions the essential part played by the British services of the SOE. The official historian of the Special Operations Executive, Michael Foot, gave his views many times over a period of at least twenty years regarding the part played by the Resistance as supported by the SOE. Each time, he became more reticent in his assertions. Foot initially perceived a new way of waging war, less costly and more efficient than traditional warfare; it owed more to sabotage than to guerrilla tactics.

Surely sabotage would have obtained more accurate results than did the bombings by the RAF. The British believed in sabotage; the Germans were surprised to find such a significant amount of plastic explosive in the equipment dropped by parachute and captured by the German forces. The weapons, despite being insufficient in number, were mostly Sten guns, renowned for their lack of precision.

Former SOE chiefs, well placed to take an overall view of the operations, were still hesitating fifteen years after the war in making a judgement on the Resistance, seriously doubting that in a future conflict the organisation could play an important strategic role.

The particular case of the *Division Das Reich* concerns the situation in the southwest of France. The question is in two parts: firstly, whether the Resistance delayed the progress of that *Division*, preventing it from reaching the Normandy front in time and, if so, whether it can be claimed that the Resistance and the SOE saved the Landings. General de Gaulle wrote:

At the end of July the French Forces of the Interior hold back eight divisions, none of which will be able to reinforce those fighting on the front ... Besides, three Panzer Divisions urgently recalled by the German Command to be engaged within forty-eight hours suffer enormous delays. ... The 2nd Panzer SS Division [is] called Das Reich. Having left Montauban on 6 June and unable to use the railway lines – all out of action – sees its elements stopped in the Tarn, the Lot, the Corrèze, and the Haute-Vienne; only on 18 June does it arrive at Alençon, exhausted and decimated.[58]

Michael Foot, author of *History of the Special Operation Executive in France*, gives the following details on the setbacks of the 2nd Panzer Division, *Das Reich*:

It was ordered to Normandy from the neighbourhood of Toulouse where it was stationed on D+1; and it did not arrive until D+17. The extra fortnight's delay imposed on what should have been a three-day journey may well have been of decisive importance for the successful securing of the Normandy bridgehead. Affairs in the bridgehead went so badly for the allies in the first few days that the arrival of one more first-

---

[58] Charles de Gaulle, *Mémoires de Guerre*, Vol. 2, *L'Unité*, pp. 346-7 (paperback edition).

class fully-equipped over-strength armoured division might easily have rolled some part of the still tenuous allied front right back on to the beaches, and sent the whole of Neptune awry. What caused this long delay? Partly, of course, the destruction of all the bridges on the Loire between Orleans and the sea, affected in the first few days of June by the allied air forces; but naturally the 2nd SS Panzer division (Das Reich) had a bridging train to see it across the Loire – it had not fought across the wider rivers of western Russia for nothing; and while there would undoubtedly have been a check at the river, Resistance or no Resistance, it would never have lasted a fortnight. What ruined the move was the incessant guerrilla activity, in which several F section circuits played a distinguished part. Before ever the order to move had reached the wretched division, some of George Starr's teams in Wheelwright were busy blowing up its petrol dumps, which Starr had had them mark down and prepare for attack weeks before. Short of petrol, the Germans turned to the railway: Pimento saw to it that only a single train went north. A single train was from the Germans' point of view practically useless; so after a further vexatious delay, hunting such reserves of petrol as they could find, they set off to march. But their march took them across Philippe de Gunzbourg's sub-sector of Wheelwright between Bergerac and Périgueux; or for those of them who took the more easterly road, through Digger's and many other audacious and well-manned ambushes round Brive and Tulle.[59]

---

[59] Michael Foot, *History of the Special Operations Executive in France*, pp. 397-8. There are some minor differences between this account and that by General de Gaulle. The dates of the departure and arrival of Das Reich differ. Also, not surprisingly, de Gaulle attributes the feat to the FFI (Forces Françaises de l'Intérieur, or French Forces of the Interior), while Foot sees it as a result of the activity of the SOE.

Is this the incontrovertible proof of the decisive role of the Resistance? Is it a fact that without the intervention of the Resistance, *Das Reich* would immediately have reached the Normandy front, thrown the Allied troops back into the sea and – by doing so – would have caused the failure of the Landing? This could possibly be confirmed by German archives, as could how the German army viewed the Resistance in France. Did the *Wehrmacht* feel sufficiently threatened to justify taking extreme measures against the "terrorists"?

Whether the Resistance in southwestern France prevented *Das Reich* from reaching the Normandy front is yet to be established. The War Diary of the 58th *Panzer Korps* to which *Das Reich* reported regularly does not seem to say so. Also, it is not totally correct to state that the *Division* left Toulouse on the day after the Landings; nor that it tried to force its way through the Dordogne, where it would have been constantly harassed, delayed and weakened by the guerrilla actions of the *maquis* and would as a consequence have been held up by many weeks.

The tanks of *Das Reich* left by railway from Périgueux station. It took them perhaps three or four days to reach Normandy and enter into action. The other vehicles left by road and took only a little longer.

For them, passing through the Dordogne was not a problem. Most of the *Division* did not have to leave from Toulouse or Montauban as it was already in the Dordogne *before* the Landings, fighting against the "terrorists". On 5 June – that is, on the day before the Landings – Lammerding, who was commanding this SS Division, wrote a memo addressed to the 58th *Panzer Korps*. In it he proposed to take the following measures to fight against the Resistance in the area around Cahors, Aurillac and Brive:

To arrest and deport to Germany 5000 suspects

To requisition 200 lorries and 400 motor cars

To hang three Frenchmen for each German wounded and ten Frenchmen for each German killed

To release one prisoner of war who is a relative or friend of any Frenchman who would betray the existence of an important cache of weapons or would inform and ensure the arrest of a terrorist chief or of at least ten terrorists. On the other hand, the Division would take care that ten able-bodied men were deported to Germany for each prisoner of war who was released.

Lammerding was convinced that if those measures were taken immediately, the area could be dominated before 15 June. In answer, the 58th *Panzer Korps* expressed its full agreement. A few days later, on 10 June, *Das Reich* acted more harshly than suggested in Lammerding's proposals: it massacred the population of Oradour-sur-Glane.

Even before the Landing, Lammerding was concerned about the situation created by the Resistance groups, which might hinder the operations of the *Wehrmacht* in the event of an "invasion". Besides, the mass of the "terrorists" was pursuing "Communist and destructive objectives";

specifically, they were raising troops by calling up those born in 1925 and 1926.[60]

On 5 June Lammerding could indeed talk of the impending invasion, for it was expected. In the autumn of 1943 the Germans obtained the key to the coded messages that would be sent by the BBC to the Resistance in the event of landing. The Germans had taken note as early as the first of June of the messages announcing that the landing was near. Finally, on 5 June, messages told that the landing was actually taking place.

The order for *Das Reich* to go to the Normandy front was received by the 58th Panzer Korps on 8 June at ten minutes past midnight.[61] Over the next few days, the *Division* continued its fight against the Resistance while preparing to leave. In his memo of 10 June, Lammerding complained of the lack of both equipment and fuel. Sixty per cent of the tanks were out of action because there were no spare parts. The

Division could not begin its march at the appointed time – except for the wheeled vehicles, which could leave by road. Repairs to the tracked vehicles, going by train, would take three or four days. It appears that the reason for the delay was a problem regarding equipment and supply, rather than the attacks of the Resistance.

---

[60] *That is, men born in 1925 and 1926, which in France would be called the classes of 1945 and 1946.*
[61] *Michael Foot was not wrong in saying that Das Reich was recalled to the Normandy front on 7 June; through the Ultra decipherings, the British were informed of the planned movement even before the unit concerned received the order to move.*

The following chronology of the movements of *Das Reich* can be given:

5 June 1944 – *Das Reich* is with armoured elements in the Dordogne-Corrèze area

6 June – The Normandy Landings take place

8 June – At 00:10, *Das Reich* receives the order to proceed to Normandy. Elements of the Division will, however, stay behind to continue the fight against the Resistance in the southwest

11 June – Lammerding takes leave from the Command of the 58th Panzer Korps, which in answer expresses its wish to have the pleasure of collaborating with him in the future

15-16 June – The tracked vehicles are loaded onto the railway at Périgueux station, on armoured train nr. 25; two trains are due to bring the 15th Panzer tanks, which will receive their crews in the night and leave for Le Mans on the sixteenth

19-24 June – The other elements (columns of munitions, vehicles, supply troops) go by road to the Normandy front (their planned route is *via* Tours, La Flèche, Laval and Fougères)

25 June – The Division is engaged in Normandy at the time of the great Allied offensive on the Caen front.[62]

The chain of events leading Foot to maintain that *Das Reich* was delayed by the SOE and the Resistance can be imagined. In London, it was learned through the Ultra decipherings that the *Division* had to leave Toulouse and reach the Normandy front. Orders were then sent to the SOE networks along the probable route to do everything possible to prevent the *Division* from arriving on time. Soon, the Pimento network would announce multiple instances of the sabotage of railway lines, in particular of the Toulouse-Paris line through Cahors; the Germans had used this for only one train after the Landing. Hence, it was reasonable to assume that the delay suffered by the *Division* was a consequence of the SOE sabotage and of the attacks by the Wheelwright network in the Dordogne.

It is worth noting that, after the transport of some armoured elements of *Das Reich* by armoured train, the Germans made no attempt to keep the Toulouse-Paris line open. The reason was simple enough. Even today, travelling on the Montauban-Cahors section shows immediately why: this part of the line is full of twists and turns, and includes a very high number of tunnels and bridges of all sorts. It is highly vulnerable to sabotage. Blowing up just one of the tunnels and causing a fall of earth would

---

[62] *Ralph Bennett, in* Ultra in the West, *gives a chronology slightly different from that suggested by the War Diary of the 58th Panzer Korps: the Division would have arrived at the front on 15 and 16 June (delayed by a lack of petrol between Poitiers and Tours) and would have been sent towards St. Lô to counter the American advance (p. 74). On the other hand, at the end of June, the Division was still without its Panzer tanks, immobilised south of Angers following the bombing of the railway by the Allied Air Forces (p. 86).*

close the line for a long period – in practical terms, for good, as far as the current operations following the Normandy Landing were concerned.

In his memo of 10 June Lammerding did not hesitate to repeat his fears concerning the 'terrorists'. He was actually much less confident than he had been five days earlier; he no longer pretended that he could put an end to the Resistance before 15 June. The area bounded by Figeac, Clermont-Ferrand, Limoges and Gourdon was, he said, firmly in the hands of the terrorists. The German troops stationed in that region were for the most part under siege and had, in some places, been wiped out. A Communist state was being formed. It governed as it liked, and was requisitioning systematically.

Lammerding's memo was written on the very day when the Division was taking reprisals in Oradour. They massacred the whole population, men, women and children. There is not one word about Oradour in the memo.

Such was the situation in the days following the landing. Lammerding thought, however, that the terrorists could be eliminated. It was not necessary to use an armoured division for the task.

A month later, on 12 July, the situation looked different. Here is the summary in a 58th Panzer Korps report:

Vast areas were controlled by the terrorists. There were two centres for their operations. One was in the Pyrénées area, south of the line Pamiers-Pau. The other lay north of the line Alès-Albi-Agen-Bergerac. In the Pyrénées area most of the terrorists were Spanish Republicans, rather badly organised, while in the other area was a strict administration exercising complete sovereignty, after having eliminated the Vichy administration; it threatened the population with reprisals if they did not openly support the terrorists. Support was liable to fluctuate sharply according both to losses and to the number of new recruits. It could be estimated that in the northern area there were at least 20,000 men, and in the southern area there could be 6,000 to 10,000 men.

The Germans found traces of the SOE when they discovered radio transmitters in those two areas where, with the help of French regular officers, several British officers were commanding *maquis*. The armaments of the terrorists consisted of light weapons, and they were comparatively short of ammunition. On the other hand, they had significant quantities of explosives. Their operations were either acts of sabotage against means of transport and communications or else surprise attacks on civilians or small groups of soldiers.

Shortly before the invasion, there was a sudden increase in the number of the operations of the Resistance. However, a few days after the beginning of the invasion, the various groups received the order to make a total withdrawal. This was so that they could take time to arm themselves and to train. Small groups were now coming to carry out raids or sabotage in the areas occupied by the *Wehrmacht*. In the zones occupied by the terrorists, roads were blocked, bridges demolished, and minefields established. The main Toulouse-Paris railway line through Cahors, Brive and Limoges, which crossed the terrorists' northern zone, had been completely cut off for some time. In the rest of the area, the number of occasions when the terrorists had blown up railway lines, bridges or electricity power lines could not reliably be counted. This had not yet greatly hindered the German units.

Mid-July in the South of France saw a sort of equilibrium between the *maquis* and the Occupation troops, as reported by the 58th Panzer Korps:

It is not possible any longer to eliminate completely the Resistance movement with the forces at our disposal, given the sheer size it has gained today without meeting any real obstacle and given also the constant support it receives from enemy powers.

Consequently, the Germans were content to keep open the main means of communication. The hostility of the population added to their difficulties. Experience showed that only small and highly mobile units could achieve notable successes against the Resistance. Counter-attacks were successful only if they intervened very quickly following information usually obtained by the SD. The report concluded with a reminder of the losses inflicted on the Resistance:

1 May – 25 June	2049 killed
3663 prisoners	
25 – 30 June	686 killed
23 prisoners	
1 – 10 July	236 killed
53 prisoners.	

Another statistic, in this case from the War Diary of Army Group G, shows that the greatest Resistance losses were inflicted after the Landing, and that the 2nd *Panzer SS* Division, *Das Reich*, was responsible for most:

Date	Unit	Location	Killed	Prisoners
4.5	2.SS-Pz-Div.	Montpezat	3 killed	20 prisoners
6.6	2.SS-Pz-Div.	Figeac	5 killed	1 prisoner
7.6	2.SS-Pz-Div.	St. Antonin		7 prisoners
10.6	2.SS-Pz-Div.	Figeac, Souillac	500 killed	1500 prisoners
10.6	2.SS-Pz-Div.	Le Fleix	50 killed	
11.6	2.SS-Pz-Div.	Limoges	337 killed	
11.6	Btl. Schreiber	region south of Toulouse	325 killed	
12.6	9.Pz-Div.Unger	Valreas	110 killed	
15.6	11.Pz-Div. Wilde	Brive	1 killed	
		[Total]	1331 killed	1564 [taken] prisoners.[63]

---

[63] *War Diary of the Army Group G on 18 June 1944, Document no. 280/44 geh.*

The entry of 11 June, which credits *Das Reich* with 337 killed, probably includes those killed at Oradour-sur-Glane, the village near Limoges. In this case, the losses allegedly inflicted on the terrorists included the deaths of innocent victims. Possibly, *Das Reich* deliberately pursued a policy of massacre to show off as a unit of the *SS* and to inflate the results of its fight against the Resistance.[64] This was all the more likely as the *Wehrmacht*'s daily communiqué had recently started to publish statistics on the losses in the Resistance. The same document gives the *Wehrmacht* losses for the same period: "70 killed, 88 wounded, 58 missing, 27 captured."

The Chief of Staff of Army Group G, von Gyldenfeldt, sending these statistics, indicated that they should be brought to the attention of the commanders of the various units and to them alone, in particular those concerning the "wiping out of the terrorists".

The figures showed that German losses in the fight against the Resistance were low, even negligible, when compared to the 62,603 German soldiers lost in Normandy about the same time, between 6 June

---

[64] *Although the General commanding Army Group G, von Gyldenfeldt, favoured harshness towards the terrorists, he on 17 July reminded his men of the Kommando-Befehl: "In accordance with my order of 17 June, I expect the innocent civilian population to be spared, especially women and children."*
It must be remembered, however, that instructions for the war on the Eastern front did not encourage qualms of conscience. Before I arrived in Nuremberg, Keitel had been taken to task by the Soviet prosecutor, Rudenko, for having countersigned Hitler's Directives on the bands of terrorists, in particular that of 16 December 1942 saying: "The army has a right and a duty in the all-out war to use all means leading to success, even against women and children." Quoted by Werner Maser, Nuremberg: Tribunal der Sieger, Duesseldorf, 1977, p. 265.

and the first of July according to the documents of the Army Group B. However, the fight between *maquis* and *Wehrmacht* appears less unequal when the number lost in the massacres of civilians, including women and children, is deducted.

Mid-July was also a turning point in the fight against the terrorists. The Germans were then preoccupied with the second "invasion" they foresaw on the Mediterranean coast. Their attitude towards the Resistance and their military preparations reflected this preoccupation. The report of 12 July by the 58th Panzer Korps on the Resistance concluded:

The Resistance movement in the South of France constitutes a danger for the rear of our troops, in particular in the area between Clermont-Ferrand, Valence, Cahors and Périgueux, but also in the Pyrénées area. The reserved observed presently by the Resistance should not delude us: in the event of enemy landing on the French coast of the Mediterranean, French forces would suddenly be engaged against our communications with the rear of the fighting troops and could constitute a serious menace for the command and supply of our troops in their fight against the invader.

Michael Foot thought that the Resistance could offer the advantage of keeping German troops away from the Front. There is little basis for this. The Germans did not hesitate to withdraw troops from the Occupied territories to throw the maximum of units into the Normandy battle, or to bring them closer to the Mediterranean coast in the expectation of a second landing. Those purely military imperatives allowed the Resistance to establish itself in vast areas. The Resistance in the south was increasingly becoming a potential threat to the rear of the *Wehrmacht*, but this was the case because of both the advance of the Allied armies and the weakening of the *Wehrmacht*, already out of breath, deprived of fuel, and low in numbers.

CHAPTER 16

To the Bitter End

The fight against the Resistance continued to the bitter end. It had become a matter of routine; killing was an acquired reflex. Since Keitel had reiterated the Commando Order, the watchword was: kill, kill, kill.

By mid-July 1944 the strategic objectives of the *Wehrmacht* had changed. Army Group G made it clear that fighting the Resistance was no longer the priority. It was decided that operations would not, from then onwards, be co-ordinated at Army Group level, as had been the case since the Normandy landing. The elimination of the terrorists was left to the initiative of the units on the spot. The effort was still encouraged, though, because it was useful for the Germans to maintain the mobility of the troops and because it entailed practice on live targets.

However, one last operation was planned at Army Group level. It was directed against an important *maquis* whose chief, the Germans discovered, was a British SOE agent.[65] The attack was planned on a large scale, involving a number of units and including the intervention of the *Luftwaffe*. At the last minute, on an order from Hitler's headquarters, some of the units were withdrawn from the attack; instead, they were sent to the southeast to meet the landing the Germans felt the Allies were planning somewhere along the coast of Languedoc or Provence.

The operation against that *maquis* took place on a reduced scale, yet the *Luftwaffe* was nevertheless involved. It ended in disaster. The Germans could find no terrorists, despite their apparently excellent intelligence. The morale of the Germans who took part was low. The *Luftwaffe* bombed the wrong château – a beautiful target, but containing no terrorists. At the end of the operation the Commander was killed by a terrorist, Walter Kapot, who had been wounded and was lying in the centre of the village square. As the Commander approached to question him, Walter pulled out his Remington and fired. The Commander died a little later in the house of the local notary. In reprisal, the Germans immediately hanged two people in the same square.

It was at around this time I entered Caffarelli. It was obvious that the end was near. The presence of the *Wehrmacht* in the South of France had become

---

[65] *He was in fact "Hilaire" (Lieutenant-Colonel George Starr), who was trying to co-ordinate Resistance operations in the southwest. After landing in France in November 1942 he had recruited in the Gers département his own maquis, composed mainly of Spanish Republican refugees. When attacked by the Wehrmacht he managed to escape to the pine forests of the Landes, from where he emerged with the Bataillon d'Armagnac*

pointless.⁶⁶ The German soldiers we saw were old and often looked exhausted. What a contrast they were to the arrival of the victorious *Wehrmacht* in June 1940: the troops then were young and alert. They had a superabundance of individual weapons, they had excellent transport, and the infantry travelled in brand-new lightweight Ford lorries built in Cologne.

At Caffarelli, the *Unteroffizier* sometimes bragged in order to raise morale. After the evening roll-call, he would ask as a kind of joke, "Who wants to come with me to fight on the Russian front?" Only the hairdresser, a former *Gestapist*, would pretend to volunteer, but nobody was fooled. Everybody knew that neither *Unteroffizier* nor the hairdresser wanted to go to the Russian front.

The Germans gave up defending the Atlantic coast altogether at the beginning of August 1944. The First German Army headquartered in Bordeaux ceased to exist as a unit, as did its command. This freed the troops, which were sent to the Loire to meet Allied tanks coming south from Brittany. As a result, a vacuum was created in the southwest.

The "land bridge" between the Atlantic and the Mediterranean was then occupied only by a thin curtain of troops. The German High Command turned to the concept of "fortresses" or "defending zones", depending on the circumstances. The rest

---

⁶⁶ *When the Normandy landing proved successful, von Rundstedt's opinion was that the southern part of France should be evacuated.*

was abandoned to the Resistance.⁶⁷ At the same time, the perception of the Resistance changed in the eyes of the Germans:

*On the whole the notion of terrorist movements is no longer accurate. Now it is rather an army organised on the rear of the Army Group. If the situation continues to worsen one can expect an insurrection of the people, which are no longer a tired French people but are made up of men with a fiery temperament.*⁶⁸

Through the period between the Normandy landing and the Liberation, the behaviour of the Germans towards the Resistance was conditioned by

---

⁶⁷ *This gave the Fuehrer, supported by his faithful aides Keitel and Jodl, to stamp here, too, his seal on the new type of warfare. From the War Diary of the Army Group G: "The Army Group G conveys to the armies this order from the Fuehrer for the information of commanders of fortresses and commanders of defended zones, an order according to which fortresses must be defended for as long as remain one man and one weapon. In the event of a revolt by the population, punish them harshly. To repress revolts and exert counter-terror give a free hand to troops from the East [former Russian prisoners of war enlisted in the Wehrmacht] whom one can trust." (KTB Armeegruppe G, 10.8.44, Anlage 614.)*

⁶⁸ *Throughout the whole period following the Normandy landing, the Germans intervened quite frequently in the Lot-et-Garonne and, more particularly, in the area between Villeneuve-sur-Lot and Monflanquin. Perhaps they were especially well informed on the existence of maquis there. A more precise reason appears in the War Diary of the 58th Panzer Korps: "In the region between the Lot and the Dordogne rivers the Resistance persuaded the farmers not to deliver their crops or their produce. As it happened the First Army (Atlantic Coast) and the 19th Army (Mediterranean Coast) depended for their supplies on the deliveries of cattle and cereals, as well as of the tinned fruits and vegetables of that region. Consequently, it was decided to mount an operation to wipe out the maquis in the area and to station a battalion between Monflanquin and the Villeréal in order to prevent incursions by maquis from the Lot or the Dordogne." (16 July 1944.)*

Who would have suspected at the time, among the French people living in that area where I had myself lived before going underground, that the deliveries of tinned fruits and vegetables from the factories in Villeneuve-sur-Lot were of such vital importance to the Wehrmacht?

the military situation. This presented a constantly changing balance of power. At no time, though, did the Resistance in the southwest sufficiently threaten the Germany Army, nor did it justify the extreme measures taken against "terrorists" and the civilian population. In June, the *Division Das Reich* headed for the Normandy front with no delaying tactics from the Resistance. By July the southwest was no longer of strategic interest to the Germans, who were withdrawing most of their fighting units. From the moment the second landing was expected on the Mediterranean coast, the Resistance ceased to constitute an important factor in the German military situation. When all was said and done, the essential military imperative in the southwest and in the south during that period was to keep open the communication route: Bordeaux – Toulouse – Carcassonne - Narbonne.

The departure of the Germans from Toulouse was relatively dramatic. At Caffarelli, the Liberation had been something of a mirage to the internees: it was believed, but no one dared say so. Rumours were circulating to match our hopes. The Allies were marching on Paris; Paris was taken, and the end of the war was in sight. Actually, Paris was still in the hands of the Germans and our guards were still here. The Gestapo was still alive. After the convoy at the end of July, there had been a lull before the arrests started again. Four or five Jewish families were brought in every day. How did the Gestapo manage to track them down? Obviously, it was through denunciation. If a Jew was imprudent enough to go back to his flat to collect a few things, the Gestapo was immediately on the spot. It seemed absurd to let oneself be caught only a few weeks before the end.

In the course of these last few weeks, the Gestapo did a huge round-up in the cafés of the Palace Wilson one Sunday at noon. It was *aperitif* time, so they had a successful haul. Dozens of suspects were brought to Caffarelli. All those who, seeing the Gestapo, had got up and hurried towards a back door to avoid the identity check had been spotted and arrested. *Gestapists* from the whole region were assembled for the operation. It was interesting to note the variety of types: young, old, puny or paunchy, poor or affluent. I still remember one of them. He was in his fifties, going slightly grey, fairly stout, wearing the black and white footwear known as "co-respondent's shoes", and he looked elegant. I could imagine him as a prosperous travelling salesman passing himself off as an industrialist, dating lonely widows who answered his small ads in the regional newspapers.

A few days later, Caffarelli was filled up again. The Gestapo brought 200 prisoners from Saint-Michel, the main Toulouse prison. Among them was a "staff captain" of the Resistance. They were locked up in two rooms, crammed full, with just enough space for each to lie down on the floor.

Then, one afternoon towards three o'clock, when the heat felt heavy and motionless, the atmosphere was torn as if by lightning. There was a commotion on the ground floor. The noise of boots was heard, climbing the stairs. I went down to see what was going on, acting as if I was on my way to chop wood for the field kitchen in the courtyard – part of my new function as kitchen hand. A soldier on guard duty whispered, "You'd better disappear!" As I passed the guardroom, I saw the *Gestapists*, now in uniform, going through the lists of the internees. Soon afterwards, they went up the stairs. I went back to the building and heard Hans the Berliner say, "*Das ist eine grosse Sauerei!*" (That's a huge nuisance!), while the *Unteroffizier* was trying to calm him down: "Not now! Not now!" I saw the Gestapo pushing into their black Citroëns four or five Jews whom I knew. They shoved them, impatient to be gone as quickly as possible. Usually, departures took place quietly. The Jews wanted to take a few things with them, a jacket or an overcoat. "No need! You'll be back tonight!" They left, and peace settled again.

Two of the Jews taken on that day remained in my memory. One, the taller one, strongly built, had been arrested only three days previously. He was in his fifties, his skull half bald and shaven on the sides. Frau Pick, always well informed, told us, "Oh! That one, it is a very ugly business ... he had fifty gold coins." The other, whom I had known much longer, was in Caffarelli before I arrived there; his double pneumonia was treated with the only medicine available, which was a little aspirin. He had been too weak to leave with the convoy at the end of the July and was placed alone in a small room. He was still weakened by the illness and very pale. He had a young wife and an eight-month-old baby, who was brought to him in the evenings. He used to sit the child on his knee and look at him, saying not a word. The father had a soft face and a small brown moustache, from under which rabbit teeth protruded. He possessed a melodious though frail voice. When he was reunited with his family, he would sing to us some evenings, "Hail, o my last morning..." I saw him coming down the staircase, wrapped up in a vast overcoat, now much too big for him. He leaned on a walking stick and rested at each step.

Several weeks after the Liberation I learned what happened on that day. There was an article in the newspaper *Le Patriot*, entitled 'The Wall of the Enfournet'. It said that the Gestapo had taken about twenty prisoners from Saint-Michel and about ten from Caffarelli. These were taken from Toulouse into the middle of the countryside. The Gestapo chose a tumbledown cottage and ordered the prisoners to build around it a thick fence with bundles of sticks. They then set it on fire. The prisoners were burned alive.[69]

A day or two later the Germans were getting ready to leave. The Gestapo went to and fro between their headquarters and the barracks. In the evening they burned their archives in the baker's oven. Tension was rising throughout the whole of Caffarelli. Men and women locked in their rooms could not sleep. A constant buzz came from inside. Towards half-past four in the morning, a few vans stopped in front of the entrance. Zarine, who had the habit of fussing around the authorities, bustled about *Unteroffizier* Muehlhausen. Suddenly, he summoned his small team, consisting essentially of Frau Pick and the Czech doctor. Adamczack summoned me together with a few other Aryans among the longest in Caffarelli.

Everything happened within only a few minutes. Muehlhausen, in full rig, helmet and all, came out of the guardroom, followed by Hans the Berliner and the three other soldiers. Zarine, Frau

---

[69] *According to Frau Pick's confidences at Nuremberg, these executions followed the order given by the General commanding in Toulouse to "liquidate" the prisons. The Gestapo had not dared to follow the order to the letter for fear of repercussions from the population. On the other hand, I learned fairly recently that the Resistance considered it likely that the Germans would liquidate the internees of Saint-Michel and Caffarelli when leaving. According to Ravanel, the Resistance chief for the R4 region, there was no way the Germans could be prevented from doing so.*

Pick and the Czech doctor lined up on one side of the corridor, Adamczack and myself on the other. Zarine said to the *Unteroffizier*, "*Alles Gute! Alles Gute!*" (All the best!) He seemed sincere and moved. The *Unteroffizier*, too, seemed moved, as if he were taking leave of old friends before a long journey. He shook Zarine's hand: "*Auf wiedersehen, Herr Zarine! Alles Gute!*" Then it was the turn of the others. We all went through it. The guard marched past us, grabbed by handshakes and under a shower of "*Alles Gute!*" and of "*Auf wiedersehen!*" I was able only with great difficulty to control myself and not burst out laughing at the absurdity of the situation, the atmosphere loaded with emotion, the drama of that moment ... and also at the thought that I could later tell the story and describe the scene. I saw Muehlhausen sit beside the driver in a small ambulance. The soldiers climbed in through the back door. A last gesture came from Muehlhausen, and the last "*Alles Gute!*" from Zarine. The ambulance moved off, overloaded, sagging at the back. That was it! We were free! We were still alive! It was the end of the Occupation which, for me, finished as it had started four years earlier – in a barracks.[70]

The Toulouse Gestapo sensed what was going to happen. During the previous week they had come one by one to Caffarelli to visit the little Jewish tailor, who had formerly run his own prosperous business and now had at his disposal a workshop fitted out in a room for the NCOs on the third floor. The Gestapo, whom so far we had seen only in plain clothes, had SD uniforms made for them urgently, in case they were taken prisoner. These gentlemen did not wish to be executed as *francs-tireurs*. Besides, the tailor on

---

[70] *In June 1940, as a young recruit, I had been taken prisoner of war in an artillery depot at La Rochelle.*

the third floor must, in the olden days, have been more adept at making caps than suits. In less than three days he produced half a dozen of these wonderful peaked caps, which placed a sort of halo around the heads of Germans belonging to the lesser fighting units of the *Wehrmacht.*

The War Diary of Army Group G shows that since mid-July the Germans were expecting a landing on the Mediterranean coast. They modified their order of battle accordingly. The War Diary also explains why the Germans evacuated Toulouse and the southwest so quickly and without a fight, leaving the Resistance controlling the area.

On 13 August the landing seemed imminent: two convoys of a hundred ships each had been sighted off Ajaccio, while the bay was cluttered with troopships and warships. The bombings by the Allied air force aimed at the bridges on the Rhône and the Var suggested the direction from which the invasion could be expected. The landing took place on 15 August. The War Diary uses an ambiguous formula, which is rather revealing: "The first attempts at landing are almost all repulsed thanks to the courage of the fighting troops." Was it possibly a way of admitting that not all attempts had been repulsed? It really does appear that the Germans offered only token resistance.

At 01:10 hours the Commander-in-Chief/West reminded his troops that he was maintaining the order to defend the Mediterranean coast by all available means; if it appeared that the enemy was trying to capture the port of Marseilles, the troops should proceed to destroy it.

After hours of bombing of the warships by the artillery and the intervention in strength by the aircraft, the Allies succeeded in gaining a foothold "east of Borme near Maxime (east of St. Raphael)" as well as at Cap Roux. Airborne troops landed east of Le Muy and in the area of Draguignan simultaneously. After that, things moved fast: Allied troops, who had landed in Normandy, were reaching the Loire without trying to cross it. Units of the First Army arriving from the southwest were on their way to meet them and stabilise the front.[71] It was obvious that all German troops south of the Loire ran the risk of being cut off from the main body of the army even if the Provence landing failed. Indeed, it could be asked why the Allies took the trouble of landing on the French Riviera, as such a move made no sense on the strategic level.[72]

Forty-eight hours after the landing, on 17 August, the headquarters of the Fuehrer gave the order to retreat. It turned into a stampede, a headlong flight from the southwest. The War Diary of Army Group G had this entry for 11:15 on 17 August:

All the troops located west of the line Orléans-Clermont-Ferrand-Montpellier, as well as the command echelons and the organisation of all of the elements of the Wehrmacht and of the Waffen-SS, as well as all of the other organisations, must begin

---

[71] *The German First Army had by then been dissolved as a command echelon.*
[72] *Lacking knowledge of the German documents, historians have attributed an important role to the Resistance in the success of the Provence landings: "When the Dragon landings took place ... and Patch's Franco-American Army began its advance up the Rhône Valley, the plain laid down the capture of Grenoble D+90, in mid-November. In fact Grenoble was captured, with Resistance help, on D+15." (M.R.D. Foot, in an article 'What good did the Resistance do?' in Resistance in Europe: 1939-1945, Stephen Hawes and Ralph White, eds.)*

immediately to withdraw behind the line Seine-Yonne-Bourgogne inasmuch as they do not have the task of holding the fortresses or the defence zones and also inasmuch as they do not belong to the fighting units of the 19th Army.[73]

This order was transmitted at half an hour past midday to the Toulouse *Kommandantur*, with an instruction for it to inform the units in its area. It was specified at the same time as its being essential to ensure – until the end – the security of the road leading from Bordeaux through Toulouse and Carcassonne to Narbonne. At 14:20 the Commander-in-Chief/West sent the text from the headquarters of the Fuehrer, with this addition: "Recipients must not wait for other instructions before applying these measures; they must take immediate action!"

Clearly, it was a cry of "Run for your life!" This explains why the departure of the Germans, in an atmosphere of panic, was so sudden. It took the Resistance by surprise in the southwest. When the Resistance decided to attack the retreating Germans, it found only a few stragglers trying to get through Toulouse. The Germans were ready to leave to their fate the units south of the Gironde. Their only preoccupation was to withdraw, along the Bordeaux-Toulouse road, the 150th Reserve Division, to which they gave as rearguard two "battalions from the East".[74]

Soon after, the German Supreme Command gave the following order: besides the troops provided for the fortresses, such as Bordeaux, Royan and La

---

[73] *The 19th Army had orders to repel the Allied troops that had landed.*
[74] *They consisted of Soviet prisoners of war who had agreed to be recruited into the Wehrmacht. The French called them "Vlassovs" after the Soviet General who had gone over to the German side after himself being captured.*

Rochelle, no element of the *Wehrmacht* should stay behind; the lack of means of transport would not be an excuse; if needs be, horses and carts had to be requisitioned from the population. This contributed greatly to the image of the German retreat as seen by the French side. Those who had witnessed the triumphal, irresistible arrival of German motorised units a few years previously now contrasted this with the desperate departure of those Germans carrying out their orders to the letter.

Such is the German background to the Liberation of Toulouse and southwest. With this in mind it is easier to understand the events that accompanied the Liberation. There is no need to labour the point; it is quite clear that the Germans did not retreat under pressure from the Resistance, nor did the Resistance pose such a military threat as to justify any measure of German counter-terror or the murder of political or Jewish internees on the eve of departure...

Now it was 19 August 1944. I left Caffarelli with my hands in my pockets. It was still night-time. The first tramways, noisy, bumpy and empty, were beginning to run. A young lady conductor asked for my fare. Lorries loaded with helmeted Germans were travelling on both sides of the road, some overtaking us. Were they entering Toulouse, or getting out? It might not be advisable to linger in the streets for they might happen to ask for my papers.

I arrived at Madame Person's. She was in her dressing-gown, nightdress and lace bonnet. She welcomed me with her enormous smile, as happy to see me again as if I had just returned from a holiday in the country. I found my bedroom as I had left it; there was the vast bed, so cold in winter, and the round armchair where I could keep warm wrapped up in a blanket. My "classical" books were still on the chest of drawers. They may well have saved my life. When, a few days after my arrest, the Gestapo had come to search the apartment, Madame Person had said, showing them my books, "Why did you arrest him? You can see! He is only interested in German literature and culture!" It might have given them something to think about. Actually, they had gone through my clothes and taken with them anything that was more presentable, saying to Madame Person, "He will need them in the winter." But I never again saw the one good suit I had during the war.

The walls of my room were still covered with the paintings done by Lieutenant-Colonel Veterinary Person, carefully painted, overly worked, and very conventional in their subjects. There was a level of perfection in the detail that in the long run became obsessive. In a corner hung the first painting done by their son, who had discovered during his military service in Morocco that he too could paint. He brought back a small canvas full of life and movement, screaming with all of its colours as if in defiance of his father's academicism.

I could not bear the idea of remaining locked up in my room. There was nothing to fear now that the Gestapo was gone. I went for my breakfast to the grimy restaurant of five or six tables just a minute away from the Rue Tolosane. On the way along the narrow streets I met a patrol of Resistants, consisting of two soldiers with Sten guns and an officer who was all smiles, joyful to have taken out his uniform, protected until this time by mothballs, and to resume his career as if nothing had happened during the last four years. All three wore the armband of the FFI. The hunting of collaborators had begun while the

Germans were still in Toulouse and still controlled the main streets. The "internal" Resistance of Toulouse was emerging from the shadows.

At the restaurant, I met a clerk employed at the city hall, a former student with whom I used to talk in that very same restaurant. He was courting the *patron*'s daughter. I had not finished my first slice of bread when a civilian in a trilby hat, who looked like a police inspector, entered. Smiling, he said as if in a joke, "Hands up!" He was followed by a young soldier aiming a machine gun at our table. I saw the clerk from the city hall turning pale and raising his hands. The inspector checked the papers of each one of us. I later learned that the clerk was arrested that same evening.

I spent the rest of the morning wandering through the streets. At each street corner I came across small groups of former internees, who were like soldiers on their first day out in a garrison town and who, as did they, had nowhere to go. They would not have found it excessively strange to return to Caffarelli if they had been asked to do so. An Armenian, whom I suspected to have "nicked" my fountain pen while we were interned, gave me a tip: "You must go to the *Secours National*. They will give you money and chocolate!" I went, and found there a number of my old pals, who were given not only money and chocolate, but also a pair of the strong, black, laced boots kept in stock in case of an emergency or a disaster. The Director of the *Secours National* was kneeling down and trying to feel their big toes, to make sure the boots were the right size. He said to them, "My poor friend! How you must have suffered!" Actually, he was well placed to know about this, as during our detention we were given food not by the Germans, but by the *Secours National*. They sent us twice a day only two containers of soup made of a few courgettes, with the result that at the end of July at least one third of the internees were suffering from dysentery.

For the Toulouse inhabitants it was a day like any other. Everyone went about their usual occupation, home for lunch at midday as usual. During the morning, an Allied plane, a Liberator, flew over the city. The flak went into action; shrapnel fell two metres away from me and broke the branch of a tree. I went to the Capitole, the main square. Until twelve o'clock German nurses, the "grey mice", were loading onto lorries everything they could take from their hotel, including the bidets. German lorries were becoming rarer and rarer. Cafés and restaurants remained open.

During the whole of the morning, the *Wehrmacht* and the Resistance co-existed in the city, avoiding confrontations and encounters. At one o'clock in the afternoon this situation ceased altogether: there were no Germans left in Toulouse. Half an hour later, troops from the *maquis* made a spectacular entrance, preceded by old, battered, front-wheel drive black Citroëns. On each front wing lay a *maquisard* armed with a machine gun. The windscreens were smashed out to allow shooting from inside. The initials 'FFI' were freshly painted – rather, white-washed – in huge letters on the doors. I saw them driving towards the Place Esquirol. There, it was said, *miliciens* were waiting in ambush in an attic, shooting at the Resistants. I saw no victims despite the firing on all sides. The *maquisards* clung to the walls, taking shelter in the corner of the *porte-cochère*, returning fire. I left, with the feeling that they were shooting randomly to dramatise the situation.

The Liberation had happened. Tongues loosened, and we could all talk freely of the secret world of the Resistance. Who could have imagined that the Resistance had penetrated everywhere? An old lady who lived on the third floor was saying, "My two granddaughters were in the Resistance. They were secretaries to Colonel Ravanel, who now commands at Toulouse. He is a very remarkable boy; he is only twenty-five years old. Besides, he is a former student of the *École Polytechnique*. My granddaughters talk about him all the time. They admire him very much." Madame Person also had revelations. She told me, "You know Monsieur Blanc, who lived on the floor above, in Madame Dussanne's flat? ... He used to come down to play cards in the evenings. Well! He was hiding. His real name is Monsieur Weiss. When I told him that you had been arrested, he wanted to organise a group to help you escape from Caffarelli, but I told him, 'Monsieur Bousquet does not want to escape!'"

After lunch, I saw a crowd gathering behind the Capitole, on the garden side, near a rendezvous traditionally named "The Oysters". I joined them. What were they waiting for? Somebody was going to appear on the balcony. What for? I remembered the crowd that had gathered in front of the Préfecture at Montpellier three years earlier[75] and had shouted, "*Vive Pétain!*" and "*Vive Franco!*" Another crowd was ready to cheer again today. Still, there was a certain tension. I was in the midst of a crowd made up of groups of five or ten; it had not unified. Uncertainty hung over us. What would the immediate future be? None of us had really thought about it until then.

[75] *In February 1941.*

Such was the Liberation of Toulouse on 19 August 1944. Toulouse had freed herself, all by herself. However, for a long time afterwards I was unable to place my personal memories within the framework of the official history of the Liberation. The date of 19 August was that of my release from prison, my own liberation. The departure of the Germans had been too sudden for the Resistance to have time to intervene. There was no armed Resistance in Toulouse, and practically no weapons – all available arms had been sent to the *maquis*, which for two or three days could not answer the call to come to Toulouse.

To the Resistance chiefs, surprised by the speed of events, 19 August was a day for dialogue and deliberation, whereas Sunday, 20 August became the official day of the Liberation and Monday, 21 August the day when the Liberation was proclaimed. This chronology explains why 19 August was not in fact the day of the Liberation, as I thought at the time. Now it is clear to me. The accepted version of the Liberation of Toulouse describes events that took place on the twentieth, the following day. It also became clear why there was neither a battle for Toulouse nor a popular insurrection, as had been envisaged in the plans of the Resistance.

It was good to remember this happy day, 19 August 1944, marking the end of a nightmare, when at Nuremberg. The Germans I was looking at, sitting in the dock, had acted as robots, letting the fight go on until the bitter end, each day adding to the burden of sufferings imposed upon the troops and the population alike. Now, Keitel, Jodl, von Ribbentrop, Doenitz and all were mere shadows of the characters they had played or pretended to play on the world stage. They did not seem like real people.

The end of the Occupation brought at last an end to the Commando Order.

At the end of September 1944, when France was for the most part liberated, the Germans recognised the members of the FFI (*Forces Françaises de l'Intérieur*) as combatants. The members of the FFI belonged to coherent formations, accompanying enemy troops, and clearly recognisable with their armbands or other insignia, must henceforth be considered as combatants and be treated according to the Hague Convention.[76] What were the causes of this change in attitude? An analogy is relevant, in that a similar situation presented itself with the Allied prisoners of German origin captured in the North African campaign. The initial German reaction was to have them executed, but the realisation that the Allies had themselves taken many Germans prisoner, and were thus in a position to make reprisals, made them think again. It could similarly be assumed that the German High Command, realising in September 1944 that sizeable numbers of soldiers of the *Wehrmacht* had fallen into the hands of the FFI, feared reprisals and they, too, changed their minds.

As Jodl explained at Nuremberg, the Fuehrer was not open to legal or moral arguments, only to "military" ones.

---

[76] *The source for this is an Ultra decryption, and not a German War Diary. It concerns Order No. 3701 of 24 September 1944, signed by the IC Section of the Army Group B, transmitting an order from the Commander-in-Chief in the West (Public Record Office, DEFE 3, p. 573).*

CHAPTER 17

The Final Summing-up by the Prosecution

The final summing up by the Prosecution began at the end of July 1946. Jackson, the US Prosecutor, was the first to stand.[77] It was a great social occasion. The courtroom was packed. Lalouette had decided that he would go. Usually, he found it more beneficial – and he was right – to read the transcript of the proceedings in his office.

That is why, for once, I remained in the office. I regretted it afterwards, primarily because I had then not seen Jackson. Since the failure of his interrogation of Goering he had lain low. He preferred to travel and visit several European capitals, Paris among them, to increase his popularity in US public opinion in preparation for a possible political career.

The main reason I regretted missing it was because his speech, which should have been brilliant, ended up as a missed golden opportunity. Indeed, the German lawyers felt that it was far inferior to the stronger pleas by the Defence.

I obtained only second-hand information, but gained the impression that Jackson had expressed

---

[77] *There was some jockeying between the British and the Americans to determine who should speak first.*

himself as a journalist writing for a newspaper with a mass circulation would have done. His immediate audience was relatively sophisticated after the months spent listening to tales of war crimes, crimes against humanity, murders and tortures. Actually, Jackson addressed himself to a wider, distant public, who would appreciate his sensationalist language and sharp comparisons. He relied on the vocabulary of the headlines of the tabloids.

A few days later an article in *The Times* confirmed for me the flavour of his speech. I was surprised at the somewhat sarcastic tone of the correspondent, and wondered whether this could be a case of *Schadenfreude* occasioned by the friendly rivalry between the delegations. *The Times* seemed to take some pleasure in reproducing Jackson's crisply delineated word-portraits.[78] These characterised the Defendants as follows:

Goering was half-militarist and half-gangster. He stuck a podgy finger into every pie. He used his SA musclemen to help bring the gang to power. To consolidate that power, he contrived to have the Reichstag burned down, established the Gestapo and founded the German concentration camps. He was equally adept at massacring opponents and at framing scandals to get rid of stubborn Generals.

The zealot Hess, before succumbing to *Wanderlust* (an allusion, supposedly light-hearted, to the solitary flight of Hess to England in 1941), was the engineer tending the Party machinery.

Von Ribbentrop, the salesman of deception, was detailed to pour wine (he was connected to a

---

[78] *I am quoting from The Times of 27 July 1946.*

champagne firm) onto the troubled waters of suspicion.

Keitel, a weak and willing tool, delivered the armed forces to the party and directed them in executing its felonious designs.

Kaltenbrunner, the grand inquisitor, took up the bloody mantle of Heydrich to stifle opposition, to terrorise followers into compliance, and to buttress the power of National Socialism on a foundation of "guiltless corpses".

Rosenberg, the intellectual high priest of the "master race", provided the doctrine of hatred that provided the impetus for the annihilation of Jewry.

The fanatical Frank, who consolidated Nazi control by establishing a new order of authority without law, exported his lawlessness to Poland.

Streicher, the venomous vulgarian, manufactured and distributed obscene racial libels, which incited the populations of Occupied territories to assist in the progressively savage operations towards "race purification".

As Minister of Economics, Funk accelerated the pace of re-armament and as *Reichsbank* president banked for the SS the gold tooth fillings of concentration camp victims – probably the most ghoulish collateral in banking history.

Schacht, beneath his façade of starched respectability, provided the temptations for the hesitant, and enabled Hitler to finance secretly the colossal re-armament programme. ("Starched respectability" refers to the famous starched collars Schacht always wore.)

Doenitz, Hitler's legatee of defeat, promoted the success of the Nazi aggression by instructing his pack of submarine killers to conduct warfare at sea with the illegal ferocity of the jungle. (Hitler in his Will had made Doenitz his successor. "Pack of submarine killers" suggests the tactics advocated by Doenitz before the war.)

Von Schirach, poisoner of a generation, initiated the German youth into Nazi doctrine. (Was Jackson suggesting that von Schirach was homosexual?)

Sauckel, the greatest and most cruel slaver since the Pharaohs of Egypt, produced manpower by driving foreign peoples into the land of bondage on a scale never previously witnessed.

Jodl, betrayer of the traditions of his profession, led the *Wehrmacht* in violating its own code of military honour in order to carry out the barbarous aims of Nazi policy.

Von Papen, pious agent of an infidel regime (he was a Catholic, and the Centre Party chief), held the stirrup while Hitler vaulted into the saddle (von Papen had been a cavalry officer).

Such images would remain imprinted on the memory.

Other epithets had a more direct meaning: Keitel, weak and willing, betrayed the armed forces, and Jodl the code of military honour. All were simplistic near-caricatures, perhaps, yet tellingly accurate.

Goering had a few months earlier made life difficult for Jackson during his cross-examination, and now laughed heartily during the whole of the US Prosecution's summing up, mocking Jackson.

In the sharing of the tasks among the delegations, Jackson chose to talk about the "conspiracy". This led him to draw a historical sketch of the Nazi Party and of its activities all the way from the origins to its taking over the German government – and after. Jackson then addressed questions of internal policy, which did not, properly speaking, concern the trial. There was no clear necessity to accuse Goering of the Reichstag fire, in which he had perhaps played no part, nor to blame him for compromising the army chiefs Blomberg and Fritsch. Goering had, admittedly, been responsible for the establishment of the Gestapo and of the concentration camps, yet these institutions had passed into Himmler's control before the war.

The German lawyers had little respect for Jackson's speech. The German *"Replik"* means the final prosecution plea, which implied that the Prosecution would answer the arguments put forward by the Defence. Jackson had, rather, preoccupied himself with repeating the accusations delivered at the beginning of the trial. This may be explained by the fact that, in the context of such enormous crimes and given the weight of the documents submitted, it seemed superfluous to waste time with legal quibbles. The German lawyers tended to see a *Replik* as a propaganda exercise.

Jackson lacked subtlety. The US Judge Biddle, a patrician and a minister in Roosevelt's former administration, held no high opinion of Jackson, whom he saw as a lawyer risen from the ranks and one who had never attended university.

Towards the time of the Prosecution's summing up, an American personality from the political milieu, LaGuardia, appeared at the trial, where he had come as a visitor. One morning, I noticed an unusual restlessness in the dock. Von Ribbentrop leaned towards his neighbour on his left to whisper a word in his ear; the latter passed it along. The words spread like a forest fire from one Accused to the next. Goering, von Ribbentrop, Hess, Raeder and Doenitz in turn looked towards and beyond me, on to the visitors' gallery. Usually, the faces of the Accused remained as impassive as profiles on medals. What was going on? LaGuardia was seated among the visitors. There was more than mere curiosity in the glances of Goering and his companions. The small Jew from New York, formerly exposed to the attacks of Nazi propaganda, was there, they thought, to savour revenge.

LaGuardia had lunch with the judges, after which he gave a press conference. He was short, Italian, bald, dumpy, smiling, self-satisfied, smoking a cigar, sitting on a table, his legs swinging well clear of the floor. How had he managed to lift himself up that high? He wore a crumpled suit. In the jokes he fired at the journalists as if from a machine gun, he projected the most disagreeable image of a victor that the Nazis, the Prussian Generals, the Gestapists and all anti-Semites could encounter.

What did LaGuardia think of the Germans during the Occupation? Did he reveal his feelings to his students during the war? He may have made indirect references to indicate that a choice existed between the Resistance and the Collaboration. He explained the word "*Schild*" (shield or carapace) by saying, "Think of the enormous plate the *Feldgendarmerie* wears on its chest!" He smiled as if to make them familiar and friendly, those thick, clumsy, helmeted characters belonging to the German military police. They patrolled the streets in threes, chosen for their bulk. They were capable of blocking off a street although, equally, were unable to pursue suspects.

Shawcross denounced the horrors of war much as Gladstone had denounced the massacres in Bulgaria. He evoked at the outset the millions of dead and the cities destroyed "from Coventry to Stalingrad".

The British had good reason to choose this particular theme as their starting point. Coventry suffered carpet-bombing and the British knew that the Germans planned similarly to destroy one city after another until Britain surrendered. A certain degree of selective blindness made it necessary, though, to ignore the ruins of the city of Nuremberg only a short distance from the courtroom.

The bombing of German cities during the war by the Allies failed to gain the sympathy of the French. After each British night raid on Germany, the Lot-et-Garonne peasants, among whom I was then living, remarked the following morning, "Well, the Germans were hit again last night!" Each German city destroyed was another reason to hope that war would one day end, and that the Germans would be beaten.

I have met only one Frenchman who deplored the bombing of German cities. This was Jean Boyer, who taught German at the Toulouse Faculty of Letters. After the war he asked, "Have you come from

Nuremberg? It's a disgrace to have destroyed the city. No one should wage war against Hans Sachs!" Boyer was an intriguing character. He suffered from an illness that forced his body into a stoop. To look at you he had, painfully, to raise his head, a head that seemed to grow larger as the illness progressed. During the war, when I was underground, I had attended some of his lectures on German literature. He was both Germanist and musicologist; his doctoral thesis was entitled *Le romanticisme de Beethoven*, and in the classroom he explained one of Hoffmann's tales, which he published for his students... He lived for his art, and this allowed him to forget about the trials of life and the ugliness of the real world. Boyer was also the music critic of the *Dépêche de Toulouse*. His column always appeared on the front page. It was incisive without being too acidic. He judged, ruled and condemned, always cheerfully, with an ironic underpinning. He never offended – as far as I know – the "authorities of Occupation" and after the Liberation was appointed Director of the Capitole.

Shawcross was the Chief Prosecutor for the British delegation. The main body of his speech dealt with "Crimes against Peace". This required, too, an understanding of war, what it was, and against whom. The RAF raid on Nuremberg signified, in the usual use of the term, a success, as the city was reduced to a heap of ashes. However, the raid of 30 March on Nuremberg was the occasion of a notable victory for the *Luftwaffe*, which inflicted enormous losses on the Allied attackers. Of the 795 bombers sent from Britain, 170 were allegedly shot down or rendered unserviceable; 500 crew members were killed in one night.

Shawcross left me unconvinced. There was no doubt in my mind that, from an historical perspective, Hitler was responsible for the war. Legally, it was less easy to pin down the Accused on that count. I was sceptical of the purpose or effectiveness of the Briand-Kellogg pact, which was supposed to have "outlawed" war. The professors of law in Paris to whom I listened during my student days, not long ago, were unanimous in saying that the Briand-Kellogg pact was a document "without sanction" thus a pact that could not be implemented. In other words, it made no contribution to positive law and could be described as an instrument of wishful thinking, however laudable the intentions of its signatories. I considered some of Jahreiss's points on the subject relevant, whereas Shawcross poured scorn on them. It was unduly simplistic to present the German professor's argumentation as conveying that the Briand-Kellogg pact had made wars "illegal" yet not criminal.

The British speech ended with a brilliant quotation said to be from Goethe:

Fate would one day strike the German people, because they betrayed themselves and did not want to be what they are. It is sad that they do not know the charm of truth, that mist, smoke and rash immoderation are so dear to them; [it is] pathetic that they ingenuously submit to any mad scoundrel who appeals to their lowest instincts, who confirms them in their vices and teaches them to conceive nationalism as isolation and brutality.

These were strong words indeed from the British advocate. However, some time later a scholar questioned the authenticity of the quotation. The Foreign Office took the matter very seriously. As the quotation was taken from a book by Thomas Mann,[79] this eminent author was approached by the British diplomatic service in the US. Thomas Mann conceded that the text was not, in fact, the work of Goethe – but added that it could have been.[80]

The British speech was moving. It showed compassion for the victims of the Nazi system. It spoke of the "majesty of death". This influenced the atmosphere of the trial, ameliorating the horror of the slaughterhouse when the extermination of the Jews and others in the gas chambers was mentioned. Himmler had studied agriculture; his preoccupation with genetics and race likely stemmed from this. Indeed, when he used Zyklon B gas to kill the Jews, he probably saw this as a form of pesticide, given that he and his SS constantly compared the Jews to vermin.

Shawcross was well briefed in the Nuremberg documents. He appeared to find it sufficient to show the horror of the crimes committed for this to establish the guilt of the Accused. He described the scene of an execution: a Jewish mother was forced to lie down at the bottom of a trench, her three children near her, to be shot in the neck. A witness describing a similar scene told of the executioner sitting nonchalantly on the edge of the trench, a machine gun across his knees, smoking a cigarette.

Was it possible that the Accused could not have known of such atrocities? There had been witnesses. Locally, the villagers knew, yet the Accused – and the German population as a whole – pleaded ignorance. On the other hand, it was nearly

---

[79] *Lotte in Weiman.*

[80] *SRO FO 371-57, 551*

impossible to determine what each actually knew, and when. Admittedly, Kaltenbrunner was photographed at Mauthausen. Doenitz used internees from concentration camps for the navy. Frank acknowledged the exterminations in Poland. Jodl, however, pretended that he knew nothing, or next to nothing.[81]

Maxwell Fyfe made a significant contribution when he called Goering back to the stand and confronted him with documents; the proof required Goering to confess that he had indeed been informed of Dr. Rascher's vivisection experiments in Dachau. Goering continued to deny, either flatly or through sarcasm, the evidence presented to him. Given all of the responsibilities he was supposed to have held (that "podgy finger in every pie", as Jackson said), Goering could not be bothered with the details of every single vacuum installation where experiments took place. For the observers in the courtroom, there was little doubt that Goering had indeed known.

It was quite apparent that the British, as the Americans, intended merely to repeat the accusations made at the beginning of the trial; they had not prepared for a thorough discussion of the legal arguments advanced by the Defence.

Professor Jarreiss launched a full attack on the principle underlying the trial itself, as well as the statistics and the crime against peace; Shawcross assumed the validity of the Paris (Briand-Kellogg)

---

[81] *At the time of his speech, Shawcross could not have known the facts about how the Final Solution had been organised at administrative level. Documentation on this was discovered only after the trial, and this explains the missing link in Shawcross's argument. He could merely assume that the Accused knew and were responsible although had no documentation to support this.*

Pact. When confronted by Jarreiss, Shawcross stood firm, stating that the Charter creating the Tribunal exists and he adhered to the Charter, which provides for the crime against peace. When he dealt with statistics covering the crimes *per se*, Shawcross was on very firm ground. He had only to mention the 50 RAF officers who had escaped from *Stalag Luft III* and when re-captured were executed.

In truth, even in Britain there was a small group of critics of the trial, foremost among them Viscount Maugham, a former Lord Chancellor. He challenged the wording of the Charter, as he considered the terms "crimes against peace" and "crimes against humanity" to have no place in a trial of "war crimes", and that the Accused could be judged only under the "laws and customs of war".[82]

Strangely, as Shawcross was reading his speech, the table of the French Prosecution team remained empty. It may have been a deliberate affront or they were busy elsewhere, perhaps preparing their own speech due for the next day.

On my way to the courtroom that morning I passed Shawcross in one of the corridors. He moved as if in a whirlwind, surrounded by a cloud of assistants and detectives, looking neither right nor left. He would have appeared arrogant were the reason for such preoccupation not known. He had come especially from London to present the British speech. He looked young, slim and elegant. At 44, he seemed much younger than Maxwell Fyfe, only two

---

[82] *Viscount Maugham, UNI and War Crimes, London, 1951. A more radical critic of the Nuremberg Charter was the well-known barrister RT Paget, KC, MP, who defended General von Manstein before a British military tribunal in Hamburg (Manstein, His Campaigns and his Trial). An early critic was Lord Hankey.*

years older. Shawcross wore a light grey suit; Maxwell Fyfe, the 'uniform' of the Bar – a black jacket and striped trousers. The contrast between the two men was rather surprising. It was not obvious on first glance whether Shawcross was Labour and Maxwell Fyfe Conservative, or that Shawcross, though upper class, was a product neither of Oxford nor Cambridge whereas Maxwell Fyfe had been at Balliol, Oxford. Also, Maxwell Fyfe served in the Scots Guards for two years during the First World War from when he was 18 years old.

Maxwell Fyfe had the profile of a prosperous businessman. He had a smooth complexion, sombre air and eyes as black as coal. Seeing him in action in the courtroom he looked, according to La Gorce, rather like an official from the Spanish Inquisition. He savaged von Papen, who, a man with perfect manners, prefaced each answer with "Sir David."

Maxwell Fyfe remained a lawyer and a politician, and it was Shawcross who later had a career associated with big business. Both had in 1945 occupied the post of Attorney General; they exchanged positions in Nuremberg when political power in Britain passed from the Conservatives to the Labour Party.

Shawcross's speech stood out for me because of one minuscule incident. I sat at the end of the table, my back towards the wall, in order to emphasise the fact that there was no representative at the French Prosecution table. Hence, there was a vast empty space between me and the main entrance. Suddenly, a small man entered the courtroom; he skimmed along the walls in his approach to the corner of the room where I sat. Slightly disconcerted, I turned towards him.

Well-documented rumours circulated some time earlier to the effect that the *SS* were preparing a coup to free the Accused and spirit them out of the courtroom. I wondered whether this little man was the vanguard of an *SS* commando unit, at its head the famous Otto Skorzeny (by the way, where was Skorzeny?), and also whether the man might fire a warning shot into the ceiling in order to divert the guards' attention. The absence of the French on that day would then reveal its full import: they knew what was to happen and had prudently failed to appear.

Actually, nothing of the sort happened. The man was probably a researcher carrying a message to the British group. By coincidence, the incident was filmed by the official ciné cameras. When the BBC in subsequent years mentioned the Nuremberg trial, it chose a clip from the film showing Shawcross giving his speech. This included the little man entering the courtroom unexpectedly, the camera following him as he walked around the room, and showed me as I turned questioningly towards him.

It would be interesting to know how Birkett, the British judge, reacted to the Shawcross speech.

He kept a diary.[83] His biographer, H. Montgomery Hyde,[84] had access to it and extracted a few acid remarks concerning questions of procedure and of administration, rather than opinion. Birkett considered that the trial was lasting too long, and that the translations from the interpreters were poor. He reproached the French with having read a long, useless speech on the looting of works of art, the

---

[83] *His son made no reply when I asked him whether it would be possible to consult the diary.*
[84] *Montgomery Hyde, Norman Birkett: The life of Lord Birkett of Ulverston, London, 1954, p. 521.*

requisition of Jewish property and the looting of State libraries, Freemasons' lodges and churches,[85] a speech, Birkett said, prepared by the Americans.

The French presentation of evidence gave rise to an angry exchange with the President of the court, snowed under by the mass of documents submitted by Dubost – who was himself losing his way in the numbering of the documents. When Dubost showed passages from a propaganda film on the Freemasons (*Dunkle Maechte*) the images were accompanied by loud German military music. The President demanded, "Can't you stop that music?"

Birkett made no attempt to hide the fact that he disliked Dubost, and perhaps the French in general. He saw with apprehension and irritation the French final prosecution plea coming.

Birkett had himself been a great barrister in the Anglo-Saxon style. He despised the Prosecution for not knowing how to question witnesses properly.

He thought the same of the German lawyers, but they had the excuse of being ill at ease in a procedure alien to them. All were doubtless serious criticisms. Maybe Birkett confided to his diary some more fundamental comments. It would be surprising if such a penetrating mind had not raised further questions...

The Prosecution's summing up was to be the crowning achievement of Dubost's career at Nuremberg. French opinion, as he saw it, required harshness from him – and he undertook not to

---

[85] *The looting of art works was undertaken by the Einsatzstab Rosenberg. Goering, too, proceeded to buy and exchange works of art. For his part Ribbentrop used the Kuensberg Commando for similar operations.*

disappoint. I found his approach rather brutal; it was not in the usual Nuremberg style, where shouting counted for nothing as what was said depended on the interpreters' versions. Even to listen in, headphones were needed. A different intonation, more intimate, such as that used by radio newsreaders, would have been advisable.

Birkett, the British judge, noted in his diary:

Dubost is at the microphone again, making his final speech. He is robust and vigorous: but such is the irony of fate that he is translated by a stout, tenor-voiced man with the 'refined' and precious accents of a decaying pontiff. It recalls irresistibly a late-comer making an apology at the Vicarage Garden Party in the village, rather than the grim and stern prosecution of the major war criminals.

Dubost adopted the following theme: the Accused are ordinary criminals given that French law and Anglo-Saxon law, as well as Soviet law, condemn murder, theft, imprisonment and slavery.[86] He asked why distinctions were drawn among the Accused. They are all guilty. They have all served the Nazi state and carried out its criminal policies. Hence, there is no need to be concerned with individual responsibilities.

---

[86] *In fact, French military courts adopted this viewpoint. This was the case when the German officers commanding at Meilhan were condemned. However, the decision on war crimes by French justice reached deadlock when it came to judging those responsible for the Oradour massacre. On the one hand Lammerding, who commanded Das Reich, was living quietly in Germany safe from prosecution; on the other hand, French public opinion discovered with amazement that the 'German' soldiers who had been brought to justice were actually Alsatians, that is, Frenchmen who had been drafted "in spite of themselves" into the Wehrmacht. In an atmosphere of panic, the French Government and Parliament brought the trial to an end.*

This was a robust thesis intended to appease French public opinion rather than to convince the Nuremberg judges. To my mind, however, Dubost went perhaps a step too far when he said that Goering and his friends were both "accomplices" and "co-authors", an interesting distinction in French law, and one that did not seem to me applicable here. I remember the example that Hugueney, Professor of Criminal Law (as was Donnedieu de Vabres) at the Law Faculty in Paris, proposed to us law students:

Let us suppose that I rape a married woman while in the next room my colleague, Donnedieu de Vabres, plays the cornet to cover her screams. Is he co-author or accomplice?" The answer seemed obvious: he was an accomplice. – But to be both at the same time! It would be quite a feat.[87]

At the end of his speech Dubost handed over, without reading it, the text against Schacht written by Gerthoffer. In it the latter's well-known hypothesis was formulated: thanks to Schacht Germany had spent ten times as much as France on its re-armament and the same ratio holds on the battlefield, that is, ten German armoured divisions against one French one. No one smiled at this renewed mention of Schacht, nor were they taken in by this reckoning, especially as the French High Command had at their disposal more tanks than did the Germans. Gerthoffer wanted at any cost his "second trial", that against industrialists and against Krupp in particular.

---

[87] *It seems that in English law the "accomplice" is associated with the commission of a crime in such a way that French law would consider him "co-author". The equivalent of "accomplice" in French law would be "accessory before the fact"*

To the French, Krupp's name appeared against an historical background belonging to a fairly remote past, as it was associated with the 1870 war, the 1914 war (Big Bertha shelled Paris) and the 1940 war. If Schacht was indeed innocent, it would be difficult to condemn Krupp. To this should be added that the French had a narrow view of Germany. France was convinced that Germany had re-armed with the sole aim of making war on France and of taking its revenge for the outcome in 1918.

Gerthoffer isolated himself at Nuremberg. He used an immense room where the walls were covered to the ceiling with shelves on which he piled up dossiers and documents against German industrialists. In July, he still believed that the second trial would take place. He said that the Americans had put together a team of 50 "researchers" to prepare it. Admittedly, by a clever manœuvre Dubost had wrested from the British on the very eve of the (current) trial the promise of a second one. In it not only the industrialists but also those "omitted from" the first trial would have been gathered to face justice.

On 19 November 1945, with the main trial due to start on the following day, the four delegations representing France, Britain, America, and Russia met. Dubost wanted to see the old Krupp replaced in the dock by his son Alfred. Dubost evoked the sufferings of the French under the Occupation, including little children dying because they were deprived of milk. He added that there were serious political reasons for adding the industrialists to the group of the Accused.

Shawcross was not accustomed to such a display of emotion in public. He was deeply moved by it. On the other hand, Dubost's reference to "serious political reasons" puzzled him. There was worse to come. The Russians requested that the opening of the trial be delayed by ten days because, they said, the chief of the Soviet delegation was suffering from an attack of malaria. At this moment, Dubost intervened to say that if the Russians were not present, the French delegation would also "out of courtesy" not appear in the courtroom.

The British were aghast. What a disastrous effect it would have on the world if the trial were to open without either the Russians or the French! This was exacerbated by the fact that the Soviets refused to say publicly that their only reason for their absence was the malaria of their chief.

Shawcross felt it necessary to make concessions. He promised that if the French agreed to attend the trial on the following day, then the British and the French delegations could immediately set to work in order to prepare the indictment for the second trial. Krupp's son would appear at this, as would the other Nazi leaders who had not been indicted in the first trial.

Dubost was jubilant. The British had until then refused to commit themselves on the issue of a second trial. The British Foreign Office was opposed in principle to the idea of judging industrialists, as they considered that war crimes could be committed only by the military.

Fortunately, the Trial began on the appointed date. In the meantime, the Quai d'Orsay, warned by the Foreign Office, had put pressure on Dubost to persuade him to withdraw his obstruction. For their part, the Soviets let it be known that they would attend on the following day, as "special medical measures" would put their leading Prosecutor back on his feet.

On leaving the meeting, which lasted two-and-a-half hours, Dubost went to Shawcross with his most conciliatory smile. He said, "You know, the real reason was that neither we nor the Russians were ready."

Had Shawcross been right in conceding the principle of a second trial? He asked himself what was the possible nature of the "serious political reasons" that made a second trial so imperative. The answer is to be found in the letter written by Dean, Lalouette's British opposite number, where he gives his account of the meeting. According to Dean, Dubost and the other members of the French delegation feared seeing a Communist government being set up in Paris. They were taking their precautions in anticipation of this contingency; hence, they supported the Soviet requests both for a delay in the opening of the trial and to include German industrialists among the Great War Criminals.[88]

Lalouette told me before I went to listen to Dubost, "Try to write a good report, to please him." I must confess that I failed. With no comment my paper was thrown into the waste-paper basket. No, I was no good at toadying. But how could I please Dubost and Lalouette at the same time? One wanted to see the Accused declared guilty and to inflict upon

---

[88] *Letter from Dean to Scott-Fox of 26 November 1945 (PRO: FO 371. 50996). Obviously, Dubost was in no way a Communist, but it was a fairly widely known fact that at that time many French civil servants of a certain rank, fearful for their careers, were anxious not to adopt positions that could be construed as anti-Communist.*

them the "supreme punishment", while the other wanted to separate the Nazis from the others, the politicians from the professionals. The latter included diplomats, generals and admirals; they should be spared, for they had done nothing but their duty.

Lalouette avoided attending the courtroom when Dubost or Champetier de Ribes were speaking: he obtained an advance copy of their speeches. Champetier de Ribes read out a brief introduction to Dubost's speech although was unable to speak for long because he had recently been seriously ill. He was very emaciated. He had a sallow, waxy complexion, running out of breath at the end of each sentence. Elegantly silhouetted, he leaned on the lectern with his arms folded, the least painful position for him.

The aristocratic profile of Champetier de Ribes could only command respect. He was close to death. To him, the elevation of thought was the main thing. From his speech I remembered only,

"One had to invent a new word – 'genocide'." I knew Lalouette would not like that. The mere fact that the word 'genocide' was mentioned meant a major victory for Professor Lemkin, who had come to Nuremberg to have "his" word adopted and to publicise his book *Axis Rule in Occupied Europe.*

After his introductory speech Champetier de Ribes left the scene to his seconds. Dubost read a speech prepared by the astute Lanoire. Nowadays, after re-reading the official transcript of the French Prosecution plea, I wonder if my initial reaction to Dubost's speech had been somewhat unfair. It is clear to me now that Dubost embarked on a demonstration, in which he somehow became entangled, in order to prove that the Accused were at one and the same time co-authors and accomplices. Then, it seemed strange, but today I can better understand why Dubost chose that path.

The reason was that de Menthon, the main French Prosecutor in the early days of the trial, had proposed the hypothesis that the Accused were "ordinary" criminals. To support his superior's proposition, Dubost argued that Goering and the other Nazi leaders may well have given orders; they themselves did not commit the crimes, but they must be considered "co-authors". As such, they were equally as guilty as the "authors".

However, one difficulty masked another. In order to justify a universal condemnation of these "ordinary criminals", and also as the concept of "co-author" was perhaps not accepted in all legal systems, Dubost said that in most countries the authors of serious crimes and also their "accomplices" were punished by the death penalty. Dubost was thus of the opinion that the Accused were both "co-authors and accomplices". His demonstration included points that to me seemed doubtful. One was that the Accused had a criminal plan. As proof Dubost used quotations from *Mein Kampf*. This was not going to make much impression on the French judge, Donnedieu de Vabres... Another, however, with which I completely agree ran thus: there was close collaboration among the various administrations headed by the Accused, rendering them equally guilty.

In Dubost's allusions to "German barbarism"[89] he reminded me of Clemenceau's provocative words when he handed over to Count Brockdorff-Rantzau the text of the Treaty of Versailles. I found it reassuring that twenty-five years later the French could treat the Germans in exactly the same way, although possibly unfairly.

Lalouette liked no better my account of the Prosecution plea by Rudenko, the Soviet representative. I must admit that I did not manage to sum it up in only a few lines. La Gorce said, "To the Russians, all the Accused deserve to be condemned, because they are Fascist." He added, "Yes, to the Soviets the Nazis are quite simply lecherous vipers. It's a hoot!" I was beginning to understand why I was unable to write the type of "diplomatic telegrams" that were expected. I was taking things too seriously. I was trying to enter into the systems of thoughts of the Prosecutors or the lawyers, whereas I should have maintained an outsider's detachment. "Well," declared Lalouette, "we shall be content with saying that the Soviet Prosecutor confined himself to a recital of invectives."

I have since read at greater leisure Rudenko's speech, in its printed German version. His hypothesis was not completely ridiculous. He maintained that von Papen contributed to the spread of Fascism throughout the *Reich*, and that Neurath played an important part by consolidating the position of the Nazi conspirators in power. The British delegation made similar comments, using nearly the same words. Maxwell Fyfe designated von Papen as the

---

[89] *On this occasion, Goering whispered "Schweinhund!" loudly enough for the guards to hear him; he was punished with a fifteen-day loss of American PX rations of tobacco and chocolate.*

man responsible for the coming of the Nazis to power. No one disputed that both von Papen and Neurath had made an error in their calculations: they had naïvely thought to adopt Machiavellian methods when bringing the Nazis to power, side by side with themselves, in order to control Hitler, Goering and company. They would then harness them to the benefit of a traditional and conservative regime, mindful of the interests of the army, the large landowners, industry and the bureaucracy.

Also, Rudenko made an interesting remark, characterising the ideology of the Nazi regime thus: the Nazi *Weltanschauung* was a sort of philosophy of action, little concerned with individuals, but seeing humanity as composed of a series of national, social and geographical groups. The Soviet Prosecutor's speech was conventional, very much along the same lines as those chosen by the other delegations. He briefly refuted the main excuses offered by the Defence of *nullum crimen nulla poena sine lege* (there is no crime nor punishment except in accordance with law) and that they had been following orders. Further, that the policies were the responsibility of the State thus not of the individuals, and there was an absence of conspiracy. Rudenko analysed the case of each of the Accused, blaming them respectively for being a "Fascist" and for having contributed to the implanting of "Fascism" in Germany.[90]

---

[90] *In the context of Frank, head of the "General Government" in Poland, Rudenko brought up the Katyn affair. At the time of my arrival in Nuremberg, the Soviets were trying to prove that the murder of thousands of Polish officers had been the work of the Germans. The Russians were not convincing, yet Dubost, again anxious to please his Soviet colleagues, for a while envisaged arranging for a special publication of the proofs put forward by the Soviet side.*

After the final summings up of the four Prosecutors came the trial of the "criminal" organisations. This provoked no great interest, although it threw a light onto the world of the Nazis – as exemplified by Juettner, a senior member of the SA. The *Sturmabteilung* (Storm Division, the Brownshirts) was organised similarly to the army.

Juettner's progress was revealing. He was originally a career officer. The German defeat in 1918 was traumatic for him; he left the army in 1920. He worked in a peat mine and soon became head of the firm. At the same time, as a good patriot he joined a nationalist party and became a member of the *Stahlhelm* (Steel Helmet), a right-wing organisation for ex-servicemen. Once Hitler had seized power the *Stahlhelm* was dissolved and its members were assigned to the SA. Juettner thus became an SA man. In 1933-34 the SA was huge: from 300,000 in 1933, membership rose to 4.5 million in 1934. If only through their numbers they represented a significant proportion of the German people, given that neither women, children, the elderly nor Left-wingers could belong to the SA.

Juettner was a typical ex-serviceman. The SA Chiefs, he explained, were honest men whose behaviour was beyond reproach, men with a sense of duty and, of course, patriots above all. The SA chiefs lived simply and modestly. Moreover, they were badly paid in comparison with civil servants.[91] They believed in a just cause and were ready to sacrifice their lives.

---

[91] *By and large, the SA became an organisation for "ordinary" people; the German aristocracy joined the SS, an "elite" corps.*

Juettner still had the physique and the bearing of the Brownshirts: square shoulders and a heavy gait. During the adjournment, he made signs of triumph to Goering, shaking his fist to show "Did you see the licking I gave them!" Goering had a good laugh and turned towards Hess and Doenitz as if to say, "Look at that damn fool, Juettner, how proud he is of himself."

There was, in the Roehm affair, more than one case of homosexuality. Roehm was an unwell man. Juettner seemed quite ready to talk about it, but the President cut him short. The fact was that Roehm had the idea of transforming the SA into an army comprised of quasi-military units and had opened negotiations with representatives of neighbouring countries. François-Poncet breathed not a word about it in his memoirs. The French military attaché seemed very much in favour to the extent of discussing it with Roehm at a time when problems of Germany's disarmament or re-armament were on the verge of becoming acute. Juettner did his best to save the honour of the SA. He had a struggle to evade the attacks of Maxwell Fyfe, who was trying to make him admit that the SA was responsible for the liquidation of 10,000 Wilna Jews. "No, it is not possible," answered Juettner, "There were no SA outside the

German borders. It could be at most that they were SA drafted in by other organisations."... Perhaps a mistake was made about the uniforms; others than the SA may have worn brown shirts.

In the long run Juettner's denials were repetitive and less convincing. He acknowledged that he was anti-Semitic, but claimed that the SA had never advocated or practised violence towards the Jews (which fails to explain the Kristallnacht).

Juettner did not know that the Party leadership intervened to stop the proceedings against the *SA*, who murdered Jews during the November 1938 pogroms – to which, he thought, Hitler, Goering and Hess were opposed. For *his* part, he was against Polish Jews, probably a question of patriotism. Apart from that, the *SA* supported freedom of religion. There were no *SA* activities at the time of church services. Did not Roehm belong to the Protestant church? Juettner himself, of the Evangelical church, was for a "positive Christianity".

Lalouette perceived irony in my writings thus did not greatly appreciate my reports...

According to Juettner, the *SA* were not a military or para-military organisation: they aimed only at educating Germans physically and morally through the practice of sport and imbuing in them a love of nature. Service in the field aimed to toughen them up while at the same time helping them discover the beauties of their country, to understand the historical meaning of the landscapes they discovered. And the shooting exercises? These were purely sporting pursuits; only small-calibre weapons were used.

To what extent was Juettner sincere? I could not forget that one of the *SA*'s activities was to "chase the Jews". There was no point in reminding Lalouette of this, as from his Berlin experience before the war he was better informed than was I.

The final pleadings by the Prosecution were a disappointment. They consisted by and large only of a summary of the evidence presented in the first phase of the trial. There was no great effort to answer the objections nor to refute the legal arguments advanced by the Defence.

Today, it seems strange that the extermination of the Jews was mentioned little more than in passing. The British speech delineated at some length the mass execution of the Jews in the East by *Einsatzkommando* A, B, or C, according to which section was then at the Front. A lengthy treatment of the extermination camps and gas chambers could have been expected, too. Was it because it was not possible precisely to allocate responsibility to any one in particular of the Accused? Or was it – less likely – because there was some doubt about the admissibility in this Trial of crimes against humanity?

Each delegation revealed something of its own national attitudes or sensibilities, and each was right in its own way. The Americans had no doubt that the Nazi chiefs were a band of gangsters, guilty from the outset. The British hated the shedding of blood. These crimes took place, though, at a distance, in far-away countries. The French considered all of the Accused to be guilty, and with them the Germans and Germany. Memories of the Occupation were still alive. The Soviets, as the French, thought all of the Accused guilty. However, whereas the French condemned them in a general, abstract and almost philosophical approach, the Soviets carefully reconstructed the *curriculum vitae* of each; and all were "Fascists", too.

CHAPTER 18

Donnedieu's Judgement

Seeing Donnedieu de Vabres perched on the Judges' dais, I remembered those early University examination days in July: a Professor with the task of invigilating over us delegated his responsibilities onto the Faculty porters (or often onto seedy-looking part-timers) while he relished the freedom of those three hours allotted to the candidates. The Professor isolated himself mentally from the rest of the world to fulfil other, more urgent and always unfinished, tasks such as writing an article, preparing lectures or reviewing a recent book.

At Nuremberg, Donnedieu remained the Professor who had taught penal law for decades at the Paris Law Faculty. The habit of teaching had helped him to retain a certain distance from the realities of this world. He similarly isolated himself from the atmosphere of the trial. He wore headphones and concentrated his attention on the French translations. He never looked up from his notebook; he wrote ceaselessly. With his long moustache '*à la gauloise*' and his old-fashioned suit, he was a man from another generation, that of my grandfather rather than of my father.

The Nuremberg old hands told me how, a few months earlier, Donnedieu addressed the Tribunal.

This caused a sensation. The foreign delegations did not expect his intervention. He raised an embarrassing problem: as one was asked, said Donnedieu de Vabres, to condemn not only individuals but also Nazi organisations such as the *SA*, the *SS*, Reich's cabinet or the General Staff, what would be the consequences if these organisations were declared criminal? Would their members automatically be criminals, thus liable to punishment with no further proceedings?

The American Prosecutor, Jackson, and after him the British one, Maxwell Fyfe, tried to allay his anxieties. It was indeed feasible to predict some of the difficulties this problem would cause to the Occupation authorities and also to the prosecuting governments, who were already beginning to lose their enthusiasm for indicting war criminals.[92] For the observers of the Trial, the intervention appeared no more than a minor hitch. Donnedieu retreated into his silence, as studious as before. His behaviour suggested that his part at Nuremberg was to represent France only as a matter of form, and no more.

That would have been a reasonable conclusion, as the trial seemed an affair led by the Americans and the British. It was if the French and Russian Judges had been called upon only to provide their moral backing, similarly to how Russian and French Generals had been invited to participate in the ceremony of the surrender of the German army in the West. The atmosphere at the Trial was decidedly Anglo-Saxon. As the city of Nuremberg was located in the American zone, the whole organisation of the

---

[92] *Donnedieu revealed to his colleagues that he had intervened on orders from his government.*

Trial was in the hands of the Americans. Even the paper and pencils I used in taking notes were supplied by the American army and were directly imported from the US. On the judicial level, all aspects were Anglo-Saxon in flavour, the procedure as well as the Statute of the Tribunal, even though the latter was formally quadripartite.[93]

However, after the event it was revealed that Donnedieu had indeed played his own part at Nuremberg. He was not always in agreement with the other Judges, yet was able to influence them. His criticisms of the trial were nonetheless a surprise. I discovered how wide-ranging they were through reading the transcript of his lectures to candidates for the Doctorate at the Law Faculty in Paris, where Donnedieu re-took his Chair immediately after the trial.[94] It would not surprise me if the students listening to him received the impression that their Professor had been totally opposed to the very idea of a trial. Donnedieu doubtless felt that crimes deserving punishment had been committed. When he examined the legal principles supporting the charges, though, he had scruples; these scruples prevailed over his wish to punish.

Donnedieu had little appreciation of the Anglo-Saxon procedure by which a defendant could plead "not guilty" and become a witness in his own case. I found this procedure, however, proper and admirable. It led to the display in full daylight, in the public eye, in front of the journalists, of the facts of which the Accused were standing trial. The debates did not

---

[93] *The Rules of Procedure had in fact to a certain extent been drawn up "by reaching compromises between the four national systems of conducting a trial". Ann Tusa and John Tusa, The Nuremberg Trial, p. 126.*
[94] *Le Procès de Nuremberg, Editions Domat-Montchrestien, Paris, s.d. 1947.*

hinge on the contents of a dossier compiled in secret by a *juge d'instruction,* and there was no question of the *secret de l'instruction.* Quite the opposite: all relevant materials were openly discussed in the presence of the Accused, the Judges, and the public. The President was not required to draw a portrait of the Accused at the outset of the Trial, which would suggest an opinion and possibly also a judgement. At Nuremberg, the Judges were expected to attend the debates with no preconceptions whatsoever.

Donnedieu deplored the fact that two of the Accused had refused to take the stand, thus that they were to be sentenced with no opportunity for the Judges to assess their characters. For the other Accused, four months elapsed before they were called to testify and before the Judges could form an opinion of their personalities. Donnedieu said, "The system by which the Accused is a witness in his own case is not justified by the experience at Nuremberg."[95] He disliked the amalgamation of the functions of Accused and witness. In French legal practice, it is expected that the Accused struggle against the Prosecution by all means available and "by lying if need be."[96] This option, allowed by the

French judicial system, becomes inconceivable the moment the Accused can plead not guilty and become a witness in his own defence, swearing to tell the truth.

Donnedieu found the indictment to be vague, the offences imprecisely worded and the sentences left almost completely to the Judges' discretion. His most acid comments concerned the charge of "conspiracy".

---

[95] *Donnedieu, Cours de doctorat, p. 220.*
[96] *Ibid., p. 247.*

This, he stated, was an Anglo-Saxon concept. French law accepts the more effective concept of "complicity".

It has suited the prosecution to present the national-socialist undertaking as the expression of a consensus of wills the immediate effect of which, after the seizure of power, was the launching of a war of aggression, while its indirect consequence was the perpetration of war crimes and of crimes against humanity.[97]

This was an absurd hypothesis in the eyes of Donnedieu, who failed to recognise in it the actual links between the events. Furthermore, he saw all too clearly how the Prosecution tried to throw dust in the eyes by using tricks such as "details of style":

While the opinion commonly held and general parlance implicate the responsibility of one man, Hitler, who when on the stage put all the others into the background, one finds often in the indictment a collective formula: '[The conspirators] provoked the withdrawal from the League of Nations; they declared to the world that they would respect the Versailles Treaty; they concluded between Germany and

Austria a treaty ...'. This tendency is probably connected with the fact that Hitler disappeared while his lieutenants became the Accused of today.[98]

Donnedieu talks of the indictment as "an interesting but rather romanticised construction". There is, he thinks, "a discrepancy between the facts and the accusation of a general conspiracy". He added, "The imputation of conspiracy adorns the

---

[97] *Ibid., p. 220.*
[98] *Ibid., p. 247.*

Hitlerite undertaking with a romantic prestige that does not fail to seduce the imagination."[99]

The French delegation had, in their small talk in the corridors of Nuremberg, spared no criticism of the conspiracy notion: "It is a purely American concept. The Americans are accustomed to thinking in cinematic terms." The French smiled indulgently. These Americans are nothing but big children; they see the world through Hollywood productions. Everything comes down to gangster films or Westerns, where the "baddies" are always members of an organised group.

As for the Prosecution, it is true to say that the conspiracy theory offered practical advantages over the French concept of complicity. It allowed the implication of Schacht and von Papen in the whole set of crimes submitted to the Tribunal, including war crimes and crimes against humanity, in which they had in fact played no part. This constituted for Donnedieu the weakness of the Prosecution's position. The Judges could be led to condemn individuals, holding them responsible for the consequences of the conspiracy – consequences they had neither known of nor wanted, and which they could not even have imagined.[100]

---

[99] *Ibid., p. 249*
[100] *However, the Prosecution could be excused for endorsing, so to speak, the mystique surrounding those who belonged to the original group of Hitler's companions in Munich (Alte Kaempfer), and more particularly to the group of those who participated in the 1923 Putsch. These old companions (and others less long-standing) occupied important posts either in the Party or in the government after the seizure of power. They were found in Nuremberg in the dock, sitting on the front bench: Goering, Hess, Ribbentrop, Rosenberg, Frank, Frick, Streicher and Funk. Some joined the Party only several years after the Munich Putsch yet nevertheless before the seizure of power.*

Donnedieu's criticism of the "conspiracy" theory was justified insofar as the theory did not seem to account for German history between the two World Wars. Conspiracy was a concept at one and the same time too wide and too narrow; too wide because it placed upon a score of Germans the responsibility for decisions that were, in the end, Hitler's own. It was also too narrow a concept because it laid on the small band of the Accused the burden of guilt for acts that required the active involvement of the whole of the State apparatus, of all of the institutions, and of millions of Germans.

I was also astonished at Donnedieu's total rejection of the notion of "crimes against humanity". To observers at the Trial, as for outsiders, Nuremberg was essentially a trial of crimes against humanity. The other crimes such as initiating a war of aggression and war crimes, no doubt deserved condemnation and punishment. However, they were, so to speak, 'ordinary' crimes committed in the context of any conflict. Concerning war crimes, in particular, all agreed that they should be condemned, but did combatants from all sides observe scrupulously the laws of warfare? Was it not the case that in difficult circumstances those involved could not be too nice as regards to the means at their immediate disposal?

It was impossible, it seems to me, to excuse crimes against humanity. Summary executions, murders, tortures, concentration camps, the Final Solution, rapes, and the gas chambers did not concern combatants at all; the victims were mainly women and children. Crimes against humanity tainted the Trial with an indescribable feeling of horror. Rather than the long speeches, the few images shown in the courtroom sealed the fates of the Accused. They were images that even some of the Accused lacked the courage to look at. The films shot when the concentration camps were liberated by Allied troops showed the emaciated faces of the internees, eyes burning with fever, bodies with no more than skin clinging to their skeletons, the corpses pushed into pits hundreds at a time by bulldozers. As they fell, the bodies briefly adopted a pose before collapsing disjointedly onto the heap.

The British judge, Birkett, was of the opinion that showing those films was in bad taste and served no purpose. I thought the opposite: that it was painfully necessary to clarify what the regime meant in practice. Indeed, pre-war films showing the glories of the Third Reich were familiar, with their mass meetings for the Party congresses at the Nuremberg stadium – which happened to be only a few steps away from the Tribunal where we sat. Faultless parades of thousands upon thousands of uniforms, including soldiers, the *SA*, the *SS* and young men from the Labour Front, each carrying a shovel over their shoulders, took place. It was imperative that the other face of Nazism as seen in the courtroom was absolutely not to be ignored.

None of the Accused tried to justify themselves as regards crimes against humanity. Goering himself, who at the start of the trial acted as if he were the loyal champion of the *Fuehrer*, wanted in his final speech to wipe out the memory of the brutalities:

I did not want war ... I did all I could to prevent it through negotiations. Once it had started, I did everything to ensure victory ... I accept responsibility for what I did, but I refuse completely to admit that my actions were dictated by the will to use the war to subjugate, murder, rob or enslave foreign peoples.[101]

I expected the Judgement to condemn, in the first instance, crimes against humanity. On reading the verdict, my first reaction was to comment that none of those condemned to death were innocent of crimes against humanity. This was perhaps literally exact, yet it misconstrued the opinions of the Judges, as Donnedieu was in a position to state: "The category of crimes against humanity, which the Statute had ushered through a very small door, vanished altogether as a consequence of the judgement."[102]

Admittedly, up to a point Donnedieu played on words, as the Judgement condemned under a different heading the most awful crimes. Nevertheless, the fact remains that Nuremberg did not accept this new concept of crimes against humanity, the application of which could have led very far – farther than the Prosecution was able at that time to consider going.

The type of criticisms formulated by Donnedieu revealed a French lawyer insistent on the precise use of technical terms. "Crimes against humanity" was a vague notion that attempted:

[T]o apply a brake on the arbitrary choice of rulers of oppressing a national, racial or religious minority, which intended in the end to ensure respect for human dignity. The task to ensure this would fall on the international community, liberated from local

---

[101] Quoted by Werner Maser in his *Nuremberg*, p. 468.
[102] Donnedieu, *Cours de Doctorat*, p. 24.

passions. It would be not merely an international but a universal safeguard.[103]

The discreet figure of the champion of the issue of crimes against humanity, the American Professor Lemkin, sat in the wings of the Tribunal. He was the author of a thick volume on the Nazi Occupation of Europe. He wanted to see the term "genocide" recognised officially. He cornered me one afternoon in the entrance of the Grand Hotel. I had to listen to him for more than an hour. Lemkin gave me a copy of his book in its blood-red cover. I handed it over to Lalouette, who told me, "There's no question of accepting the term of 'genocide'."[104]

Donnedieu disliked, in the Statute, the formulation defining crimes against humanity, which contained reference to "murders, exterminations, enslavement, deportations and other inhuman acts committed against the civilian population, before or during the war, or the persecution for political, racial or religious motives". He disliked in particular seeing a crime defined by its *motive*, for this could lead into the realm of the arbitrary. In such a context Donnedieu expressed a curious consideration, one that perhaps revealed one of his deep preoccupations:

Social minorities are not mentioned. By reasoning a contrario must we admit that penal protection is

---

[103] *Ibid.*, p. 239.
[104] As early as in 1933, Lemkin, then a lawyer in Warsaw, published an article where he defined the notion of crimes against "humanity": to protect the rights of the individual as a member of an ethnic, national, religious or social group. The word "genocide" was not yet mentioned. Raphael Lemkin, Staatsanwalt in Warschau, *Akten der Barbarei und des Vandalismus als delicta juris gentium*, Vienna, 1933. Sonderabdruck aus dem Internationalen Anwaltsblatt.

denied to them? The past – a recent past – shows, does it not, that the class struggle can be just as murderous as the racial or the religious one.[105]

Donnedieu may have been referring to the 1917 Russian Revolution, of which the *bourgeoisie* was the victim. More likely, he was thinking of the relatively recent events accompanying the Liberation in France. I thought I understood reasonably well the mentality of the Professors at the Faculty of Law in Paris, having listened to their lectures over a period of three years. They were deeply *bourgeois* and, as such, the keepers of a tradition that stretched back through the generations to the beginnings of the nineteenth century. As bourgeois, their main preoccupation seemed to be in offering unquestioning respect for the State, whether liberal or authoritarian. It disturbed their personal equilibrium if social stability was in any way threatened.

At the time of the Liberation, the Paris bourgeoisie felt threatened by the Resistance, which to them related to revolutionary forces taking as their inspiration the "class struggle". Actually, the first version of Gaullism, dating from London and the Liberation, may appear disconcerting. In an important speech at the Albert Hall on 8 June 1942, General de Gaulle declared:

For France ... where the disaster, treason and the waiting game have discredited most of the leaders of the privileged few and where, by contrast, the popular masses in their depth remained the most courageous and the most loyal, it would not be admissible that the

---

[105] *Donnedieu, Cours de Doctorat, p. 244.*

terrible ordeal could leave standing a social and moral regime that worked against the nation.[106]

Donnedieu also remarked that the indictment had "mixed together" war crimes with crimes against humanity and had made an indiscriminate mass of the two. Under "war crimes" fell every single action or event that happened during the war, such as the deportation of civilian workers. He said:

Under heading No. 4 in the indictment, Crimes against Humanity ... all that remains to be addressed are atrocities committed before the war in concentration camps ... and the persecution for political, racial and religious reasons, that is, the persecution of the Jews.[107]

Against this new crime, "in the avant-garde of international law", he raised an objection to the principle of *nullum crimen nulla poena sine lege*, which was addressed by Rudenko. The effect of this is that, if at the time of an act no law exists specifying it as a crime, later laws could not be applied retroactively.

Such retroactivity would shock French tradition. This tradition condemns also the elasticity of terms characterising all of the definitions of the crimes against humanity so far encountered. The terms 'persecution', 'enslavement' and 'violation of liberty' ... may take their place as headings within a code, but they may not enter as the definition of a crime.[108]

---

[106] *Quoted by Pierre Bertaux in his La Libération de Toulouse, p. 153.*
[107] *Donnedieu, Cours de Doctorat, p. 222.*
[108] *Ibid., p. 243.*

Moreover, Donnedieu noted that the Statute itself introduced only discreetly the concept of crimes against humanity, which at the trial was accepted merely incidentally. It required a relation between, on the one hand, the notion of crimes against humanity and, on the other, the crimes specifically addressed by the Tribunal. That is why Donnedieu concluded, with some satisfaction:

Thus the category of crimes against humanity which the Statute had ushered through a very small door vanished into thin air as a result of the judgement. Nowhere can the judgement be criticised for having charged the Accused with inhuman acts committed independently of the circumstances of war.[109]

The elimination of the concept of crimes against humanity was indeed problematic. It raised the issue of how Schirach and Streicher, not accused of war crimes, could be sentenced. In the case of Streicher, Donnedieu noted that during the whole period of the hostilities he had consistently urged the extermination of the Jews, and such was considered in the Statute as a war crime. As for Schirach, *Gauleiter* of Austria, a territory incorporated into Germany, he did not seem *a priori* to be guilty *per se* of crimes within the competence of the Tribunal. However, the Judgement disposed of this objection by remarking that Austria was occupied as a consequence of a concerted plan of aggression.[110] Hence, the Occupation of Austria was well and truly a crime within the competence of the Tribunal.

---

[109] *Ibid.*
[110] *The concerted plan of aggression was the "conspiracy", a charge Donnedieu did not take very seriously, as we have seen. At Nuremberg the Occupation of Austria was considered an element of the conspiracy and not of a war of aggression.*

Donnedieu in no way denied the existence of war crimes with which the Accused could be charged. Over the years and the centuries, a law of warfare had developed. Custom played its part; the equivalent of a Code existed with the Hague Convention of 1907. War crimes, it could be assumed, would form the solid foundation supporting the Nuremberg Judgement.

However, for no immediately apparent reason, Donnedieu expressed reserves here, too. He noted that applying the Hague Convention had encountered certain difficulties, given that this provided only a "civil sanction" against a State under the jurisdiction of which the Accused belonged. It was therefore impossible to condemn individuals and also impossible to impose a penal sanction. Besides, the Hague Convention included a clause of "general participation", which meant that it could take effect only if all of the countries at war had ratified it. Neither Italy nor the USSR had either signed or ratified the Hague Convention. Could it then be stated that the Hague Convention lacked weight in the context of the Second World War? Also, added Donnedieu, the Hague Convention had been overtaken by the conditions of modern warfare, for which it could not possibly have provided comprehensively at the time of signing. The Convention prescribed that the countries at war were required to come to the rescue of the crews and passengers of ships they had sunk. Doenitz ordered the submarine commanders to abandon to their fate the survivors from enemy ships. Whether Doenitz's order could lead to his prosecution for this was in doubt. Given the existence of aircraft chasing submarines, argued Donnedieu, the German submarines would have been exposed to excessive danger if they had surfaced to rescue those who had been shipwrecked.[111]

This was also the opinion of the Tribunal, although another factor had contributed. Doenitz had an excellent Counsel for his defence, Kranzbuehler, formerly an Admiralty judge in Germany, who succeeded in obtaining from the American Admiral Nimitz a declaration according to which American submarines operating in the Pacific had received a similar order.[112]

Donnedieu's objections seemed to me then of little importance as far as the relations between France and Germany were concerned, for the two countries had committed themselves at least tacitly to acknowledging the Hague Convention, a codification of existing practice. Jodl said that during the whole war he kept on his desk the text of the Hague rules. From my reading many years later of the archives of some of the *Wehrmacht* units stationed in France during the Occupation, it became quite obvious that the German Generals considered that the Hague Convention applied.

However, I wondered whether Donnedieu's objections hid a preoccupation he did not wish to express openly. By weakening the import of the law

---

[111] *The Laconia affair was brought up at Nuremberg. The U-156 had on 12 September 1942 sunk the Laconia, a transport ship of the British Admiralty, in the South Atlantic. The Commander of the U-156 had made every effort to save the survivors, with the help of other U-boats. An American Liberator bombed the U-boats five times. Consequently, on 17 September, Doenitz gave the order not to attempt any future rescues.*

[112] *Kranzbuehler brought off a remarkable coup, for the Tribunal decided that this type of argument (tu quoque, or 'the same applies to you, too') was not admissible. Doenitz was thus to escape the death penalty; however, the Tribunal discussed whether Doenitz's order implied that the shipwerecked enemy forces should be massacred.*

in force concerning war crimes, was he attempting to influence a moderate judgement? In actual fact, he considered that the French Resistance failed to respect the laws of war; consequently *maquisards* were to be seen as *francs-tireurs*. It begged the question whether the charge of war crimes allegedly committed by the Germans could be enforced. In other words, Donnedieu considered that the methods applied by the Resistance constituted extenuating circumstances for the Germans.[113]

It seems almost logical to assume that the Accused at Nuremberg would have been charged with having started World War II. Some historians afterwards believed that the Judgement held the Nazi leaders responsible for the war. They were charged with the wars of aggression, including those against Poland, Norway and the USSR. There was the sense that the mistake of saying to the Germans at the time of the Treaty of Versailles "You are responsible for the war" should not be repeated. The nightmare of the controversies between historians after the First World War persisted. Nuremberg could have become an arena where historians would again have confronted each other *ad infinitum*. But embarking on an analysis of the economic, political, social and military causes of the war and then writing the complete history of the period between the two World Wars was simply not feasible.

The Tribunal took certain well-considered precautions and warned the Accused, "It would be a waste of your time in claiming that the Treaty of Versailles was the cause of all of Germany's misfortunes and ultimately the cause of the 1935-45 war." In order also to cut short any discussion that

---

[113] *See Bradley-Smith, op. cit. p. 146.*

could easily have become endless, the Tribunal declared, "It would not be acceptable to argue that the Allies had done the same thing." Many Germans told me later: we are blamed for creating concentration camps, but the English were the first to do so – during the Boer War.

The wars of aggression, considered individually as a series of isolated events, seemed to offer an arena in which the Nazi leaders could with confidence be challenged. After all, since Hitler came to power, Germany had committed a whole series of bids for power and acts of aggression, and was always on the eve of another coup: their attack on Poland, the invasions of Denmark and Norway, followed by operations against Yugoslavia and Greece, culminating in the attack upon Russia. It was a long list. Germany had few excuses. Moreover, Germany could not be accused of having caused a world conflict as Germany had always tried both to mount raids on her neighbours one at a time and to avoid fighting the whole world simultaneously, in particular France and Britain.

The good conscience of the Tribunal was, though, seriously shaken when Grand Admiral Raeder requested that he present, among the documents for his defence, the *White Book*. This was published by the Germans during the war, and concerned the invasion of Norway. This *White Book* contained documents from the French General Staff – documents that were captured at La Charité-sur-Loire in June 1940 during the German advance. They had been found in three trucks abandoned on a railway siding. These proved that the French and the British had themselves long planned an invasion of Norway. How, then, could Raeder or von Ribbentrop be charged with having committed an act of aggression against Norway? This indictment would collapse on the evidence in the *White Book*.

It is rather strange that Shawcross should have been taken so completely by surprise by the Norway affair. Obviously, he knew nothing of it thus was oblivious of the existence of such a potentially devastating pitfall. He asked the Foreign Office to tell him what had really happened, then proposed to adopt a new line of argument. He wrote to Sir Basil Newton on 19 February 1946:

Thank you for your letter of the 8th February about Admiral Raeder's application to the Tribunal at Nuremberg that the White Book of the German Foreign Office in regard to the Norwegian campaign should be produced in evidence of his defence.

I am bound to say that your letter discloses an unfortunate state of affairs, which may have repercussions of which, I am inclined to think, the Secretary of State should be informed. The first essential in the conduct of this prosecution is that the true facts concerning all relevant matters should be fully disclosed to me. I am quite unable to accept any responsibility if I am instructed by the Foreign Office to put the case forward on a basis which, as the Foreign Office ought to have known if there had been proper consultations with the Service Departments concerned, is quite inconsistent with the facts and, moreover, with the facts likely to be within the knowledge of the defendants and to be brought out by them. In preparing and presenting the cases against the Defendants in regard to Germany's so called aggressive war against Norway, we naturally proceeded in the belief that there were no concrete plans for military operations by ourselves against Norway of the kind which it now appears in fact existed, and that the matter could properly be dealt with on the basis indicated in Dean's letter of the 17th October. On that assumption we stated in terms in presenting our case that the allegation made by the Germans that we were about to invade Norway and that their action was taken in consequence of this was patently false.

In the circumstances disclosed by the documents contained in the Geheimakten, we shall, I think, now have to take the line (a) that German preparations for the invasion of Norway commenced substantially earlier than and were independent of our own, and (b) that, in any event, our own plans are irrelevant to the charges before the Court, and that the theory that he who gets his blow in first is thrice blessed is not accepted in international law.

It remains true, however, that these documents may prove very embarrassing not only in connection with the Trial itself, but also in their bearing on our relations with the U.S.S.R. I do not see, however, how we can prevent Admiral Raeder having access to them.[114]

This line of argument was to reveal itself a poor weapon when the Foreign Office opened its files to determine the facts. As early as in February 1940, a British intervention in Norway had been envisaged. It was then designed to come to the help of Finland and to ensure the supply of Swedish iron ore. Unfortunately, Finland collapsed on 12 March, when it signed the Moscow Peace Treaty. This allowed Finland to retain its independence, but ceded parts of Finnish territory to the Russians. (It was ratified by both sides nine days later.) On 15 March the French

---

[114] *PRO, FO, 371-57540, Doc. U-2127.*

embassy in London put forward a plan for the invasion of Norway. On 28 March Norwegian territorial waters were mined by the Allies, although on the first of March Norwegians and Swedes had turned down the idea of an Allied intervention.[115]

It would seem that Allied preparations for an invasion of Norway preceded the German ones, however slightly. My memory is that German plans were drawn up with all possible speed during the three weeks preceding their attack of 9 April. Lalouette asked me to prepare a letter using the German documents available at Nuremberg on the invasion of Denmark and Norway, although he did not let me suspect the importance of the request – nor did he reveal to me the existence of consultations on the subject between the Foreign Office and the Quai d'Orsay a few months before I arrived in Nuremberg.

The Foreign Office proposed that Britain and France adopt a common line and agree on the facts. The French diplomats at the *Secrétariat des Conférences*, Fouques-Duparc and Ruffin, following the Nuremberg trial, took a somewhat detached attitude, tossing the ball back to the British by quoting a speech by Churchill. According to this, the traditional concept of neutrality lost any meaning once the German aggression took place.[116]

Donnedieu's opinion of Germany's wars of aggression, of the crimes against peace, was hard to predict. We have seen that he considered conspiracy inadmissible as a charge, that he found unacceptable the very notion of crimes against humanity, and that

---
[115] *See PRO, FO 371-58540 and 57544*
[116] *Telegram from Duff Cooper (Paris) to the FO of 25 March 1946, in PRO, FO 371-57544, Doc. U-3182.*

he had doubts about the concept of war crimes. So, what was left in the end? It was the crime against peace. Was he going to discard this too, and adopt a fully negative attitude towards the Charter of the Tribunal and the trial itself?

No, not at all. This gives us the opportunity to discover what he really thought. Indeed, Donnedieu had his doubts. He did not agree with the definition put forward by Shawcross, who saw in the war of aggression the violation of a treaty condemning war: "The war of aggression can only be defined by contrast with the defensive war, which itself has no legal criterion."[117]

Besides, as I had anticipated, Donnedieu was struggling with the argumentation of Professor Jarreiss, which could not easily be brushed aside. Jarreiss, I noted, invoked the constitutional system of the Third Reich, based on the *Fuehrerprinzip*. In this way all of the Accused of Nuremberg were proved innocent, as in the whole of Germany there was but one person responsible: Adolf Hitler. Donnedieu, as we have seen, was close to sharing that opinion not only for abstract reasons, but also because it corresponded to the facts: "(Public) opinion, as well as common knowledge, implicates the responsibility of one man, Hitler, who on the stage relegates the others to the background."[118]

On the issue of the war of aggression, Jarreiss elaborated at length. Without wanting to defend or justify the use of war as 'legitimate means', he tried to prove that the Accused neither had nor could have

---

[117] *Donnedieu de Vabres, Cours de Doctorat, p. 227.*
[118] *Ibid., p. 247.*

had the mental element (*mens rea*) necessary for the existence of a crime.

In actual fact, no treaty existed forbidding war. The collective security system set up under the ægis of the League of Nations had collapsed and, if it had ever existed, its disappearance was not solely Germany's fault. The Kellogg-Briand Pact, so often invoked at Nuremberg against the Defendants, was only a declaration of principle, and was not accompanied by any sanctions.

Jarreiss made a point that Donnedieu was unable to dismiss. From the perspective of collective security, a war of aggression could be designated a "crime" only through a misuse of this term. If it were the violation of a contract, the sanction could be only a civil sanction and not a penal one. If it incurred a penal sanction, it could concern a State only and thus not individuals, who are not parties to the relations of public international law. The law in force cannot ignore the existence of the State.

In the field of positive law, Donnedieu felt ill at ease in responding to Jarreiss' arguments. After all, the German Professor's criticism over conventions forbidding war was rather similar to that formulated by Donnedieu concerning the Hague Convention in the matter of war crimes. Nevertheless, on the issue of the crime against peace, Donnedieu held a very firm stance. He lent it great importance, for in his view all other matters stemmed from there. He did not approve of the system through which Germany was accused of a series of wars of aggression. He thought that Germany should indeed be held responsible for the Second World War, which would in turn have allowed consideration of the other acts of aggression as mere episodes. Against Jarreiss,

Donnedieu resumed the arguments put by French lawyers in an age-old quarrel with German lawyers, who maintained that "the fact creates the law". In order to support the accusation of the crime against peace, Donnedieu went so far as to call upon the existence of a collective conscience that, beyond international conventions and beyond international realities, would create henceforth links between the Community of States and individuals. Such a collective conscience was a vague and almost indefinable notion. As for the Community of States, where was it to be found in 1939?

In order to justify the existence of the crime against peace, Donnedieu apparently accepted everything the French prosecutor de Menthon said in the early part of the trial: Hitler's premeditation in this series of aggressions was established, and the proof of it was *Mein Kampf*, where one could see Hitler's Grand Design "was to reconquer the territories lost in 1919, war to annihilate French power."[119] Yes, war to annihilate French power; this was for Donnedieu the essential crime. We will find it confirmed by his interventions during the judges' deliberations at the end of the trial.[120]

It is worth mentioning here that for the purpose of strengthening the validity of the crime against peace (thus crime against France),

---

[119] *Ibid., p. 224.*
[120] *Premeditation, according to Donnedieu, was also borne out by Hitler's Secret Conferences with his generals: among others, that of 5 November 1937, where he announced the conquest of Austria and Czechoslovakia; of 23 May 1939 where he announced the attacked against Poland, and that of 23 November 1939, where he announced further acts of aggression. By acknowledging the importance of Hitler's Secret Conferences in order to prove Germany's warlike intentions, Donnedieu was close to contradicting himself. Earlier, he denied them any significance in the alleged crime of "conspiracy".*

Donnedieu without hesitation throws overboard the principle of legality, which he had himself invoked to discredit the charges of conspiracy or of crime against humanity.[121] Suddenly, he takes a dynamic view of the evolution of the law, saying, "[t]he principle of the legality of offences and penalties must not be separated from the historical context in which it was born."[122] He went so far as to say that the principle did not apply to international public law, "the ceaseless evolution of which is subjected to the evolution of an often unpredictable groundswell, perturbing the Society of States."[123]

---

[121] *Donnedieu de Vabres, Cours de Doctorat, p. 232.*
[122] *Ibid., p. 233.*
[123] *Ibid., p. 233*

CHAPTER 19

The Judges' Deliberations

Donnedieu expressed himself with surprising frankness in front of his students,[124] given that memories of the Occupation and the horrors of the Nazi regime were still fresh in the minds of all French people. Any attempt to delimit German responsibilities could hurt French feelings and appear insulting to the memory of all of those who had fallen victim to the *Wehrmacht* or the Gestapo, or who died in concentration camps. Moreover, Donnedieu had, to my mind, failed to reveal to his audiences what he really thought. He expressed himself more frankly in the course of the judges' deliberation as he discounted the American attitude towards official secrets and the Americans' belief that everything can and must be published. The papers of US Judge Biddle have been opened to research, and historian Bradley F. Smith has been in a position to reveal both how the Judgement was elaborated and which position each of the Judges adopted.[125]

It is interesting to note the serious differences between, on the one hand, what Donnedieu

---

[124] *In a series of lectures at the Académie de Droit International he had been very careful not to criticise the trial, being content with analysing and justifying the Judgement.*
[125] *Bradley F. Smith, Reaching Judgement at Nuremberg, London, 1977. The papers of Francis Biddle are kept at Syracuse University, Syracuse, New York.*

proclaimed from his Chair at the Paris Faculty of Law and, on the other, what he confided to his colleagues in the intimacy of their conversations behind closed doors. For example, during his lectures he identified himself with the remarks of the French Prosecutor de Menthon on Hitler's aggressive intentions towards France, as well as the premeditation as demonstrated by *Mein Kampf* and the famous Secret Conferences. At Nuremberg, Donnedieu had taken a much more uninterested attitude, saying that he did not take seriously the idea that the Prosecution should go and look in *Mein Kampf* or in the Party programme for proof of a criminal plan. There had been no definite Nazi plan, Donnedieu had said, adding that the seizure of power in Germany and the expansion in Europe were the result of a series of improvisations.[126]

In spite of his old-fashioned appearance, Donnedieu preceded by several decades the views advanced by "revisionist" historians such as AJP Taylor in Britain in his work on the *Origins of the Second World War*. As did Taylor, Donnedieu expressed doubts on the level of importance of the Secret Conferences. Hitler announced to his generals his intention of using force, which may or may not constitute a dialogue among conspirators. The existence of a conspiracy required a certain level of equality among participants. But those Conferences were monologues, in which Hitler simply informed those present of his intentions of absorbing Austria *et al.*[127] After all, said Donnedieu, Nazi Germany was a *Fuehrerstaat*, in which only the Fuehrer held power, and held actually all of the powers. Here, we can recognise the hypothesis of Professor Jarreiss.

[126] *Ibid., p. 122.*
[127] *Ibid., pp. 123-4.*

Criticisms formulated by Donnedieu in his lectures addressed the general conception of the trial rather than the Judgement itself. This position could seem paradoxical. The fact was that Donnedieu could defend the Judgement in all good conscience, as in the course of the deliberations he had won over his colleagues on all of the points he considered essential. Under his impetus the "conspiracy" was limited in its application to the case of wars of aggression, and the "crime against humanity" rendered irrelevant. In the question of the "criminal organisations" he succeeded in winning the American Judge, Biddle, over to his side. Biddle was originally responsible for the trial of the organisations. In the end, though, he was impressed by Donnedieu's objections – all the more so as in a public discussion with the member of the Prosecution Biddle had not been convinced by Jackson, the US Prosecutor. Jackson, when cornered, said, "It is the advantage of the jury system. Juries do not have to be logical and the prosecution does not need to be logical either." Biddle had not been impressed by Maxwell Fyfe, the British Prosecutor, who, on the contrary, adopted a position of extreme rigour in legal logic and accepted the cumulative character of the effects of the "conspiracy" and of the membership of a "criminal organisation". In answer to a question from Biddle, Maxwell Fyfe admitted that a German who had become a member of the SA in 1921 then left it in 1922 would be just as guilty of belonging to a conspiracy aiming at a war of aggression.[128]

---

[128] *Maxwell Fyfe's position was perhaps not as absurd as it seemed. The activities of the Nazi party in Bavaria in the 1920s and in 1922-3 in particular, in connection with some elements of the Reichswehr, were aimed at preparing a resumption of hostilities with France. (On this, see my book* Le Putsch de Hitler à Munich en 1923.)

Biddle was ready to give up completely this aspect – of declaring "criminal" the Nazi organisations – of the procedure. However, Donnedieu was not disposed to play the Professor to the bitter end, again showing his ambiguity. In some cases he took his inspiration from practical considerations. For example, he refused to exonerate among the criminal organisations the SS or the Gestapo because, as he said, there was no village in France where the distinction between the SS and the regular army was not known. He gained only very limited satisfaction as regards individual sentences. He had to compromise, and obtained only rarely a mitigation of the punishments.

Donnedieu was opposed to the charge of crimes against humanity, thus he pleaded in favour of Frank, Frick and Rosenberg, who counted among the less likeable among the Defendants. Frank had been Governor of Poland, where German Occupation had displayed the most despicable cruelty with, for instance, the concentration camps and the extermination of Jews. Alone among his colleagues, Donnedieu wanted to spare Frank the death penalty.[129] Frick was an old Nazi, Hitler's accomplice at the time of the Munich Putsch of 1923. At least at the administrative level he had been the head of the whole apparatus of repression, including the police, Gestapo, SS, and concentration camps. Was Frick a mere bureaucrat? Donnedieu expressed his reserves about the death sentence, which his colleagues had no hesitation in passing on Frick.[130] Rosenberg had

---

[129] *Bradley F. Smith, Reaching Judgement at Nuremberg, p. 196. How to explain this? Frank had been a lawyer; he had invited Donnedieu to Berlin before the war. Was it a case of professional solidarity?*
[130] *Ibid., p. 199. In this case the reason was perhaps that Donnedieu deplored the fact that Frick had refused to testify in his own defence. As a consequence, it had been impossible to gain an impression of his character. It could be that,*

been to some extent responsible for the Occupation policies pursued in the East. Donnedieu would not have hanged him.[131] It is perhaps worth noting that those three cases were about crimes committed in the East, thus did not concern France directly.

On the issue of "classic" war crimes, Donnedieu was also in favour of a mitigation of the penalties. He wanted Grand Admiral Doenitz to receive a lighter pently because he wondered whether submarine warfare lay within or outside international law.[132] Similarly, Donnedieu proposed to condemn Grand Admiral Raeder merely to twenty years' imprisonment, but failed. Raeder received life imprisonment.[133] In the cases of Raeder and Doenitz, as in that of Jodl, Donnedieu would have preferred to hand down an "honourable" punishment because both belonged to the armed forces. His colleagues neither understood nor were persuaded. What did Donnedieu have in mind? Detention in a fortress with the privileges granted to political prisoners? If the death penalty, the firing squad instead of the gallows?[134]

It is revealing that Donnedieu had no hesitation in condemning Sauckel to death whereas he was in favour of saving the lives of Frick, Frank, and Rosenberg. Sauckel organised the deportation to

---

seeing among the members of the US Prosecution team one of his former civil servants. Robert Kempner (who had been forced to emigrate and was now instructing in the case against him), Frick may have thought that under those conditions there was little chance of pulling the wool over the eyes of the Tribunal. (See also Robert M.W. Kempner, Anklaeger einer Epoche, p. 248.)
[131] *Ibid., p. 194.*
[132] *Ibid., p. 260*
[133] *Ibid., p. 247.*
[134] *The Inter-Allied Control Council in Berlin rejected all requests from those condemned to death to die by shooting instead of hanging.*

Germany of French workers through the STO. It was a war crime that affected France, even if Sauckel was not considered ultimately responsible. Moreover, the deportation had taken place only thanks to the collaboration of the French, who launched the *gendarmes* on the heels of the *réfractaires*.[135]

Equally, those accused of participating in the crimes against peace, essentially Hess and von Ribbentrop, found no favour with Donnedieu, for this was a crime affecting France directly. He wanted, though, to condemn Hess only to twenty years' imprisonment, too short for the other judges, who were guided by other criteria. Accordingly, Hess, the madman, was sentenced to life imprisonment. Von Ribbentrop, held responsible for World War II, received no mercy: Donnedieu voted for the death penalty.

In those cases where Donnedieu leaned towards severity, the aspect of whether the Accused had participated in the crimes against peace was important. Non-involvement in a war of aggression was, in contrast, an argument favouring the Accused. Funk, Schacht's successor as President of the *Reichsbank* was charged with harbouring precious objects and gold taken by the SS from the Jews in concentration camps. The Judges hesitated about sentencing him to death. Donnedieu, too, hesitated, but in the end opted for life imprisonment, because Funk "had never participated in a war of aggression."[136]

---

[135] *It must be said that, in my own and many other cases, the good gendarmes pursued their investigations for form's sake and were not at all anxious to arrest the réfractaires.*
[136] Bradley F. Smith, p. 206.

His attitude towards Schacht was particularly interesting. Donnedieu's initial reaction was to find him guilty. Schacht was responsible for re-armament, and re-armament meant preparation for a war that turned out to be disastrous for France. The British judges, however, succeeded in making Donnedieu understand that there was no causal link between re-armament and war. Re-armament was justified as it gave greater weight to Germany on the international scene.

The von Papen case preoccupied Donnedieu for reasons that had nothing to do with legal technique yet everything to do with French interests, however indirectly. From the moment the Tribunal decided to abandon the theory of "conspiracy", it was very difficult to condemn von Papen; he had played no part in either the wars of aggression, the war crimes or the crimes against humanity. American and British judges recognised early on in the proceedings that von Papen's acquittal was inevitable. They were perhaps influenced by Falco, their French opposite number, who wanted to inflict ten years on von Papen. The reasoning was that von Papen played a part in the *Anschluss*, considered by Falco to be an act of aggression and could thus be assimilated under a war of aggression. Donnedieu wanted von Papen to be sentenced, describing him as an immoral creature and a corrupter, who throughout his career had displayed his deceitfulness. This was notably so in the US, where von Papen was linked with spying during the 1914 war, and also in Vienna where, as Ambassador, he worked towards the *Anschluss*. Donnedieu asked, "Why are we here if not to introduce morals into international law?"[137] Donnedieu was in fact inspired by practical

---

[137] *Ibid., p. 289.*

considerations: if von Papen were acquitted, could Schacht, whom the judges at first agreed to find guilty, be condemned? To find von Papen guilty would have made it possible to find Schacht, whose fate was of prime significance to the French at Nuremberg, also guilty.

Fritzsche, the man from the Ministry for Propaganda, was one of the Accused because Goebbels had committed suicide. Donnedieu hesitated, changing his mind several times, about Fritzsche's guilt. Was propaganda reprehensible? Yes, said Falco, if it was at the service of a criminal regime. At first Donnedieu supported a severe sentence. Fritzsche was acquitted, although for reasons of the internal equilibrium of the Judgement. From the moment von Papen was acquitted, there was no question of inflicting a more severe sentence on Fritzsche, a rather colourless character and unknown to the Allies.[138] By agreeing to these more lenient punishments, Donnedieu joined the American judges who had, from the start, advocated acquittal in the name of the freedom of expression.[139]

As for the other Accused, Donnedieu seems not to have intervened, possibly because of his national or personal prejudices. Certain cases had never been in doubt: Goering, for one;[140] Kaltenbrunner, the man from the Gestapo and the concentration camps, or Seyss-Inquart, responsible for the Occupation

---

[138] *Ibid., p. 296*

[139] *The Soviet judge had tried in vain to persuade the Americans that they misunderstood the principle of the freedom of expression. (Ibid., p. 296.)*

[140] *Here, as elsewhere, Donnedieu expressed reservations about Goering's participation in the conspiracy and, as in the case of Jodl, would have preferred to have Goering shot rather than hanged because of his rank of Marshal. (Ibid., pp. 176-7.)*

policy in Holland.¹⁴¹ In these cases, the death sentence was inevitable from the start of the trial, as it was for Keitel, second only to Goering in the military service hierarchy, and for Streicher, the anti-Semite. There was little discussion about the principle of the sentencing of von Neurath, not only because of his position as Minister for Foreign Affairs before von Ribbentrop but also because he was Protector of Bohemia and Moravia during the war. He was probably lucky to get away with a fairly light prison sentence, partly thanks to the intervention of Donnedieu.¹⁴²

Two points on which Donnedieu failed to persuade his colleagues have been mentioned. Firstly, why did he see an "honourable punishment" for military defendants as being important? Secondly, he wanted to insert into the Judgement a section about the methods of the Resistance, methods that would have justified the barbarous repression by the *Wehrmacht*.¹⁴³ As Smith wrote, a certain courage was needed to formulate in 1946 this opinion of the Resistance, when they and the Occupation were so fresh in the minds of all, given the political atmosphere in France at the time. Donnedieu was to breathe no word of his views on the "methods of the Resistance" to his students at the Law Faculty in Paris.

---

¹⁴¹ *Donnedieu came down in favour of life imprisonment instead of the death sentence.*
¹⁴² *A legal discussion may have turned to von Neurath's advantage: had Czechoslovakia become German territory following the Treaty, signed by Hacha, or had it become Occupied territory, where the laws of war applied with their attendant restrictions? More likely, the element deciding in his favour was the fact that he had never been a convinced Nazi. (Ibid., p. 228.)*
¹⁴³ *Ibid., p. 146.*

CHAPTER 20

The Judgement of History

Donnedieu's writings were not used by the opponents of the trial for an all-out attack on Nuremberg. Former Nazis and neo-Nazis could hardly have failed to notice that Donnedieu was neither pro-Nazi nor pro-German. As a French judge, he could, in the name of positive law, condemn the principle of the trial yet refrain from formulating fundamental criticisms of the Judgement itself. He could pass for "moderate" when it came to sentencing individuals. In an extreme case, Biddle reproached him with being too soft.[144] Was Donnedieu a man guided by his feelings?

The key to his attitude seems to be sought elsewhere. He had a certain view of history, that of Germany as well as of France. He confided one day to his colleagues what he really thought; Smith, reporting his remarks, found them so fantastic that he could not believe his ears. Essentially, Donnedieu considered that the real guilty party was Germany and that Hitler was to a lesser degree the man truly responsible; much lower down the scale of responsibility came the Accused at Nuremberg. Such, when all was said and done, was the reason for not punishing the Nazi leaders too harshly, except when

---

[144] *Ibid., p. 266.*

the direct consequences of their actions were blindingly obvious.

That Hitler possessed supreme power and authority was confirmed by the witnesses in the courtroom. The notion that, beyond Hitler, Germany was the real culprit was a view commonly held by the French at the time. Historians and Germanists from the Sorbonne demonstrated that the whole course of German history led to Hitler. The book by Vermeil, *L'Allemagne, Essai d'Explication*, was authoritative. This was the same Vermeil whom Lalouette had attempted, in the foyer of the Grand Hotel, to convert to a less determinist and more optimistic view of the future.[145]

According to Vermeil, one had only to follow the various stages of German history: Lutheran reformation, followed by the ascent of Prussia; romantic nationalism; Bismarck and his empire; the industrial revolution, followed by the intellectual and moral crisis that included Nietzsche and pan-Germanism and, finally, Hitler's *Reich*, sandwiched between the Weimar Republic and the Second World War. It was coherent. All elements were linked. Vermeil portrayed Germany over a period of four centuries, going back to before Luther:

The dream of the coming Reich and the whole culture were moving towards the 'Volkstum' and later on towards the Race ... Prussia became with Bismarck the real Germany ... The alliance between Prussia and pan-Germanism was the 'true' German Revolution. Its elements took shape in the course of the four centuries opening in front of us. On the one hand, Luther,

---

[145] I am referring to the fourteenth "edition" dated Autumn 1944. The first edition was from September 1939. It shows that Vermeil's views really were contemporary.

Leibnitz, classicism, romanticism, and the racialist pan-Germanism. On the other, the territorial policy, the conquests of Frederic II, the wars of independence, Bismarck, William II and Weimar. After this long historical preparation, the Third Reich will be a mixture of racial mysticism and dictatorial discipline, a terrible and overwhelming mobilisation of minds and bodies.[146]

Nothing is omitted from Vermeil's fine analyses. Religious life, theology, philosophy, music, Bach, Mozart, Beethoven, political and social life, family life – everything is mentioned and labelled. The whole contributes to a psychological portrait of the German people. Vermeil was a Germanist in the tradition inaugurated by Charles Andler, who recommended the study of Germany from every angle. By this he meant from the perspective not only of literature, but also the others mentioned. Vermeil's first book was published pre-1914 and had as its subject *Romantic Theology in Wuerttemberg and Germanic Origins of Modernism*.

Historians belonging to the next generation, such as Jacques Droz, may have adopted a more modern viewpoint, emphasising the importance of social history and deploring the absence in Germany of an influential *bourgeoisie* over the course of the centuries. They reached identical conclusions, tracing the same phases in Germany's history. Jacques Droz, too, went back as far as Luther, absorbing on the way Weimar, Bismarck and the Kings of Prussia. It all hung together:

Is there not in fact a better explanation of the whole German history than the attitude of the monk Luther

---

[146] Vermeil, *L'Allemagne, Essai d'Explication*, pp. 70-1.

who, having proclaimed the complete freedom of the Christian to enter into a relationship with God, later enslaves the German population under an authoritarian yoke within the confines of the territorial States? Who understands this apparently strange antinomy succeeds in unravelling the secret of the German community.[147]

Starting from the Lutheran position, one eventually reaches "this disjunction of culture and politics which is the key to the whole history of modern Germany".[148] Concerning more particularly politics, the contribution of Frederic the Great was as follows: "He relies entirely on his army and his bureaucracy to ensure the power and the material prosperity of his people."[149] Hitler acted no differently, in that "[t]he alliance of Prussian militarism and big industry, under the control of the National-Socialists, has placed Europe under its supervision and imposed a new status."[150]

Small wonder, then, that beyond the Accused of Nuremberg and even beyond Hitler, Donnedieu was aware that the true responsibilities lay with Germany – and not merely the Germany of today, but a German tradition going back at least four centuries. In the judgement of History, were there such a thing, Germany would be convicted.

As a Professor of Law in Paris, Donnedieu could be excused for reasoning in historical terms. Before the war, in France, legal studies aimed not towards training practitioners, but towards

---

[147] Jacques Droz, *Histoire de l'Allemagne*, Paris, 1948. Collection Que Sais-Je?, p. 7.
[148] *Ibid.*, p. 12.
[149] *Ibid.*, p. 1.
[150] *Ibid.*, p. 131.

demonstrating how every law, every rule, and every institution was the outcome and product of History. However, as early as in 1948, a respected non-Nazi German historian, Gerhard Ritter, published a book in which he undertook to refute in detail the type of hypothesis proposed by Vermeil and Droz.[151] To Ritter, Hitler and Nazism had not been unavoidable; History was not a one-way street. It comprised a multitude of paths running along and among each other. Far from being a series of necessary links, History was the field in which men could act freely. Germany's destiny was sufficiently varied and rich in sudden innovations and developments that there was more than only one route to follow. The route leading into the abyss was not the sole possible conclusion.[152]

Ritter disputed the assertion that Luther was the source of all calamities for Germany, pushing the Germans into obeying their princes blindly and reducing the sphere of influence of morals and religion into the field of private morality while political leaders retained the right to exercise their powers without controls. Luther encouraged soldiers to refuse obedience to their masters if the latter espoused a cause that was not "just."[153] Besides, one has only to look abroad to see what happened with other religions. Absolutism found its greatest triumphs not in Germany but at the very Catholic courts of Madrid, Vienna and Paris.[154]

Droz wrote that, for Luther, "to obey was to conform to divine authority."[155] Ritter, on the other

---

[151] Gerhard Ritter, *Europa und die deutsche Frage*, Munich, 1948.
[152] *Ibid.*, p. 200.
[153] *Ibid.*, p. 14.
[154] *Ibid.*, pp. 15-16.
[155] Droz, p. 9.

hand, rejects the suggestion of servility, for German history offers enough examples of independence of mind and strength of character. Admittedly, on one point French and German histories have differed: Germany did not experience the frequent revolutions France did. But is the label of 'servility' necessary? There is nothing unhealthy, explained Ritter, in loyalty, which manifests itself in the multiple States that are part of Germany. Such loyalty meant that the average citizen believed that his or her government wished him or her well, and that they felt protected by an equitable judicial system.[156]

Finally, Ritter proposed a rather down-to-earth explanation for more recent times. Germany became Nazi because of its loss of affection for political parties and its government. The Germans underestimated the merits and the achievements of the Weimar Republic, which had now gained entry into the League of Nations, and the end of reparations, thus was on the verge of obtaining the right to re-arm. However, the Germans were impatient to recover their freedom and their dignity, stripped of both by the Treaty of Versailles. They formed "national fronts" against their own government.[157]

Ritter mentioned in his biographical note that he had been arrested towards the end of the war as a member of the Goerdeler circle; he was due to appear before the sinister People's Tribunal, which judged the conspirators of 20 July 1944. He seemed to be an intellectual who had dedicated his life to History rather than a man of action. I appreciated his judgement on Nazism, which he described in an

---

[156] *Ritter, pp. 194-5.*
[157] *Ritter, pp. 196-7.*

expression difficult to translate with its nuances: "National Socialism seen from here appears as 'a romantic cramp', not as the expression of a calm and firm will."[158] Was Nazism, rather, a spasm? Ritter nevertheless encapsulated what he wanted to convey. Nazism lived in a condition of instability, of excitement; "romantic" because it appealed to the emotions rather than to reason, and it submerged itself in bluster and conceit – gesticulating and posturing, unafraid of appearing ridiculous.

I never knew Nazism in Germany either before or during the war, although I was familiar with disturbing agitation in France of the milieu of the extreme Right; here, enthusiasm was the prime virtue, allied to the desire to embark blindly on an adventure with a vague plan of fighting against the *communards*.

It is doubtful whether the judgement of History will be satisfied with Ritter's explanations: impatience, and the wish to recover the dignity and freedom lost through the Treaty of Versailles. The judgement of history will be written by historians, each with his or her own nationality and national prejudices – just as the Nuremberg Judges. I can hardly see French historians accepting that through the Treaty of Versailles the Germans had lost their freedom and dignity; at that time, at least for the French, freedom and dignity entailed individual freedom and individual dignity, unassailable even while making tanks or war plans. For the Germans, at question was their national freedom and national dignity, an

---

[158] *Ibid., p. 198.*

issue of foreign policy, as it were.[159] Words did not carry the same weight of meaning for the French and the Germans respectively at that time.

Historians will probably perceive the conflict of influences in Europe. While reading the German diplomatic archives, I was particularly struck by the sudden and complete change of attitude of the smaller states in eastern and south-eastern Europe as soon as Hitler came to power. Did they act out of prudence or of fear, or simply to safeguard their interests? At a single stroke, without the German army's having to cross any border, Germany's influence, political and economic, was restored; the system of alliances entered into in the wake of the Treaty of Versailles crumbled or became no more real than a theatre set.

Actually, Donnedieu and the French Prosecutor de Menthon acknowledged that the main accusation levelled at Germany was that it eliminated French influence; also, that it did so up to and during the war. In this respect, the lawyers agreed, sharing the same conception of History. The grounds for the Judgement of Nuremberg differ according to whether the French interpretations of Vermeil and Droz of German history, or Hitler's interpretation, are favoured.

Following the train of thought of the French hypothesis, Germany and the Germans are all

---

[159] *Strangely, at Nuremberg questions of foreign policy received only very superficial treatment. Von Neurath was condemned rather for his part as Protector of Bohemia. Von Ribbentrop was found responsible for the wars of aggression. There was no discussion of these and consequently no discussion in depth of German foreign policy or of the origins of World War II. This was not due solely to the fear of reminding all present of the Nazi-Soviet pact of 1939.*

condemned; the individual responsibilities of the Accused appear diminished, as these are merely an ephemeral expression of permanent tendencies. On the other hand, Ritter's theory wishes to pardon Germany and the Germans of past generations. He refuses to consider Hitler as a necessary outcome of German history, which leads to a hardly flattering moral judgement on the Germans who were Hitler's contemporaries:

The general decline of the cultural tradition in Europe and in the West does not excuse the fact that millions of Germans turned to Hitler before 1933, without being shocked either by the absence of intellectual and moral merit of his companions, which should have been noticed, nor by the spirit of savage hate, untruthfulness and violence of the worst kind.[160]

Hence, to Ritter, Hitler's ascent was not "irresistible".

---

[160] *Ritter, p. 200.*

CONCLUSION

In the presence of a hideous crime, public opinion demands an exemplary punishment. An investigation by a judge in France, at least, requires due process; by the time the case is heard, public opinion has somehow calmed down. It is even liable to turn in favour of the accused, who sits alone in front of the judges and may give the impression of being a victim.

The Nuremberg Trial was rushed, as if an emergency. It suffered no lengthy delay as the investigations took place during the hearing. It was a trial in a Germany still in ruins, still as defeat had found it; a trial organised by the victors; a political trial before a military tribunal; a trial where the Accused were already condemned by world public opinion, and where the Prosecutors, be they French, American, British or Russian, were expressing global popular outrage.

My first surprise when I arrived in Nuremberg was to discover that the political adviser did not consider it his task to do all he could to have all of the Accused condemned. He represented, I believe, the attitude of the diplomats at the Quai d'Orsay, who found it flattering that France should be present at a great international event; however, their long-term objectives were located far beyond the walls of the Palace of Justice. Aristocrats by birth or by adoption, French diplomats had become immune, through a long tradition and constant practice, to the impulses of popular sentimentality. They had in mind the place of France in History and in the future. To them, the real difficulty lay in the relations between France and Germany. It was of course necessary to judge and punish the most abhorrent among the Nazis because this was unavoidable. Nevertheless, Franco-German relations had to resume from the point where the war and Nazism had broken them, and in such a way that the two countries could henceforth live in harmony. The war would, as it were, be parenthesised, the Vichy files buried in the archives and forgotten.

A distinguished British diplomat, Lord Strang, had at that time a different approach to the German problem. He had been appointed political adviser to the British Commander-in-Chief. In the summer of 1945, while touring the British zone, he enjoyed a long conversation with the mayor of Hamburg, Dr. Petersen ("a 'good German' if there were any such"):

The mayor was complaining of economic difficulties, saying that the Germans might in despair turn to Communism; I interrupted this exercise in self-pity and covert blackmail to say: the primary purpose of the [Allies' current] occupation was to disarm and demilitarise Germany and to uproot the Nazi party, not to promote Anglo-German friendship or to bring about the economic revival of Germany.[161]

To the diplomats, the serious business was transacted at the Conference of Foreign Ministers in Paris in early July 1946, at the very moment when I was making my way to Nuremberg. At the Paris

---

[161] Lord Strang, *Home and Abroad*, pp. 234-5.

Conference, Bevin requested Molotov to transfer to the British occupied zone in Germany some of the agricultural surplus produced in the Soviet zone. The British taxpayer, he said, could not continue paying the whole food bill for the Germans in 'their' zone. Molotov flatly refused. Bevin then declared he would therefore stimulate the economic activity of the British zone. Immediately, the American representative added that he would propose that the American-occupied zone would join the British zone and pursue the same policy. The idea of the 'bi-zone' was launched, and the partition of Germany already consummated.

The French would have preferred not to break with the Soviets, all the more so as Molotov, pandering to their wishes, advised them to do as the Russians themselves were doing in their zone and capitalise upon their occupation: "Of course! Why don't you take the coal from the Ruhr?" he said to the French, disposing generously of something that did not belong to him.

I discovered only after the Trial that Donnedieu de Vabres was opposed on principle to the Tribunal of Nuremberg. His opposition was the counterpart of the diplomats' opposition; in his case, it was the opposition of the bourgeoisie to the legists. Admittedly, in the writings of Donnedieu de Vabres is found an occasional remark placing morals above formal law, or accepting that international public opinion could make the laws of war more progressive. Still, I do not think I am mistaken in saying that he would have liked to insert the trial into the context of a legal tradition, thus to integrate it into an existing system.[162] Donnedieu de Vabres wanted to see in the State, or the States, the sole source of law. He adhered to the so-called "volontarist" system which is the rule in France, as it is in all countries with a developed judiciary system.

In contrast, the French Justice Minister at that time, Pierre-Henri Teitgen, felt that he could write how the Nuremberg Judgement established "fully" the abandonment of the "volontarist" system

---

[162] *After the First World War, the US Representatives at the Commission on Responsibilities adopted a similar line:*
[T]he American members declared that there were two classes of responsibilities, those of a legal nature and those of a moral nature, that legal offences were justiciable and liable to trial and punishment by appropriate tribunals, but that moral offences, however iniquitous and infamous and however terrible in their results, were beyond the reach of judicial procedure, and subject only to moral sanctions.
While this principle seems to have been adopted by the Commission in the report so far as the responsibility for the authorship of the war is concerned, the Commission appeared unwilling to apply it in the case of indirect responsibility for violations of the laws and customs of war committed after the outbreak of the war and during its course.
'Memorandum of Reservations presented by the Representatives of the United States to the Report of the Commission on Responsibilities, April 4, 1919' in Violation of the Laws and Customs of War, Carnegie Foundation, Division of International Law, Pamphlet No. 32, Oxford, 1919, pp. 58-9.
Actually, the Americans were opposed to the creation of an international tribunal to judge the Kaiser. They were opposed to the doctrine of "indirect responsibility", which held the Kaiser responsible even if he had not directly ordered the violations. Donnedieu de Vabres considered that the most awful Nazi crimes should receive a traditional label instead of being presented as new categories of crimes.

concerning the source of international law.[163] How was this possible? Both were Professors of Law, yet Teitgen, a Christian-Democrat, was a critic of the *bourgeoisie* and of the *bourgeois* concepts Donnedieu de Vabres was defending.

For my part, I could not forget the war years, still so very recent. I lacked, as did the diplomats, the ability to bounce back so quickly; I possessed neither the lawyers' lucidity nor their realism. I was unable to achieve their *sangfroid*. It seemed to me shocking to envisage a policy of close friendship with Germany at the very moment everything Germany had done since 1933 – and even before, from the time of the Nazi party – received worldwide condemnation. I remained curious about Germany and the Germans, yet could not place myself at a level of politics on a grand scale. The absurdity of these I could, since the outbreak of war, only measure better than ever.

I had my doubts about the legal foundations of the Trial after listening to Professor Jahrreiss' speech, while still not quite identifying myself with the position of Donnedieu de Vabres – then unknown

---

[163] P.-H. Teitgen, 'Le Jugement de Nuremberg' in *Revue de Droit International, de Sciences Diplomatiques, Politiques et Sociales*, Octobre-Decembre 1946, p.161. Another Law Professor, Paul Reuter, who paid several visits to the French delegation at Nuremberg, wrote in 1946 in the same vein: "The tribunal has ruled out unquestionably the theory which makes the will of the State the only foundation of the law."

As proof, he quoted this passage from the Judgement: "The condemnation of the war of aggression demanded by the conscience of the world, finds its expression in the series of pacts and treaties which have just been revoked." Paul Reuter's article 'Nuremberg 1946: Le Procès' was published in La Vie Intellectuelle, December 1946, pp. 56-77.

To say that the conscience of the world expresses itself through pacts and treaties is to apply a formula that makes possible a reconciliation of opposing viewpoints and which was probably penned by the clever British Judge, Birkett. The volontarists, for their part, will note that the "conscience of the world" is found nowhere but in pacts and treaties.

to the general public. In the end, traumatised by my war experiences, I shared the perhaps rather simplistic feelings of the people and felt myself closer to Dubost's position. I considered, nevertheless, that it was not enough to agree with Dubost that the Accused were at one and the same time "co-authors" and "accomplices". I saw them simply as "co-authors". The reason is that when I thought of the slave labour policy, a matter that concerned me more particularly, it seemed to me that Sauckel was not the only one responsible. The forced recruiting of workers was also attributable to Speer, for it was he who formulated the requests for foreign labour. Furthermore, Kaltenbrunner had some responsibilities when the Gestapo arrested the *réfractaires*. Keitel and Jodl similarly bore their share of responsibility when the *Wehrmacht* guarded those *réfractaires* who had been arrested, and would shoot them if they were discovered in a Resistance group. Von Ribbentrop played a part inasmuch as the *Auswaertiges Amt* supported Sauckel's "negotiations" in Vichy to obtain the deportation of French workers. Seyss-Inquart was involved with the workers' deportation in the context of Occupied Holland. Frick should be charged among those responsible for this business, as he was in general terms responsible for the machinery of repression and the concentration camps.

There was thus a complementary nature of responsibilities from the Fuehrer down to the last underling. But did the middle and lower grades of the hierarchy feel responsible? At Nuremberg, Sauckel could not understand what was happening to him when he was condemned to death. He believed there had been a misunderstanding, for he was conscious of having done his best to ensure that the French workers in Germany were well treated. Seyss-Inquart had to explain to him that the mere fact of sending the civilian population to work in Germany constituted a war crime.

My own feeling was that in order to give a fair account of the way the Germans had conducted the war, the notion of "collective responsibility" should have been proposed from the outset. The concept seemed to the Allies unacceptable for practical reasons, first and foremost. The Nazis used the method of "collective" punishment against innocent victims such as Jews and French hostages. This was, though, a misapplication of the concept of "collective". Collective responsibility is normal in civil or commercial law. At the Trial, Speer caused a sensation in his acknowledging the collective responsibility of the Nazi leaders. This did not make him popular among the other Accused, but it contributed towards improving his image in the eyes of the Judges.

The Tribunal could not accept the principle of collective responsibility while simultaneously condemning the use the Nazis had made of it. The principle was inherent in certain aspects of the trial, such as the condemnation of criminal organisations, and even in the choice of the Defendants – they were there as representatives of social groups, including party leaders, generals, diplomats, administrators, financiers, and police officers. The Judgement distributed an impossible justice, attempting to vary the punishment according to the proven action of each Defendant, and thus preserved the principle of individual responsibility.

EPILOGUE

I left Nuremberg soon after the end of the public sessions. At the Quai d'Orsay I saw again the man with the sad face, who throughout the trial had followed Lalouette's correspondence. He asked me, "What will be the judgement?" I answered that there would probably be eleven death sentences. He looked dismayed. "French public opinion will be disappointed," he commented. He was already envisaging all of the possible repercussions.

This forecast had actually been made by Lalouette. It was confirmed by the event. Precisely eleven, approximately half of the Accused, were sentenced to death. Out of these eleven, eight sat in the front row.[164] Their group consisted of the tough nuts of Nazism and included all those who had participated in the Munich *Putsch* of 1923, with the exception of Hess. The death sentences were

---

[164] *They were Goering, von Ribbentrop, Keitel, Kaltenbrunner, Rosenberg, Frank, Frick and Streicher. The three in the second row who were also condemned to death were Sauckel, Jodl and Seyss-Inquart. Bormann was condemned in his absence; he was the twenty-second defendant.*

expected. The only surprise was Doenitz, whose neck was saved although he had from the beginning of the trial been regarded as a loser.

Jodl's conviction was regretted, it seems, by some of the Allied Generals, who saw in him a colleague and knew the dilemma they had to face in their profession. His condemnation rested on the *Kommando Befehl*, which was the order to execute members of the Commando. Jodl denied having agreed with this order; nevertheless, he had been required to transmit it to the army. The Tribunal considered that he could not be exempted from blame.[165]

The Accused accepted their fate – except von Ribbentrop, who did not resign himself easily. However, his system of defence was disastrous. During the trial he had continued to identify himself with Hitler. He lacked the cunning of Speer who, without denying the existence of his close relationship with Hitler, succeeded in distancing himself from the monster and acknowledged that he had been led astray. Speer charmed his judges by telling how he had tried to murder Hitler and his entourage by introducing a deadly gas through the air inlet of the Bunker in the Chancellory where Hitler took refuge during the final weeks of the war.

---

[165] *Actually, as we have seen earlier, the text of the Order was aimed also at the Resistance and in particular at the British, who were helping the Resistance. Jodl, on the witness stand, did not hide the fact that he thought that Resistants ("rebels") should suffer the same fate as francs-tireurs. On 19 July 1946 General von Falkenhorst, who commanded in Norway during the Occupation, was condemned to death by a British Military Tribunal at Brunswick, for having implemented the Kommando Befehl. His sentence was commuted to 20 years' imprisonment.*

Goering sprang a last-minute surprise on the Allies by committing suicide a few hours before his hanging was to take place. He used a capsule of [potassium] cyanide he had managed to keep with him despite regular searches by his gaolers. His death received widespread publicity in Germany and throughout the world. Through this last act of defiance he somehow overshadowed the executions of his companions. The Allies, the Control Commission for Germany, did not reveal the result of their enquiry into how it happened. However, I was recently able to read the report of the Commission of Enquiry. Before dying Goering wrote a letter in English to his gaoler, Colonel Andrus:

Nuremberg, 11 October 1946

To the Commandant,

I have always had the capsule of poison with me from the time that I became a prisoner. When taken to Mondorf I had three capsules. The first I left in my clothes so that it would be found when a search was made. The second I placed under the clothesrack on undressing and took it [with me] on dressing. I hid this in Mondorf and here in the cell so well that despite the frequent and thorough searches it could not be found. During the court sessions I had it on my person in my high riding boots. The third capsule is still in my small suitcase in the round box of skin cream, hidden in the cream.[166] *I could have taken this twice in Mondorf if I had needed it. None of those charged with searching*

---

[166] *The "small suitcase" was a vanity case containing what he needed for skin care and doing his nails. It seems clear that he must have used the second capsule that he kept on his person. The Board of Enquiry discussed at length the question of which orifice of his body he might have used. On the other hand, he could have hidden it in the toilet.*

is to be blamed for it was practically impossible to find the capsule. It would have been pure accident.

Hermann Goering

Dr. Gilbert informed me that the Control Board had "refused to change the method of execution to shooting."[167]

A short while before Goering committed suicide, the Lutheran chaplain, Pastor Gerecke, had refused to give him Communion, even though Goering considered himself still to be a Christian, as he had not formally left the Church. But Pastor Gerecke justified his decision by saying that Goering did not accept the teachings of Jesus Christ; he was a rationalist, a materialist and a modernist.[168]

Colonel Andrus saw Goering's suicide as a personal failure; he and his men had done their best in dealing with all of the Accused in such a way as "to protect their dignity and help them to conduct themselves manfully", hoping at the same time to reduce the possibility of suicides.[169]

---

[167] *According to Gilbert, Goering killed himself because he was afraid of hanging.*

[168] *According to a source that cannot be authenticated, Pastor Gerecke reported that during the last meeting with his family Goering remained unmoved by his little daughter's pleading, "Please, Daddy, trust Jesus because I want to see you in heaven, Daddy!"*

[169] *On the copy of the official report, opposite Andrus' testimony, is found a marginal comment on Andrus, probably from a British source: "A pompous, very conceited little man, alert and suspicious but essentially stupid. The Quadripartite Commission had to make the best use of him but would have never selected him."*

What was to remain from the Trial and the Judgement of Nuremberg? A warning to statesmen and generals who may be tempted into ignoring the laws and conventions of war? A lesson to the Germans? They had not been Judges at the Trial; however, they admitted that they had not believed the Allies capable of producing such important documentation, which unmasked the most hidden activities of the Nazis during the war. The long and meticulous presentation of the documents at the hearings, which sounded monotonous and was, frankly, boring, constituted for German public opinion the singular interest of the Trial.

Jackson, the American Prosecutor, must be credited with this. Donovan, who headed the OSS (the Office of State Security) during the war and was originally a member of the US delegation at Nuremberg, had been in favour of a different way of proceeding: to call witnesses instead of reading documents aloud, and to persuade some of the Defendants to turn State evidence. This would have made for a livelier trial, one closer in accordance with Donovan's character. The Foreign Office described him as being endowed with the "Irishman's wit and mercurial temperament".[170]

There were signs that some of the Defendants would indeed have been prepared to testify against the Nazi regime. Schacht's lawyer wrote to Donovan that his client could supply "a brief summary of the underlying reasons and conditions".[171] Keitel, too, in an early interrogation by Thomas Dodd, had envisaged offering the Prosecution a full confession. Even Goering might have agreed to denounce the

---

[170] *FO 371.51022, quoted by Ann and John Tusa, p. 70.*
[171] *Quoted by Ann and John Tusa, p. 258.*

Nazi regime, but there would have been a price to pay: Goering preferred execution by firing squad to being hanged, which he feared more.

Soon after the end of the war, the Allied services in Germany discovered masses of documents, tons of archives, which had been evacuated from Berlin because of the bombings and were under orders to be destroyed. In the case of the diplomatic archives in particular, archivists simply disobeyed orders and retained their papers intact. This, to Jackson, justified conducting a trial based on the use of documents rather than on witnesses. He told Donovan, "We do not see alike concerning the defendants such as Schacht. I do not think he will help us convict anyone we do not have already convicted on the documents."[172] Donovan maintained, though, that no bargain needed to be struck with the Defendants. Eventually, he left Nuremberg in a huff, which resulted in abandoning the whole idea of involving the Defendants in each other's prosecutions. Goering and his companions adopted an attitude of systematic denial. The documents supplied the proofs of guilt.

Relying on the documents was effective, yet the method had its own limitations. There was always the risk of missing an essential piece of paper. This happened in the case of the extermination of the Jews. Few have realised that in actual fact this issue was not addressed at Nuremberg, the reason being that the key document was discovered only in October 1946, thus *after* judgement had been passed and the main Defendants hanged. The Final Solution

---

[172] *See Ann and John Tusa, p. 259. The book by the Tusas is the best source to date on the way the documentation was gathered for the trial. Their main source was KMH Duke, who played an important role in collecting the documents eventually submitted by the Prosecution.*

is recorded in notes on the Wannsee Conference of 20 January 1942.[173]

Admittedly, in the course of the Trial, the Final Solution was indeed mentioned, in particular by the witness Dieter Wisliceny; he was very well informed on what had happened. The former Commandant of the Auschwitz concentration camp, Hoess, was another witness. During the summer of 1941 he was summoned by Himmler, who explained: "The Fuehrer has ordered the Final Solution of the Jewish question and we have to carry out this task. For reasons of transport and isolation I have picked Auschwitz for this. You now have the job of carrying it out."[174]

Observers such as Lalouette then at the Trial concluded that the Final Solution was the work of the SS in the concentration camps, and that the whole issue concerned very few individuals outside the camps: Himmler, who talked to Hoess, and probably Hitler himself. No more. It was then possible to believe the Germans – even those in exalted positions – when they said they had known nothing about the extermination of the Jews.

However, the record of the Wannsee Conference gives its true dimension to the Final Solution on the administrative level [unfortunately only discovered after the final judgement had by passed]. State Secretaries and the top civil servants from a number of Ministries participated in that Conference. They were informed that the Final Solution had its origin in an order given by Marshall Goering. It required the involvement of the

---

[173] *It was found by Major KMH Duke, a former member of the British delegation at Nuremberg, in the diplomatic archives then stored at Berlin-Tempelhof.*
[174] *Quoted according to Gilbert, Nuremberg Tagebuch, 9 April 1946.*

Government and the administration as a whole. Hence, it was not such an awesome secret shared only by a few at the top of the Party hierarchy.

The document was submitted at one of the subsequent trials, the so-called "Trial of the Wilhelmstrasse" (Case 11, i.e., US trials). Here it was shown, for example, that the very respectable State Secretary of the *Auswaertiges Amt*, von Weizsaecker, had to give his approval to the deportation of Jews from Hungary, although he did so very reluctantly. This showed how Hitler led decent, conservative circles to participate in undertakings contrary to traditional morality. If the record of the Wannsee Conference were known at the time of the first Nuremberg Trial, the Judges would possibly have adopted a more severe stance and accepted more readily the notion of solidarity among the Defendants.

The documentary method held a further disadvantage. Not only might some essential and relevant documents be unavailable because of being undiscovered; other documents were unavailable because the Allied governments had, for political reasons, decided to keep them secret – as some of them remain to this day.[175]

---

[175] *From time to time comes a glimpse of what is missing or withheld, such as in the case of documents on Rudolf Hess used by Eugen K. Bird, Prisoner No. 7: Rudolf Hess, New York, 1974.*

HISTORY OF THE RESISTANCE

The Resistance in the Southwest of France

Archives

The S.O.E. archives are not open to private research; parts have been destroyed. Michael Foot, as an official historian, had access to what was left of them.

German military archives may, though, be consulted in Freiburg. In practice, it is convenient to use the microfilms available from the National Archives in Washington. We have used essentially the War Diary of the 58th *Panzerkorps*; Sections Ia (Operations) and Ic (Intelligence) kept one diary. The War Diary of the Army Group G has been consulted. This German documentation offers the advantage of being coherent and well structured. It gives a useful chronology and makes it possible in particular to differentiate between the various phases of the fight against the Resistance.

By contrast, French sources on the Resistance are, as is the nature of such things, either fragmentary or non-existent. Exceptionally, the Armagnac Battalion had well-organised archives. However, Colonel Monnet handed them over to the State, which means that [*at the time of writing*] they remain closed under the fifty-year rule.

The Ultra decipherings provide in some cases a useful complement to the German archives. There is at the Public Record Office in London a selection of the most important decipherings covering a long period. They are of particular interest for the last weeks and the last days of the Third Reich, when the German leaders could communicate only by radio: PRO>DEFE 3. 573; it is actually the C series of documents sent by telex from "Hut 3" of Bletchley Park, documents considered as particularly confidential. In this series is found the 1944 version of the *Kommando Befehl*, as well as the Order of 24 September 1944 henceforth to treat the F.F.I. as regular troops. It is interesting in this respect to note that, long before the end of hostilities, British and Americans were well informed about the *Kommando Befehl*. The documentation from the Ultra decipherings has its limitations: it covered only communications by radio; letters, memos and general reports on the situation are found in German files.

In recent years there has been a spate of books on the Ultra operation, two of which are:

Winterbotham, F.A. (1974) *The Ultra Secret*. London.

Calvocoressi, Peter (1980) *Top Secret Ultra*. London.

Printed Sources

British Perspective:

Foot, Michael (1966) *S.O.E. in France*. London: this deals at some length with the southwest of France and the Wheelwright network headed by "Hilaire". It is difficult to appreciate the actual extent and the value of his documentation as some references are vague, e.g. "an SOE" file. It is at the same time indispensable as it is comprehensive.

Cave Brown, Antony (1976) *A Bodyguard of Lies*. London... Also on the Resistance in the southwest of France

Bennett, Ralph (1979) *Ultra in the West*. London... The author was party to the work of "Hut 3" at Bletchley Park. He confirms that Ultra, soon after the landings in Normandy, deciphered the order given to the 2nd SS Division, *Das Reich*, to leave Toulouse for the Normandy front.

Lieutenant-Colonel George Starr ("Hilaire") has not published memoirs, yet he talked to a journalist.

Lucy, Geoffrey (1978) 'George Starr's secret war'. *Reader's Digest*, June, p. 179.

A FINAL CONSIDERATION

In the account you have just read my father passes over the encounter I am about to describe so fleetingly that one does not give it a second thought. This, I would suggest, is largely due its significance becoming apparent only much later.

The book begins with my father's arrest in Toulouse. My father at this time was a man of habit. Most days, at more or less the same time, he would leave for and return from the library. He would go to the library to study and do his research, apart from for any other reason than it was warm in the library.

As he left his building he was approached by a man in the street. The man introduced himself by saying: "Bonnin, remember me? We were at school together in Vannes." Not that they had been friends when they had attended that same school in Vannes, Brittany. Nor were they even in the same class and neither had they had contact since about the age of eleven or twelve.

At that moment the Nazis arrived and took the two of them away. After that day my father never saw this gentleman again, neither in the prison nor after the war.

This is the backstory to how my father ended up in the prison camp and former barracks *Caffarelli*, in Toulouse. For quite a time after my father's capture for no discernable reason, at least not discernable to my father at the time, none of his fellow inmates would converse with him. This, he eventually discovered, was due to his having been apprehended along with a lorry-load of gangsters, pimps, drug dealers, and general unsavoury types. His fellow inmates, assuming he was also a hardnosed criminal, did not wish to associate with a dodgy member of the underworld; 'best to play it safe and keep one's distance'.

The reason for this rounding-up of racketeers by the Nazis was that they thought that it should be they who controlled these operations; if there was money to be made it was they, they felt, who should make it.

That would have been that: my father got arrested by the Nazis simply while strolling along a road. Up until approximately five years prior to his death, that indeed *was* that.

However, five years before he died here in southwest Wales, my father received a letter. The letter was from my father's former school colleague, the one with whom he had been arrested all those years before.

The man, a devout Catholic, was on his deathbed, suffering from terminal cancer. The final words in his letter were: "Pray for me. Forgive me."

Jean Bonnin
Pembrokeshire
12th July 2016

BIBLIOGRAPHY AND NOTES

The Trial
Archives and Interviews

French diplomatic archives were, when I started writing, still closed under the 50-year rule. However, it seems that this has recently been relaxed, except for particularly sensitive files. In practice, I was told that three files of the main series on War Crimes corresponding to the period of the Nuremberg Trial had been misplaced. At the time of writing, the search is on.

British archives on the Trial are open. The Cabinet papers are useful regarding the decision not to continue with the War Crimes trials after the major Nuremberg Trial. Foreign Office papers document the origins of the Trial, negotiations with the Americans and internal discussions.

In recent years the studies into the Nuremberg Trial have received a boost from authors' access to the private papers of participants, in particular those of the US Judge, Francis Biddle (Syracuse University). These form the background to the books by Bradley F. Smith and Robert E. Conot in the US and, to a lesser extent, to the book by Ann and John Tusa in the UK.

These authors have also interviewed a number of personalities connected with the trials. The Tusas list no fewer than thirty-two, including Sir Patrick Dean, retired from the Foreign Office. I would have been interested to talk to Sir Patrick, especially as he was Lalouette's counterpart in the British Delegation. He felt, though, that there would be no purpose in meeting me, especially as he had left Nuremberg in March 1946, several months before I arrived. Just the same, I read with interest in the FO archives the letters he sent from Nuremberg.

I should mention here the name of Kenneth Duke, of the British Delegation, who has greatly helped the Tusas and who has an unparalleled knowledge of the way documents were collected for the Trial. This aspect of the Trial did not fit chronologically with the subject of the present book. I am obliged to add that Kenneth Duke was a very close colleague of mine for the best part of twelve years, when we worked together on the publication of the German Diplomatic Documents. Although I did not consult him before writing the current book, over the years I enjoyed many occasions to talk with him about the Trial.

I have quoted in the course of this book from the following files at the Public Record Office:

Lord Chancellor's Office, file 2–2981;
Foreign Office, file 371–50996;
War Office, file DEFE 3-573.

On archives in Germany see Otto Puchner, 'Der Bestand "Nuernberger Prozesse" im Staatsarchiv Nuermberg' in *Wehrw. Rundschau*, 6 February 1956, pp. 93-7.

ALEXANDER, Charles W. and KEESHAN, Anne (1945) *Justice at Nuernberg*. Chicago.
It contains many photographs by Charles Alexander.
ALEXANDROV, G.N. (1965) 'Looking Back to Nuremberg'. *New Times* **43** 16; **44** 20; **47** 16.
ANDRUS, Burton (1969) *The Infamous of Nuremberg*. London.
 The Jailer's memoirs.
APP, Austin J. and FOUS, J. (1960) *Crimes de guerre des Alliés*. Paris.
APPLEMAN, J.A. (1954) *Military Tribunals and International Crimes*. Westport, Conn.
ARENDT, Hannah (1963) *Eichmann in Jerusalem: A report on the banality of evil*. New York.
Eichmann's mentality – was he a real Nazi?
ARNDT, Karl (ed.) (1949) *Alphabetical Index of All Witnesses and Defence Counsel Heard in the Twelve Nuremberg War Crimes Trials, with pages of the Official Transcripts of the Proceedings*. Bremen.
ARONEAU, Eugene (1954) 'Le Juge Jackson et la justice pénale internationale'. *Revue de Droit International*. (Sottile-Geneva) October-December **32** 361-72.
ARZINGER, Rudolf (1953-4?) *La Réhabilitation des criminels de guerre hitlériens et le project "d'Armée Européene"*. Brussels.
ASSMANN, Kurt (1953) 'Der Deutsche U-Bootkrieg und die Nuernberger Rechtsprechung'. *Marine*

Rundschau **50** 2-8. In this, Assmann gives information on Doenitz.
- (1956) 'Hitler and the German Officer Corps'. *United States Naval Institute Proceedings* May **82** 509-20.
- (1961) 'Grossadmiral Dr. hc. Raeder und der Zweite Weltkrieg'. *Marine Rundschau* February **58** 3-17.

AZIZ, Philippe (1974) *Les Criminels de Guerre*. Paris.
BADER, Karl S. (1946) 'Nuernberger Prozess'. *Deutsche Rechtszeitschrift* November **1** 140-142.
BALL, George W. (1982) *The Past Has Another Pattern*. New York.
BARDÈCHE, Maurice (1948) *Nuremberg, ou la Terre Promise*, Paris.
BARDENS, Dennis (1962) *Lord Justice Birkett*, London.
BAUM, Walter (1960) 'Der Zusammenbruch der obersten militaerischen Fuehrung'. *Wehrwissenschaftliche Rundschau*. **5**. Frankfurt.
BEDFORD, Twelfth Duke of (1946) *Failure at Nuremberg: An Analysis of Trial Evidence and Verdict*. London.
   Published by the "British People's Party".
BEIN, Alexander (1958) 'Der moderne Antisemitismus und seine Bedeutung fuer die Judenfrage'. *Vierteljahrshefte fuer Zeitgeschichte* October **6** 340-60.
   Bein mentions the role of Streicher.
BELGION, Montgomery (1946) *Epitaph on Nuremberg*. London.
BENTON, Wilbourn and GRIMM, Georg (1955) *Nuremberg: German Views of the War Trials*. Dallas.
   Includes contributions from German lawyers who were at the trial.
BERNAYS, Murray C. (1946) 'Legal Basis of the Nuernberg Trials'. *Survey Graphic* January **35** 4-9; November **3** 390-391.

BERNSTEIN, Victor H. (1947) *Final Judgement: The Story of Nuremberg.* New York.

BERTAUX, Pierre (1973) *La Libération de Toulouse et de sa Région.* Paris.

BETZ, Dieter Hermann (1970) *Das OKW und seine Haltung zum Landkriegs-voelkerrecht im zweiten Weltkrieg.* Bamberg.

BIDDLE, Francis (1946) 'Report to President Truman'. *Department of State Bulletin.*

Biddle (with Parker) was one of the American judges at the Trial.

- (1947) 'The Nuremberg Trial'. *Virginia Law Review* November **33** 679-96.

- (1962) 'Nuremberg: The Fall of the Supermen'. *American Heritage* August **13** 65-76.

- (1947) 'The Nuremberg Trial'. *Proceedings of the American Philosophical Society* **91** 294-302.

- (1948) 'Le Procès de Nuremberg'. *Revue Internationale de Droit Pénal* **19** 1-19.

- (1962) *In Brief Authority,* New York.

BIRD, Eugene K. (1974) *Prisoner No.7: Rudolf Hess,* New York.

BIRKETT, Norman (1947) 'International Legal Theories Evolved at Nuremberg'. *International Affairs* July **23** 317-25.

Birkett and Lord Oaksey were the British judges at the Trial.

Extracts from Birkett's diary at the time of the Nuremberg Trial are contained in his biography by H. Montgomery Hyde (1964) *The Life of Lord Birkett of Ulverston,* London. In those extracts Birkett shows himself critical of a number of aspects of the trial.

(1957) 'Right Honourable Sir Norman Birkett' in *Law Journal* 18 January, 107.

BISHOP, William W. Jr. (1955) 'Robert H. Jackson – Obituary'. *American Journal of International Law* January **49** 44-50.

BOEDDEKER, G. and WINTER, R. (1979) *Die Kapsel, das Geheimnis um Goerings Tod*, Duesseldorf.
BOEHM, Herman, General Admiral (1951) *Die Grossadmirale*, Nation Europa, December, 41-44.
  Boehm mentions Raeder.
BOISSIER, Pierre (1953) *L'épée dans la balance*, Geneva.
BOSCH, W.J. (1970) *Judgement on Nuremberg: American Attitudes towards Major German War-Crime Trials*, University of Carolina Press.
BOWER, Tom (1982) *The Pledge Betrayed: America and Britain and the DeNazification of Germany*. New York.
BRACHER, Karl Dietrich (1970) *The German Dictatorship: The Origins, Structure and Effects of National Socialism*. New York.
BRAND, G. (1949) 'The War Crimes Trials and the Law of War'. *The British Yearbook of International Law*.
BRANDT, Willy (1946) *Nuernberg-Norge-dommen*. Oslo.
BROSS, Werner (1950) *Gespraeche mit Hermann Goering waehrend des Nuernberger Prozesses*. Flensburg, Hamburg.
CALVOCORESSI, Peter (1947) *Nuremberg: The Facts, the Law and the Consequences*. London.
  Calvocoressi was part of the British delegation.
CANOT, Robert E. (1983) *Justice at Nuremberg*. London.
  Canot used the documents of the American prosecution to write the story of the Nazi regime.
CARJEU, P. (1951) *Le jugement du Tribunal Militaire de Nuremberg*. Paris.
CARTIER, Raymond (1947) *Les secrets de la guerre devoilés à Nuremberg*. Paris.
  Cartier was, as a journalist, present at the trial.
CASAMAYOR, Serge Fuster (1985) *La guerre en process*. Paris.

Casamayor was part of the French delegation.
Catalogue of Nuremberg Documents. London, Wiener Library, 1961.
CHALUFOUR, A. (1958) 'Le procès de Nuremberg et le droit international'. *Annuaire de l'Association des Auditeurs et des Anciens Auditeurs de l'Académie de Droit International de la Haye* **28** 26-38.
Chalufour was Dubost's assistant.
COOPER, R.W. (1947) *The Nuremberg Trial.* London.
Cooper was a journalist present at the trial; this is one of the first accounts.
DAVIDSON, Eugene (1959) *The Nuremberg Trials and the World in Issues and Conflicts, Studies in Twentieth Century American Diplomacy.* George L. Anderson (ed.). Lawrence, University of Kansas Press.
- (1966) *The Trial of the Germans.* New York.
DEAN, Gordon (1955) 'Mr Justice Jackson: His Contribution at Nuremberg'. *American Bar Association Journal* October **42** 912-15.
DESCHEEMAEKER, Jacques (1947) *Le tribunal militaire international des grands criminels de guerre,* Paris.
DODD, Thomas J. (1947) 'The Nuremberg Trials'. *Journal of Criminal Law and Criminology* January **37**.
Dodd was a member of the American delegation.
DOENITZ, Karl (1968) *Mein wechselvolles Leben,* Goettingen.
Memoirs written after his release from prison. He still thought that his being found guilty was by and large unjustified. The Tribunal focused on "secondary" points, such as his transmitting the order to kill captured commandos, who anyway constituted a form of illegal warfare. He knew nothing about the extermination of the Jews. When he approved of the internees of concentration camps' working for the navy, he thought he was doing them a favour as they would therefore receive better food rations. Besides, he did not know that some

concentration camp inmates came from occupied countries. In an appendix, Doenitz gave at length his reasons for still thinking that the 20 July plot against Hitler was an act of high treason.
- (1917) *Die Fahrten der "Breslau" im Schwarzen Meer*. Berlin.
- (1943) *Die U-Bootswaffe* (4th edn.). Berlin.
- (1959) *Memoirs: Ten Years and Twenty Days*. London.

DONNEDIEU DE VABRES, Henri (1946-47) 'Le procès de Nuremberg (Exposé fait le 27 février 1947 a la Conférence du Jeune Barreau)'. *Revue de Droit Pénal et de Criminologie* **27** 480-90.

Donnedieu was the French judge at the Trial.
- (1947) 'Le procès de Nuremberg'. Cours de Doctorat professé à la Faculté de Droit de Paris, Paris.
- (1947) 'Le procès de Nuremberg devant les principes modernes due droit pénal international'. *Recueil des Cours de l'Académie de Droit International de la Haye* **70** 477-582.
- (1947) *Le procès de Nuremberg: Le statut du Tribunal Militaire International, les débats, les chefs d'accusation, le jugement*. Paris.
- (1947) 'Le jugement de Nuremberg et le principe de légalité des délits et des peines'. *Revue de Droit Pénal et de Criminologie* July **27** 813-33.
- (1947) 'Le procès de Nuremberg' in *Revue de Science Criminelle et de Droit Pénal Comparé* **2** 171-83.
- (1947) *Traité de droit criminel et de législation pénale comparée*. Paris.
- (1948) *La justice pénale d'aujourd'hui*. Paris.

The work that established Donnedieu de Vabres' reputation before the war was: *Principes modernes de droit pénal international*, Paris, 1928. As reviewed by Donnedieu's colleague at the Faculty of Law in Paris, Louis Hugueney (1948) 'Le procès de Nuremberg devant les principes modernes du droit international' in *Revue Internationale de Droit Pénal*, p. 277.

Donnedieu's viewpoint is not shared by Pierre-Henri Teitgen, French Justice Minister at the time: (1946) 'Le Jugement de Nuremberg' in *Revue de Droit International, de Sciences Diplomatiques, Politiques et Sociales* October-December **24** 161-173.

DROZ, Jacques (1948) *Histoire de L'Allemagne.* Paris.

DUBOST, Charles (1946) 'Les Crimes des Etats et la coutume pénale internationale'. *Politique Etrangere* December.

Among the French delegation at the Trial.

EHRENBERG, Ilja (Erenburg) (1945) 'History's Morality: The Nuremberg Trial'. *USSR Embassy Information Bulletin* 8 December **5** 1-3; 7.

- (1965) *Menschen, Jahre, Leben.* Translated from Russian by Alexander Kaempfe. 2 vols. Munich.

(1946) 'Eisenhower Reports on ETO Tour'. *Army and Navy Bulletin* 26 October **2** 2.

This mentions Jodl's involvement.

ERHARDT, Hans (1949) 'The Nuremberg trial against the Major War Criminals and International Law'. *American Journal of International Law* April **43**.

FAIRMAN, Charles (1955) 'Robert H. Jackson: 1892 – 1954 Associate Justice of the Supreme Court'. *Columbia Law Review* April **55** 445-87.

FEST, Joachim C. (1974) *The Face of the Third Reich.* New York.

- (1974) *Hitler,* New York.

FISHMAN, Jack (1954) *The Seven Men of Spandau.* London.

FRANK, Hans (1953) *Im Angesicht des Galgens.* Munich.

Frank's official diary is on microfilm: U.S. National Archives, World War II Crimes Records. Record Group 238. Publication T.354. 12 rolls.

FRANKFURTER, Felix (1975) *From the Diaries of Felix Frankfurter.* New York.

Extracts from January to June 1943, pp. 141-261.

FRIEDRICH, W. (1960) 'Nuernberg und die Kollektivscham'. *D. Quelle*, 9 December 1960.

The viewpoint of Neo-Nazis.

FRITZSCHE, Hans (1953) *The Sword and the Scales, as told to Hildegard Springer*, London.

In these memoirs Fritzsche tells that his first reaction was to recognise "the plain absurdity of any accusation that I had influenced Hitler or entered into a conspiracy with him. Hitler scarcely knew me." Actually, Fritzsche, a well-known radio commentator, was present at the trial as a substitute for his boss, Dr. Goebbels, whom he hardly mentions in the book.

FUHRMANN, Peter (1963) *Der hoehere Befehl als Rechtfertigung im Voelkerrecht*. Munich.

Fuhrmann discusses war crime and blind obedience.

GALBRAITH, J.K. (1981) *A Life in Our Times*. London.

GANSHOF VAN DER MEERSCH, W.J.O.L.M. (1961) 'Justice et droit international pénal'. *Revue de droit pénal et criminel* October pp. 1-42.

GAULLE, Charles de (1959) *Mémoires de Guerre*, Paris.

GEMZELL, Carl-Axel (1965) *Raeder, Hitler und Skandinavien*. Frankfurt-am-Main.

GENDREL, Michel and LAFARGE, Philippe (1965) *Eléments d'une bibliographie mondiale du droit pénal militaire des crimes et délits contra la sûreté de l'Etat et du droit pénal international*. (Concludes on 31 December 1961) Paris.

GEOUFFRE DE LAPRADELLE, A. (1946) 'Une révolution dans le droit pénal international'. *Nouvelle Revue de Droit International Privé* No. 2.

- (1951) 'La répression des crimes de guerre en France'. *Ecrits de Paris*, May, 74-80.

GERECKE, Henry F. (1951) 'I Walked to the Gallows with the Nazi Chiefs'. M. Sinclair (ed.). *Saturday Evening Post*, 1 September 1951, 17-19; 57-58.

GERHART, Eugene C. (1958) *Robert H. Jackson, America's Advocate*, Indianapolis and New York.

GIBB, Andrew Dewar (1954) *Perjury unlimited; a monograph of Nuremberg*. Edinburgh.

A Professor of Law in the University of Glasgow shows that the defendants were obviously lying.

GILBERT, G.M. (1948) *Nuremberg Diary*. London.

Gilbert was the official psychologist, and had permanent access to the defendants.

- (1948) 'Hermann Goering: Amiable Psychopath'. *Journal of Abnormal and Social Psychology* April **43** 211-29.

GISEVIUS, Hans Bernd (1947) *To the Bitter End*. Boston.

Gisevius addresses the role of Schacht.

GOERING, Emmy (1972) *My life with Goering*. London.

GOERLITZ, Walter (1967) *Keitel: Verbrecher oder Offizier?* Goettingen.

GOODHARDT, A.L. (1946) 'The Legality of the Nuremberg Trials'. *Juridical Review* April.

- (1947) 'Questions and Answers concerning the Nuremberg Trials'. *International Law Quarterly*.

GRANET, Marie (1954) 'La déportation au procès international de Nuremberg'. *Revue de la Deuxieme Guerre Mondiale* **15-16** 99-113.

GRAVEN, Jean (1967) 'Vingt ans après: la libération des prisonniers de Spandau: Quelques reflexions actuelles et rétropectives sur le sens du procès de Nuremberg'. *Revue de droit pénal et de criminology* February 431-460.

The author is President of the Geneva "Cour de Cassation".

GRIMM, Friedrich (1955) *Nun aber Schluss mit Rache und Vergeltung. Eine erste Betrachtung zehn Jahre nach dem Zusammenbruch*. Goettingen.

GROS, André (1945) 'Le Châtiment des Crimes de guerre'. *Cahiers Politiques* April **9** 49-58.

The author was one of the two French delegates at the London preparatory conference.

GRUNDLER, Gerhard E. and MANIKOWSKI, Arnim von (1969) *Nuremberg ou la justice des vainqueurs.* Paris.

HAENSEL, Carl (1946) 'Nuernberger Probleme'. *Deutsche Rechtszeitschrift* September **1** 67-69.

Haensel was Counsel for the Defence of the SS.

- (1947) 'Zum Neurnberger Urteil: Schuldprinzip und Gruppen-Kriminalitaet'. *Sueddeutsche Juristenzeitung* **2** 19-25.

- (1948) 'Das Urteil im Neurnberger Juristenprozess'. *Rechtszeitschrift* February **3** 40-43.

- (1950) *Das Gericht vertagt sich: Aus dem Tagebuch eines Nuernberger Verteidigers.* Hamburg.

- (1963) 'The Nuremberg Trial Revisited'. *De Paul Review* **13**.

HAERTLE, Heinrich (1965) *Freispruch fuer Deutschland, Unsere Soldaten vor dem Nuernberger Tribunal.* Goettingen.

HANKEY (Lord) (1950) *Politics, Trials and Errors.* Oxford.

Hankey was opposed in principle to the trial of the German leaders.

HERF, Jeffrey Charles (1981) *Reactionary modernism: reconciliation of techniques and unreason in Weimar Germany and the Third Reich.* Brandeis University.

HERZOG, Jacques Bernard (1946) 'Les organisations nationales-socialistes devant le Tribunal de Nuremberg'. *Revue internationale de droit pénal* **3-4**.

- (1957) *Nuremberg, un échec fructueux?* Paris.

Herzog was part of the French delegation.

HESS, Ilse (ed.) (1952) *England-Nuernberg-Spandau: Ein Schicksal in Briefen.* Leoni-am-Starnberger-See.

- (1954) *Prisoner of Peace.* London.

- (1965) *Gefangener des Friedens: Neue Briefe aus Spandau.* Leoni-am-Starnberger-See.

HEYDECKER, Joe J. and LEEB, Johannes (1958) *Der Nuernberger Prozess. Bilanz der tausend Jahre.* Cologne, Berlin.
HOEGNER, Wilhelm (1959) *Der schwierige Aussenseiter: Erinnerungen eines Abgeordneten, Emigranten und Ministerpraesidenten.* Munich.
IRVING, David (1979) *Der Nuernberger Prozess.*
JACKSON, Robert H. (1941) 'The Challenge of International Lawlessness'. *International Conciliation* November **374** 683-91.
  The American Prosecutor at the Trial.
- (1945) 'The Rule of Law among Nations'. *American Bar Association Journal* June **31** 290.
- (1945) 'War Criminals and International Law: Judicial Proceedings must not be tied to predetermined policy'. *Saturday Review of Literature* 2 June **28** 7-8.
- (1945) 'Atrocities and War Crimes: Report to the President'. *Department of State Bulletin* **12** 1071-8.
- (1946) 'The Trial of War Criminals'. *American Bar Association Journal* June **32** 319-21.
- (1946) 'The Law under which Nazi organisations are accused of being criminal'. *Temple Law Quarterly* 371.
- (1946) 'The Significance of the Nuremberg Trials to the Armed Forces'. *Military Affairs* Winter **10** 3-15.
- (1947) 'Nuremberg Trial of the Major Nazi Leaders'. *New York Bar Association Bulletin* **70** 158.
- (1947) 'A Country Lawyer at an International Court'. *Virginia State Bar Association Proceedings* **58** 190-200.
- (1947) *The Nuremberg Case, as Presented by Robert H. Jackson,* New York.
- (1949) 'Nuremberg in retrospect'. *Canadian Bar Review,* 761.
- (1950) 'Trial of the Trials: Nuremberg'. *Common Cause* **3** 285-94.

JAHRREISS, Hermann (1949) 'Die Fortentwicklung des Voelkerrechts'. *Jahrbuch fuer internationals und auslaendisches oeffentliches Recht* 658.

Assistant Counsel for Jodl and spokesman for the Defence Counsel to present the legal arguments.

JAROWSKI, Leon (1961) *After Fifteen Years: The story of the Nazi War crimes trials.* Houston, Texas.

JASPERS, Karl (1947) 'Significance of the Nuremberg Trials for Germany and the World'. *Notre Dame Law Journal* 150.

JESCHEK, Hans-Heinrich (1952) *Die Verantwortlichkeit der Staatsorgane nach Voelkerstrafrecht: Eine Studie zu den Nuernberger Prozessen.* Bonn.

The legal basis of the trial is to be found in German law, i.e., Law No. 10 of the Control Commission. The Nuremberg principles cannot be introduced directly into international law.

JODL, Luise (1976) *Jenseits des Endes: Leben und Sterben des General-oberst Alfred Jodl.* Vienna, Munich, Zurich.

JONES, Sir Elwyn (1971) *Nuremberg 25 years on: A retrospective analysis.* London.

This was given as the Noah Baron Memorial Lecture.

KALNOKY, Countess Ingeborg, with Ilona Heisko (1974) *Guest House: A Nuremberg Memoir.* Indianapolis.

KATZENBERGER, K. (1947) 'Das Korps der Politischen Leiter im Urteil von Nuernberg'. *Neue Juristische Wochenschrift*, 371.

KEITEL, Wilhelm (1965) *The Memoirs of Field Marshal Keitel.* London.

KELLEY, Douglas M. (1947) *Twenty-two cells in Nuremberg.* New York.

Kelley was psychiatrist to the Nuremberg jail.

KELSEN, Hans (1948) 'Collective and Individual Responsibility for Acts of State in International Law'. *Jewish Yearbook of International Law.*
KEMPNER, Robert W. (1950) 'The Nuremberg Trials as Sources of Recent German Political and Historical Material'. *The American Political Science Review* June **44** 447-59.
- (1961) *Eichmann und Komplizen.* Stuttgart.
- (1964) *SS im Kreuzverhoer.* Munich.
- (1969) *Das Dritte Reich im Kreuzverhoer: Aus den unveroeffentlichen Vernehmungsprotokollen des Anklaegers Robert M.W. Kempner.* Munich.
These memoirs were dictated in conversations with Joerg Fridrich. Kempner, who had under Weimar been a lawyer and civil servant in Berlin, played an important part within the U.S. Delegation; he has many publications to his credit, a fairly comprehensive list of which is to be found at the end of his book, pp. 463-466.
- (1983) *Anklaeger einer Epoche.* Frankfurt, Berlin, Vienna.
KIRKPATRICK, Ivone (1959) *The Inner Circle.* London.
KLESSMANN, Cristoph (1971) 'Der Generalgouverneur Hans Frank'. *Vierteljahrshefte fuer Zeitgeschichte* **19** 245-60.
KNIERIEM, August von (1953) *Nuernberg. Rechtliche und menschliche Proleme.* Stuttgart.
The author, legal adviser to I.G. Farben, was acquitted at Nuremberg in one of the subsequent trials.
KOGON, Eugen (1951) *The Theory and Practice of Hell.* London.
For many years Kogon was a concentration camp inmate.
KRANZBUEHLER, Otto (1949) *Rueckblick auf Nuernberg.* Hamburg.
Kranzbuehler was Defence Counsel for Doenitz.

- (1950) 'Nuernberg als Rechtsproblem'. *Um Recht und Frieden*, Festgabe fuer Erich Kaufmann, Stuttgart-Cologne.
- (1964) 'Nuremberg, Eighteen Years afterwards'. *De Paul Law Review* **14**.

KRAUS, Herbert (1948) *Gerichtstag in Nuernberg.* Hamburg.

Kraus was Defence Counsel for Schacht.
- (1948) *Kontrollratgesetz Nr. 10*, Hamburg.
- (1963) 'The Nuremberg Trial of the Major War Criminals, Recollections after Seventeen Years'. *De Paul Review* **13**.

LACHS, Manfred (1945) *War Crimes: An attempt to define the issues*, London.

Lachs was a Polish barrister and had fought on the British side.

LANTERN, Mark (1950) *Das letzte Wort ueber Nuernberg. Fassade und Sumpf in den Kriegsverbrecher-Prozessen*. Buenos Aires.

LATERNSNER, Hans (1946) *Plaedoyer vor dem internationalen Militaergerichtshof zu Nuernberg.* Nuremberg.

Laternsner was Defence Counsel for the General Staff and High Command.
- (1950) *Verteidigung deutscher Soldaten: Plaedoyers vor alliierten Gerichten*. Bonn.

LAUTERPACHT, Sir Hersh (1944) 'The Law of Nations and the Punishment of War Crimes'. *British Yearbook of International Law* **21** 58-95.
- (1944) 'The Law of Nations and the Punishment of War Crimes'. *British Yearbook of International Law* **21** 58-95.

LAZARD, D. (1947) *Le procès de Nuremberg: Récit d'un témoin*. Paris.

LEMKIN, Raphael (1933) *Akten der Barbarei und des Vandalismus als* Delicta Juris Gentium. Vienna.

LEVENTHAL, Harold *et al.* (1947) 'The Nuremberg Verdict'. *Harvard Law Review* July.

LEWIS, John R. (1970) *Uncertain Judgement: A Bibliography of War Crimes Trials*. Santa Barbara, Oxford.

This volume contains 3,352 titles; items 674 to 1445 concern more specifically the Nuremberg Trial of the major War Criminals.

LICHTENSTEIN, Heiner (1981) *NS-Prozesse: viel zu spaet und ohne System*. Bonn.

LIPPE, Viktor von der (1951) *Nuernberger Tagebuch Notizen: November 1945 bis October 1946*. Frankfurt am Main.

LIPPMANN, Walter (1946) 'The Meaning of the Nuremberg Trial'. *Ladies Home Journal* June **63** 32; 188-90.

LOMBOIS, Claude (1979) *Droit pénal international*. Paris.

This is a textbook for law students. It is interesting on the subject of the Oradour trial.

LUEDDE-NEURATH, Walter (1953) *Regierung Doenitz: Die letzten Tage des Dritten Reiches*. Goettingen.

MANN, Aleby (1962) *Jugement à Nuremberg*. Paris.

MARTIENSSEN, Anthony K. (1948) *Hitler and His Admirals*. London.

MASER, Werner. (1979) *Nuremberg, a Nation on Trial*. London.

This is the result of extensive research. The German title was *Tribunal of the Victors*.

- (1981) '1946: Der Nuernberger Prozess. Seine historischen und voelkerrechtlichen Probleme'. *Damals, Zeitschrift fuer geschichtliches Wissen* **10/11** 831-847; 939-954.

MAUGHAM, Viscount (1951) *UNO and War Crimes*. London.

The book contains a long list of criticisms addressed to the trial; Lord Hankey contributed a few pages.

MAXWELL FYFE, David Patrick (First Earl of Kilmuir) (1956) *Nuremberg in retrospect*. Birmingham.

This was given as a Presidential address to the Holdsworth Club.

- (1964) *Political adventure*. London.

Political memoirs, of which two chapters deal with Nuremberg.

MENDELSOHN, B. (1965) 'Les infractions commises sous le régime nazi sont-elles des "crimes" au sens du droit commun?'. *Revue de Droit International* October-December **4** 333-341.

MENTHON, François de (1946) *Le procès de Nuremberg, son importance juridique et politique: Conférence prononcée le 7 mars 1946*. Paris.

De Menthon was among the French delegation.

MERLE, Marcel (1949) *Le procès de Nuremberg et le châtiment des criminels de guerre*. Paris.

MIALE, F.R. and SELZER, M. (1975) *The Nuremberg Mind: the psychology of the Nazi leaders*. New York.

This book used documents of Gilbert and the American psychologist at the trial.

MOLL, Otto E. (1962) *Die deutschen Generalfeldmarschaelle, 1939-1945*. (2nd edn.) Rastatt.

MONNERAY, Henri (1946) 'L'appréciation des responsabilités individuelles par le Tribunal de Nuremberg'. *Le Monde*, 16 October.

Monneray was one of the French delegation.

MUELLER, Gerhard O.W. *et al*. (1965) *International Criminal Law*. London.

NADLER, Fritz (1955) *"Ich sah wie Nuernberg unterging!..." Tatsachenbericht und Stimmungsbilder aus bittersten Notzeiten nach Tagebuchaufzeichnungen*. Nuremberg.

NEAVE, Airey (1955) *They have their Exits*. London.

Neave was part of the British delegation.

- (1978) *Nuremberg, a personal record of the Trial of the Major Nazi War Criminals in 1945-1946*. London.

NELTE, Otto (1947) *Die Generale: Das Nuernberger Urteil und die Schuld der Generale*. Hannover.

Nelte was Defence Counsel for Keitel.

OAKSEY, Lord (1947) 'The Nuremberg Trial'. *International Affairs* April **23** 151-59.

Oaksey and Birkett were the two British judges at the Trial.

- (1947) *The Nuremberg Trials and the Process of International Law* Birmingham.

PANNENBECKER, Otto (1964) 'The Nuremberg War Crimes Trial'. *De Paul Review* **14**.

Pannenbecker was Defence Counsel for Frick.

- (1947) *Geheim! Dokumentarische Tatsachen aus dem Nuernberger Prozess.* Duesseldorf.

PAPEN, Franz von (1952) *Der Wahrheit, Eine Gasse.* Munich.

PARKER, John J. (1946) 'The Nuremberg Trial'. *Journal of the American Judicature Society* December **30** No. 4, 109-15.

Parker (with Biddle) was one of the American judges at the Trial.

- (1947) 'The Nuremberg Trial'. *Kentucky State Bar Journal* June **11** 157-65; 185.

- (1951) 'The International Trial at Nuremberg: Giving Vitality to International Law'. *American Bar Association Journal* July **37** 493-96; 549-55.

'John J. Parker: Senior Circuit Judge – Fourth Circuit'. *American Bar Association Journal* December **32** 856-59; 901-903.

PEILLARD, Leonce (1963) *The Laconia Affair.* New York.

This mentions Doenitz's involvement.

POLEVOI, Boris (1978) *The Final Reckoning.* Moscow.

Polevoi was the *Pravda* correspondent at the Trial.

POLIAKOV, Léon (ed.) (1971) *Le procès de Nuremberg.* Paris.

POLIANSKY, N. (Poljankij) (1946) 'The Soviet Prosecution's Case at Nuremberg'. *New Times* **4** 3-6.

POLTORAK, Arkadi (n.d.) *Le Procès de Nuremberg.* Moscow.

Poltorak was a member of the Secretariat.
- (1971) *The Nuremberg Epilogue*. Moscow.
Published in Russian in 1965: *Niurembergskii epilog*.
- and SAITSEV, V. (1961) *Remember Nuremberg*. Moscow.
This book denounces West Germany and the monopolies.
RAEDER, Erich (1960) *My Life*. Annapolis, U.S. Naval Institute.
RAUSCHENBACH, Gerhard (1954) *Der Nuernberger Prozess gegen die Organizationen, Grundlage, Probleme, Auswirkungen auf die Mitglieder und strafrechtliche Ergebnisse*. Bonn.
REITLINGER, Gerald (1953) *The Final Solution: The Attempt to Exterminate the Jews of Europe, 1939-1945*. London.
The key book on the subject.
REUTER, Paul (1946) 'Nuremberg: Le Procès'. *La Vie Intellectuelle* December.
- (1947) 'Nuernberg 1946: The Trial'. *Notre Dame Lawyer* November **23** 76-97.
RIBBENTROP, Joachim von (1954) *Zwischen London und Moskau. Erinnerungen und letzte Aufzeichnungen*. Leoni-am-Starnberger-See.
RITTER, Gerhard (1948) *Europa und die Deutsche Frage*. Munich.
ROSENMANN, Samuel (1952) *Working with Roosevelt*. New York.
ROSENTHAL, Ludwig (c. 1979) *"Endloesung der Judenfrage". Massenmord oder Gaskammerluege. Eine Auswertung der Beweisaufnahme im Prozess gegen Hauptkriegsverbrecher vor dem Internationalen Militaergerichtshof Nuernberg vom 14. November bis 1. Oktober 1946*. Darmstadt.
RUECKERL, Adalbert (1962) *NS-Verbrechen vor Gericht: Versuch einer Vergangenheitsbewaeltigung*. Heidelberg.

RUDENKO, Roman A. (1946) *Die Gerechtigkeit nehme ihren Lauf! Die Reden des sowjetischen Hauptanklaegers R.A. Rudenko im Nuernberger Prozess der deutschen Hauptkriegsverbrecher.* Berlin.
 Rudenko was part of the Soviet delegation.
- (1947) *Die Gerechtigkeit fordert fuer alle Hauptkriegsverbrecher nur eine Strafe, die Todesstrafe; General Rudenkos Schlussrede in Nuremberg.* Berlin.
- (ed.) (1957-1961) *Niurnbergskii process nad glavnymi nemete kimi voennymi prestupnikami: Sbornik materialov v vermin tomakh pod obschchei.* 7 vols. Moscow.
- (1970) *Niurnbergskii process.* Moscow.

RUGE, Friedrich (1957) *Der Seekrieg: The German Navy's Story 1939-1945.* Annapolis, United States Naval Institute.

RUSSELL of Liverpool, Baron (1954) *The Scourge of the Swastika: A Short History of Nazi War Crimes.* London.

SAUER, Willhelm (1947) 'Zum Begriff der Kollektivschuld'. *Deutsche Rechtszeitschrift.*

SAUREL, Louis (1965) *Le procès de Nuremberg.* Paris.

SCHACHT, Hjalmar (1931) *Das Ende der Reparation.* Oldenburg.
- (1948) *Abrechnung mit Hitler.* Hamburg.
- (1953) *Sechs-und-siebzig Jahre meines Lebens.* Bad-Worishofen.
- (1968) *1933: Wie eine Demokratie stirbt.* Duesseldorf.

SCHIRACH, Baldur von (1967) *Ich glaubte an Hitler.* Hamburg.

SCHIRACH, Henriette von (1956) *Der Preis der Herrlichkeit.* Wiesbaden.

SCHMIDT, Matthias (1984) *Albert Speer: The End of a Myth.* London.

SCHMIDT, Paul (1951) *Der Statist auf der Galerie 1945 bis 1950: Erlebnisse, Kommentare, Vergleiche.* Bonn.
SCHRAMM, Wilhelm von (1974) *Geheimdienst im Zweiten Weltkrieg.* Munich.
SEIDL, Alfred (1949) *Die Beziehungen zwischen Deutschland und der Sowjetunion 1939-1941.* Tuebingen.

Seidl was Defence Counsel for Hess and Frank. The book reproduces documents on the Nazi-Soviet treaty of 1939.

SHAWCROSS, Hartley (1969) 'Tribute to Jackson'. *New York Bar Association.*
SIGGERT, Karl (1953) *Repressalie, Requisition und hoeherer Befehl. Ein Beitrag zur Rechtfertigung der Kriegsverurteilten.* Goettingen.
SMIRNOV, L.N. (1959) 'Njurnbergskij process i egovol v razoblacenii prestuplinij germanskogo imperialism' ('The Nuremberg trial and its part in disclosing the aims of German imperialism'). *Socialist zak.,* August **8** 49-56.
- (1966) 'Njurembergskij process'. *Soviet gosudartstvo i pravo* **2** 3-11.
SMITH, Bradley F. (1981) *The Road to Nuremberg.* New York: Deutsch.
SPEER, Albert (1970) *Inside the Third Reich.* London.
- (1976) *Spandau: The Secret Diaries.* London.
SPRINGER, Hildegard (1949) *Es sprach Hans Fritzsche: Nach Gespraechen, Briefen und Dokumenten.* Stuttgart.
STEINBACH, Peter (1981) *Nationalsozialistische Gewaltverbrechen: Die Diskussion in der deutschen Oeffentlichkeit nach 1945.* Berlin.
STEINBAUER, Gustav (1950) *Ich war Verteidiger in Nuernberg.* Klagenfurt.

Steinbauer was the Defence Counsel for Seyss-Inquart.

STEINERT, Marlis G. (1969) *Twenty-three Days: The Final Collapse of Nazi Germany*. New York.
  Doenitz's role is also discussed.
STEINIGER, Alfred *et al.* (1956) *Der Nuernberger Prozess*. Berlin.
STEINIGER, Peter Alfons (1968) 'Der OKW-Prozess in Voelkerrechtlicher Sicht'. *Zeitschrift fuer Militaergeschichte* **2** 183-196.
STEVENS, E.H. (ed.) (1949) 'The Trial of von Falkenhorst'. *War Crimes Trials* **VI** London.
  Von Falkenhorst was condemned for implementing the "*Kommando Befehl*" in Norway.
STIMSON, Henry L. (1947) 'The Nuremberg Trial, Landmark in Law'. *Foreign Affairs* January 25.
STOREY, Robert G. (1946) 'Legal Aspects of the Trial of Major War Criminals at Nuremberg'. *Louisiana State Bar Association Journal* October **5** 67-81.
- (1946) 'The Nuremberg Trials'. *Tennessee Law Review* December **19** 517-25.
- (1958) *The Final Judgement*. San Antonio.
TAWFIK, Hazan, E. (1951) 'Etude critique du jugement de Nuremberg'. *Revue de droit international, Moyen Orient* June 33-43.
TAYLOR, Telford (1949) *Final Report to the Secretary of the Army*. U.S. Government Printing Office, Washington D.C.
- (1949) *Nuremberg Trials, War Crimes and International Law*. Foundation Carnegie, No. 450, New York.
- (1948/1950) 'The Nuremberg War Crimes Trials: An Appraisal'. *Proceedings of the Academy of Political Science* **23** 239ff.
- (1953) *Sword and Swastika: The Wehrmacht in the Third Reich*. London.
- (1955) 'The Nuremberg Trials'. *Columbia Law Review* April **55** 488-525.
- (1970) *Nuremberg and Vietnam: An American Tragedy*. Chicago.

- (1974) 'The Use of Captured German and Related Records in the Nuremberg War Crimes Trials'. *Captured German and Related Records: A National Archives Conference*, edited by Robert Wolfe. Athens, Ohio University Press 92-100.

THOMPSON, H.K., Jr. and STRUTZ, Henry (eds.) (1976) *Doenitz at Nuremberg: A Reappraisal: War Crimes and the Military Professional*. New York.

This contains 400 opinions on the condemnation of Doenitz.

TRAININ, A.N. (1946) *Responsabilité pénale des Hitlériens*. Paris.

Professor Trainin was one of the two Soviet delegates at the 1945 London preparatory conference.

- (1946) 'La procédure à Nuremberg'. *Revue de droit international, de sciences diplomatiques et politiques* April-September 77.

- (1946) 'Le Tribunal militaire international et le procès de Nuremberg'. *Revue Internationale de Droit Pénal* **17** 263-76.

TUSA, Ann and John (1983) *The Nuremberg Trial*. London.

A comprehensive study by BBC journalist and her husband. The equivalent of a British official history of the trial.

VERCEL, Michel C. (1966) *Les rescapés de Nuremberg: Les "seigneurs de la guerre" après le verdict*. Paris.

VERMEIL, Edmond (1938) *Doctrinaires de la Révolution Allemande, 1918-1938*. Paris.

VULLIEZ, A. (1957) 'Le "cas Doenitz"'. *Revue des Deux Mondes*, 15 September 297-312.

WARLIMONT, Walter (1964) *Inside Hitler's Headquarters, 1939-1945*. New York.

Warlimont mentions Jodl's role.

WARREN, Earl (1958) 'John J. Parker'. *New York University Law Review* May **33** 649.

WATKINS, H.E. (1958) 'A Great Judge and a Great American: Chief Judge John J. Parker'. *American Bar Association Journal* May **44** 448.
WECHSLER, Herbert (1947) 'Fortune Letters – Nuremberg Defended'. *Fortune* April **35** 29-32.
- (1947) 'The Issues of the Nuremberg Trial'. *Political Science Quarterly* March **62** No.1, 11-26.
WEST, Rebecca (1955) *A Train of Powder*. London.
 It contains brilliant pages on the Trial by an observer.
WESTPHAL, Siegfried (1978) *Der deutsche Generalstab auf der Anklagebank. (Nuernberg 1945-1948)*. Mainz.
WHEELER-BENNETT, Sir John (1976) *Friends, Enemies, Sovereigns*. London.
 He was part of the British delegation.
- and NICHOLLS, Anthony (1972) *The Semblance of Peace: the Political Settlement after the Second World War*. New York.
WOETZEL, Robert K. (1962) *The Nuremberg Trials in International Law with a Postlude on the Eichmann Case*. London, New York.
WRIGHT, Quincy (1946) 'The Nuremberg Trials'. *Chicago Bar Review* **27** 201-09.
- (1947) 'The Nuremberg Trial'. *Journal of Criminal Law and Criminology* March-April **37** 477-78.
- (1948) 'Legal Positivism and the Nuremberg Judgement'. *American Journal of International Law* April **42** 405-14.
- (1945) 'War Criminals'. *American Journal of International Law* **39** 257.
 By the President of the UN Commission on war crimes.
ZIEGLER, Hans Severus (ed.) (1972) *Grosse Pruefung: Letzte Briefe und Letzte Worte Todgeweihter*. Hanover.

Official Publications

Accord du 8 août 1945. Statut du Tribunal Militaire International, articles et documents. Nouvelle Série No.348, Paris, Ministry of Information, 1945.

Der Prozess gegen die Hauptkriegsverbrecher vor dem Internationalen Militaergerichtshof, Nuremberg, 1947–9 (42 volumes). A massive publication. Approximately half of the volumes cover the stenography of the debates; the other half covers documents submitted. The German edition is probably the more reliable for declarations made by the Accused. However, for practical purposes, quotes from the English edition are used here.

History of the United Nations War Crimes Commission and the Development of the Laws of War, London, 1948.

History Survey of the Question of International Criminal Jurisdiction. Memorandum submitted by the Secretary General. New York, 1949.

Nazi Conspiracy and Aggression, Washington DC, U.S. Government Printing Office, 1947 (10 volumes). German documents translated into English, concerning the two counts for which the U.S. Delegation had made itself especially responsible.

Report of Robert H. Jackson, U.S. representative to the International Conference of Military Tribunals,

London, 1945. Department of State, Publication 3080, Washington, 1949.

Violation of the Laws and Customs of War. Reports of Majority and Dissenting Reports of American and Japanese Members of the Commission of Responsibilities, Conference of Paris 1919; Oxford, 1919. Published by the Carnegie Foundation.

OBITUARY

[as published in *The Guardian* newspaper Friday 2nd January 2009]

In 1944, my father, Georges Bonnin, who has died aged 88, was imprisoned by the Nazis in Toulouse. Each night he fell asleep to the screams of comrades being tortured. There were regular convoys of inmates to concentration camps. One day he was informed that he was to be killed, but the next day the Nazis instead opened the gates as the Allies advanced, and waved the prisoners goodbye.

After the war Georges was an official French observing lawyer at the Nuremberg trials, and at the time of his death he was revising an autobiography, to be entitled *The 14th of July at Nuremberg*. After the war he moved to Whaddon Hall, in Buckinghamshire (1947-59), as an editor of the German diplomatic archives.

He then went on to become an internationally respected historian. One of his most well-respected books, *Bismarck and the Hohenzollern Candidature for the Spanish Throne* (1957), combined documents and commentary to lay bare the Chancellor's scheme in 1870 to substitute the exiled Queen Isabella with the German Prince Leopold. *Le Putsch de Hitler à Munich en 1923* (1966) drew on transcripts of the future Führer's trial after his abortive coup, which up until that point had not been fully explored by historians.

Georges was a solicitor's son, born in the Vendée in western France and educated by Jesuits at Vannes. He took a Doctorate in law from the Sorbonne. With the outbreak of war he served in the army. He was arrested during the Occupation while evading forced labour.

After Whaddon Hall he studied at St Catherine's College, Oxford, and researched in Bonn, Ohio and St Antony's College, Oxford. He also worked as a fruit farmer in Lot-et-Garonne and taught at Leeds University and Thames Polytechnic. He was a generous and drily amusing tutor who wore odd coloured socks - because the first two socks at the top of his drawer would be the ones he would put on. Once, by accident, he wore a matching pair - and one of his students asked whether he was feeling all right.

In the mid-1980s he retired to Wales, although for the last eight years he suffered from Parkinson's disease. At his funeral his coffin was draped in the tricolore, and the *Marseillaise*, *La Vie en Rose* and *Je ne Regrette Rien* were played. His last words were "Let's have champagne and oysters in Arcachon".

Jean Bonnin

NOTES AND ACKNOWLEDGEMENTS

We would like to thank the following people:

Paddy Long – Thank you so very much. My mother and I can honestly say that without you and without your advice, researching, re-typing, encouragement and friendship this book would not exist. We cannot thank you enough... For so many reasons this account needed to be published. But one important reason was that it is another piece of the jigsaw which reveals to us more of the story and the truth surrounding the Second World War. Hence, apart from anything else, we have to thank Paddy for helping another historical gap to be filled. It is only a shame that you never got to meet Georges.

Denise Llewellyn – Thank you, Denise, for your help with this manuscript and for your encouragement with what Lyn and I were embarking upon. And we thank you for your friendship and love.

David Evans – Your friendship to Georges, and to Lyn and me, and your help and advice with Georges' computing, will always be remembered. Thank you.

Jean and Morfydd

~

Jean Bonnin is an author, poet and translator of literary texts. He was born in France but now resides in Wales, UK. And is the son of Georges Bonnin. www.jeanbonnin.com

Morfydd (Lyn) Bonnin, having resided at various times in numerous locations around the world, now lives by the sea in southwest Wales. She is a writer of short stories, and was the wife of Georges Bonnin.

Both Jean and Morfydd edited and smoothed the edges of this most important of manuscripts that is an invaluable contribution to the body of knowledge concerning World War II.

V3

www.redeggpublishing.com

www.ingramcontent.com/pod-product-compliance
Lightning Source LLC
Chambersburg PA
CBHW071647090426
42738CB00009B/1449